PLANTING
A NEW PERSPECTIVE

Piet Oudolf and Noel Kingsbury

PLANTING

A NEW PERSPECTIVE

TIMBER PRESS

LONDON • PORTLAND

►► (Pages 6–7) *Angelica gigas* seedheads stand like spectres amongst a range of late flowering perennials in Piet and Anja Oudolf's garden.

All planting plans discussed and featured in the book can also be studied in detail online. You can find them on www.oudolf.com and www.noelkingsbury.com

Published in 2013 by Timber Press, Inc.

The Haseltine Building	2 The Quadrant
133 S.W. Second Avenue, Suite 450	135 Salusbury Road
Portland, Oregon 97204-3527	London NW6 6RJ
timberpress.com	timberpress.co.uk

Project coordination by Hélène Lesger – Books, Rights & More, Amsterdam
Book design by Gert Jan Slagter
Printed in China

Library of Congress Cataloging-in-Publication Data

Oudolf, Piet.
Planting : a new perspective/Piet Oudolf and Noël Kingsbury. — 1st ed.
   p. cm.
Includes index.
ISBN 978-1-60469-370-6
1. Planting design. 2. Plants, Ornamental. 3. Gardens — Design. I. Kingsbury, Noël.
II. Title.
SB472.45.O92 2013
715 — dc23   2012032341

A catalog record for this book is also available from the British Library.

CONTENTS

PLANTING DESIGN FOR THE TWENTY-FIRST CENTURY

Plants are increasingly being recognized as a vital part of our urban and domestic environments, not just a luxury or an unnecessary – if pleasant – bit of decoration. It has long been established, for example, that the mere view of plants through a window has a beneficial effect on the human psyche, and that plants can play an important role in cleaning and purifying the air of buildings and built-up environments.

Gardening, whether on the most intimate private level or the most extensive and public, involves an appreciation of and involvement with the natural world. For many people, plants may be their only point of contact with nature apart from feeling the effects of the weather. Private gardens offer the opportunity for personal choices to be made about what plants to grow and how to manage them, while designers of civic landscapes have always had the responsibility of serving the wider public interest. There is, however, a new and additional agenda for gardeners, both private and public: sustainability and the support of biodiversity. Sustainability demands that we minimize irreplaceable inputs in gardening and reduce harmful outputs, while the support of biodiversity brings a demand for wildlife-friendly planting and practices.

The use of long-lived perennials in conjunction with woody plants – the approach Piet Oudolf and I, Noel Kingsbury, have always supported – genuinely offers improved sustainability and support for biodiversity. Reducing the amount of regularly mown lawn and the unnecessary trimming of woody plants for unclear motives is surely a step forward. Creating rich garden habitats offers natural beauty close at hand, provides resources and homes for wildlife, and improves the sustainability of management.

Deciding what plants to use and how to arrange them is covered by the field of planting design, which

◀◀ (page 8)
A green roof around a conference facility: Moorgate Crofts, Rotherham, Yorkshire, designed by Nigel Dunnett (2005). A variable 10–20 centimeter deep substrate supports a wide variety of plant life (around 50 species), selected to maximize the length of the flowering season. This is an example of a semi-intensive green roof, where visual appeal is important as well as functionality.

▲
The former nursery at Piet and Anja Oudolf's at Hummelo in the Netherlands. It is now a boldly experimental area where robust perennials grow amidst a sown mix of wild pasture grasses along with various spontaneously arriving species. Only time will tell how it will work out. The pale mauve-blue is *Aster* 'Little Carlow', the dark red *Eupatorium maculatum* 'Riesenschirm'.

brings together a combination of technical knowledge and artistic vision. This book looks at some of the recent trends within planting design, and is aimed primarily at home gardeners, garden design and maintenance professionals, and landscape architects. It has important lessons for others, such as architects, who do not use plants directly but often have to situate their work in close proximity to them, or ecologists, whose profession does not involve much design but who increasingly have a role to play in the creation and management of designed plantings.

While the role of plants – and therefore planting design – is well established in the domestic garden, and is indeed absolutely crucial to its aesthetic and functional success, it has not been so well established in landscape design. Or perhaps more accurately, plants have often played a minor role in urban landscape design. Histori-cally, for centuries the only plants used in cities were av-enue trees; the nineteenth century saw the growth of ur-ban parks, the late twentieth a much wider use of plants in urban areas – a practice to a large extent pioneered in the Netherlands. Now, however, the use of plants is in-creasing, particularly that of perennials and ornamental grasses, requiring greater access to technical informa-tion about plant establishment and management, and to ideas about the visual aspects of their use. It is perhaps worth looking at these new trends.

Green roofs

While green roofs have captured the public imagina-tion, the technology involved in their construction is also being used in many other situations, often not immediately recognisable as roofs. Increasingly, high-density urban environments are creating artificial grow-

▲

A randomized perennial mix designed by Nigel Dunnett at Sandvik Tools, Warwickshire (2007), designed to capture and hold water during periods of high rainfall and so prevent flooding. The dark purple is *Aster novi-belgii* 'Purple Dome'.

▲

This swale, designed by Nigel Dunnett for London's Olympic Park, illustrates well a basic concept of sustainable drainage schemes. Drainage water is collected in the lowest part of the site and allowed to drain slowly into the water table, with only the excess being taken off site. A diverse community of British native plant species are used; clearly visible are white *Leucanthemum vulgare* and pink *Lythrum salicaria*.

ing situations which require soil or artificial soil-like substrates above impermeable surfaces. An example of such a green roof which is not a green roof might be Chicago's Lurie Garden – built over a parking garage.

Green roofs are often categorized by the use to which they are put: extensive roofs are functional and usually have a shallow substrate; intensive are more likely to be roof gardens with conventional planting; semi-intensive ones are somewhere between and are developed for their visual appeal as well as functionality. Extensive and semi-intensive roofs tend to be planted up with plant 'communities' – combinations of plants selected for the conditions which coexist well and survive with minimal maintenance, often species from dry meadow habitats. In this sense there is a real distinction between these and conventional plantings, where plants are placed individually.

Water management

A major environmental problem in cities concerns the management of water, especially the control of excessive run-off during storms, which can cause flooding and associated pollution. Sustainable urban drainage schemes (SUDS) are designed to capture water, and either store it or release it slowly into the water table or streams or allow it to be evaporated back into the atmosphere. Domestic gardeners in some cities are encouraged to develop rain gardens where the same objectives are reached, with no drainage water leaving the property and the minimum amount of irrigation water brought in. Green roofs, with their capacity to store rain as it lands, often play a role in integrated SUDS. SUDS often involve swales – detention basins where water can be held temporarily before slow release into natural drainage systems. Often these are planted up with a carefully selected vegetation, usually locally native species which can survive periodic inundation but dry conditions too. More ornamental planting combinations are, however, also possible. Again, the emphasis is on mixtures of species.

Biofiltration

Biofiltration is the reduction of polluting chemicals in the environment through the use of plants. Street trees, green roofs and living walls are all examples of plant life which can be effective at trapping dust, and breaking down complex hydrocarbons (often known as Volatile Organic Compounds – VOCs) into harmless CO_2 and water. Plants differ in their ability to break down specific VOCs, so combinations are often more effective than just one species.

A more targeted biofiltration technique is in the idea of the natural swimming pool, developed in Germany, where plants act in conjunction with beneficial bacteria to break down or trap nitrogen and phosphorus compounds, so denying nutrients to disease-causing bacteria. The plants used are often grown as a mixed community, as different species have different roles to play in a complex set of biochemical reactions.

Spontaneous vegetation

Post-industrial societies often leave behind large areas of wasteland: abandoned industrial facilities, railways, mines, military training grounds and the like. These are often overrun with plants with remarkable speed, bringing home to us very forcefully how rapidly and thoroughly nature can recover lost ground and heal polluted and damaged environments. Such places often develop a fascinating and unique flora, a combination of locally native species, weeds and escaped garden plants. So often 'redevelopment' means the destruction of these unique plant communities. Recent years have seen a more positive interpretation of these places; led by Germany, areas of post-industrial wasteland are being managed more respectfully and creatively to preserve something of their special character.

One of the most famous examples of such plant conquest of abandoned land is the New York City High Line, an elevated freight railway line last used in the 1960s. The last part of the line was closed in 1980. Its redevelopment as a park had to involve complete rebuilding so the flora was lost, but Piet Oudolf's collaboration with landscape architects James Corner Field Operations is intended to evoke the wild feeling of the old High Line. The remarkable success of the project is now inspiring other projects in the USA, and highlighting the importance of post-industrial landscapes.

What is striking about many of these new and distinctly technological and engineering approaches to planting is that communities of multiple species are being used – relatively stable groups of plants which can be managed altogether as a unit. This is part of the zeitgeist of contemporary planting design – a slow move away from precise individual plant placement to combinations of species, designing and planting something which is greater than the sum of the parts, developing a vegetation rather than planting a mass of individuals.

Key to the idea of combinations of plants is the intermingling, mixing or blending of species, as opposed to the use of blocks or groups. This creates an effect which is visually more complex and naturalistic. This also means that there is more interaction between plants, and so more competition – as a consequence there is a need for a greater knowledge of ecological issues or at least a greater awareness of long-term performance.

This book aims to explore the new emerging planting design based on intermingling combinations. It is centered around the work of Piet Oudolf, a Dutch landscape designer who works on private and public commissions in northern Europe and North America. It also includes some material about other practitioners working with plant combinations in several different countries: landscape architects, academic researchers and public space managers. I – Noel Kingsbury – have written the text, but this has been very much a joint project between Piet and myself, so for most of this book I am writing on behalf of both of us. Chapter four, 'Long-term Plant Performance', however, has been the result of research as part of a doctoral thesis with the Department of Landscape at Sheffield University followed by some further formal research work; consequently, I have written this with my voice.

What unites the two of us is our passion for and close involvement with plants. Just as the best potters have an intuitive understanding of clays and glazes and master cabinet makers a deep feeling for every type of wood they use, skilled planting designers have a knowledge of the plants that make up their repertoire. Piet's work as a designer is based on 35 years of not just using plants in designs but growing them himself and, from 1982 to 2010, running a nursery with his wife, Anja. I have a background in nursery work myself (albeit for a very much shorter period) – there is nothing like it for gaining an intimate knowledge of how plants behave, what they do and when they do it, and – crucially – what goes on underground: how roots behave. The knowledge needed to propagate plants and then grow them on is that of plant performance – such experience is then invaluable for understanding how they will perform over many years. This surely is a major part of the Oudolf success story.

It is helpful to think about the material in this book as covering two gradients: from macro to micro and from order to spontaneity. The first chapter, 'Planting – The Big Picture', looks at the context of plantings and the gradient from order to spontaneity. The second chapter, 'Grouping Plants', considers the middle level: how plants can be put together in different ways. This is very much about Piet's work, for he is a true designer, in contrast to many professionals whose work is also featured in the book, who could perhaps be better described as ecological engineers. Piet's plants are precisely placed, and indeed much of this chapter is given over to a study of his planting plans. Over time, his plants may move about – which is fine – but the intention is that such changes will only very slowly degrade the original design concept.

Chapter three, 'Combining Plants', comes down to a lower level, looking at combination and juxtaposition: why one plant looks good next to another, how combinations can be made to look good at particular times of year, why one grouping may change with time faster than another. I pay particular attention to plant 'architecture' – their shape and structure. This chapter will be of most interest and use to the new gardener or designer and to those with only small spaces. Chapter four on performance looks at issues crucial to the long-term survival and spread of perennial plants, but also at death and disappearance. Such issues are vital to understand, not just for the ongoing management of plantings but also at the planning stage.

A fifth chapter covers the work of others who are at the naturalistic cutting-edge in planting design. Whereas Piet's work can be seen as an artistically stylised version of natural habitats, most other practitioners in the field are more concerned with a randomizing of individual plants from a carefully researched selection. The term 'ecological engineers' describes their approach, which combines a technical knowledge of plant performance with visual appeal to create relatively stable and highly decorative plant communities.

Garden and landscape making is increasingly becoming a globalized business. There was a time when the vast majority of ornamental or amenity plant growing happened in the cool temperate climates of north-west Europe, North America, their southerly Mediterranean climate fringes and Japan. Anything done beyond these areas tended to be quite 'colonial' and derivative in character. This is now changing. As the so-called emerging markets generate more resources for public and private garden making, immense new possibilities are opening up. One is for the ongoing development of garden traditions which became stalled – either through cultural decline or the impact of imperialism – notably Islamic, Chinese and Thai. Another is working with plant palettes which have never before been utilized in design.

►► (pages 14–15)
A spontaneous meadow garden at Carrie Furnace, Pittsburgh, Pennsylvania, with spikes of *Echium vulgare* particularly prominent. Post-industrial landscapes can be remarkably biodiverse and even beautiful. Landscape consultant Rick Darke is involved with managing this abandoned industrial area, describing his role as 'to identify the useful components of the existing spontaneous vegetation on the site and ways of integrating this in the eventual designs . . . which will have the historic ironworks at the core of mixed-used residential, professional, retail and trailways development.'

This latter approach, the use of novel plants, is tremendously exciting. Much garden design in non-industrial or emerging economies in the past has used a limited flora, repeated all over the world across appropriate climate zones; the monotony of endlessly meeting bougainvilleas, yuccas and *Ficus benjamina* wherever you travel in the tropics is deeply disappointing. The garden, landscape and nursery professions are now increasingly turning to their own floras rather than this global lowest common denominator mix. The reasons are many: a desire to celebrate regional diversity, patriotism, a wish to support biodiversity, and a need for species which are guaranteed to survive the onslaught of difficult local climates.

One example illustrates how this process can work. Amalia Robredo is a garden designer who practices on the coast of Uruguay, an area with a number of interesting plant communities, now seriously endangered by development. Over the last few years she has systematically made herbarium specimens, got them identified by botanists at the University of Montevideo, collected seed, grown and trialled plants in her garden, persuaded local nurseries to start growing them, and then used them in projects. For a coastal climate, with frequent high-velocity and desiccating winds and sandy soils, the use of such plants makes sense, as well as replacing lost habitat and encouraging people locally to value their environment. For us there will be further advantages, as new species adaptable to other climates make their way into global commerce – not as in the past as species introduced directly from the wild, but already tried and tested by local nurseries and gardeners. Piet's work in

◀◀ (pages 16–17)
The *Salvia* and *Achillea* planting at Hermannshof, Weinheim, in Germany's Rhine Valley, is an example of a naturalistic planting designed for color and structure and to thrive on dry alkaline soils. The blue-purples are seedlings of *Salvia nemorosa* and *S.* ×*superba* cultivars, the blue a hybrid of *Veronica longifolia*. The tall yellow is *Verbascum speciosum*, a self-seeding biennial. In the foreground is grass *Festuca mairei* from the Atlas Mountains in north-west Africa, where the climate is similar to regions with steppe or short-grass prairie habitats.

▲
Amalia Robredo in Uruguay is one of the pioneering plant-oriented designers using locally native species for the first time in their regions. The wild flora of the Uruguayan coast has many attractive plant species. Here the grass *Andropogon lindmanii* grows alongside silver *Achyroline satureoides*.

▲
A green roof on the Uruguayan coast designed by Karina Hogg, with planting by Amalia Robredo uses a mix of native (recently introduced into cultivation) and non-native species. Conditions are extreme with salt spray and exposure; the substrate is 5–7 centimeters. The silver is a native sand dune species, *Senecio crassiflorus*; the yellow daisy is a rare local endemic, *Grindelia orientalis*; the blue is *Plectranthus neochilus*. The grass in the foreground is locally native *Stipa filifolia*.

With the High Line now so popular, many other communities are looking at abandoned rail lines as potential public spaces. Like many former industrial sites, their poor and sometimes polluted substrate, which hardly earns the name of 'soil', is actually very good for encouraging a wide range of plants; it is a counter-intuitive fact of ecology that stressful environments often support more species diversity than fertile ones. Here, in Reading, Pennsylvania, garden escapes *Macleaya cordata* and a species of *Verbascum* are prominent. In other locations rare natives may find a niche.

►► (pages 20–21)
The design for New York City's High Line was intended to evoke the spontaneous vegetation of the old abandoned railway line. Here, in October, are seedheads of the grass *Sporobolus heterolepis* and *Eupatorium maculatum* 'Gateway' alongside the yellow flowers of *Rudbeckia subtomentosa*.

the United States and his collaboration with native plant specialists such as Roy Diblik of Northwind Perennials in Wisconsin have already contributed to a growing interest in North American perennials among garden and landscape professionals in central and northern Europe.

Practitioners in this field tend to be very collegiate. We swap ideas, images and plants. We may produce very different results but share many of the fundamental beliefs, which are also being increasingly shared by others beyond our field, both amateur and professional. We are all passionate about wild plants and wild plant communities, and about the need for gardeners and landscape professionals to create environments which support biodiversity as well as nourishing the human

spirit. This book will inspire, encourage and enable others to join us.

We live in interesting times for planting design. There are a great many areas where the integration of plants with architecture and the wider urban fabric is taking plants beyond their merely ornamental or amenity use. Planting design has long been something of a 'Cinderella' within landscape design, and even in the booming profession of garden design it enjoys surprisingly little discussion. Now landscape architects and designers are paying it more attention, and with a growing acceptance of the need for plants to be woven more deeply into the fabric of our lives, I hope this book will make its contribution.

►►► (pages 22–23)
Chicago's Lurie Garden, part of the Millenium Park project, opened in 2004, is an example of a new kind of urban public garden. It is in fact a giant green roof, as it is built over a parking garage, yet reads as part of a ground-level landscape. Offering a stylized version of the Midwest prairie, its combination of native and introduced perennials and grasses is symbolic of a blend of nature and culture. Such a blend is easily understood by city dwellers, some of whom will be tempted to find out more about wildflowers and so be drawn into wider issues of conservation and biodiversity.

ONE

PLANTING – THE BIG PICTURE

Traditionally, the way plants were organized in parks and gardens reflected a culture that liked to order and discipline nature. Contemporary planting design is not only freer, but also seeks to reflect nature. It also addresses our concerns about how we garden sustainably and in partnership with nature.

Even someone who takes the quickest glance at a wild or semi-natural habitat will see that it is a blend of different plant species. Someone who has no interest in wild plants and lives most of their life in a city standing in front of an average field in spring or early summer – by which we mean a traditional low-intensity pasture or hay meadow – will rapidly appreciate that several different kinds of wildflower are present, and that they are all mixed up. Ask them to pay a bit more attention to the grass, and they will soon appreciate that more than one kind can be seen; some in the field form obvious tussocks, others which appear to be spreading on to some bare ground are particularly fine, whereas still others just seem to form an even-textured mass. The flowering plants present (in Europe, most likely to be meadow buttercup, *Ranunculus acris*, and red clover, *Trifolium pratense*) are scattered all over the field but not evenly – clearly in places the concentration of flowers is greater than in others. Areas of abandoned agricultural or other land can be even better sites to appreciate this complexity of plant life. In much of North America the diversity can often be visually very impressive, particularly later in the growing season, with a range of grasses, wildflowers and wildflower seedheads scattered across a wide area.

◄ Perennials self-seeding at Pensthorpe.

Early spring is a very good time to appreciate the layout of perennial combinations. In the planting below (left) species are in blocks – although most designers would not plant out in straight lines like this (carried out here by the New York City parks authority). The planting below (right) shows a more naturalistic intermingled style (on the High Line) – blocks may still be used, but they are more likely to bleed into each other and some plants are more scattered.

BLOCK OR BLEND?

Looking at a semi-natural grassland is a good place to start thinking about the visual qualities of natural plant communities. Similar patterns occur in woodland, but we famously cannot see the wood for the trees and a good vantage point can be hard to find. Thinking about what we are looking at, it is helpful to focus on the following qualities:

• Intermingling – a wildflower meadow where all the buttercups are neatly organized into one patch, the clover in another and the thistles in another is plainly absurd. Plant communities are very obviously made up of densely intermingled species.

• Diversity – the range of species varies greatly from one sort of community to another, but in most cases there is more diversity than meets the eye. The more

you look, the more you see, particularly in grassland habitats.

• Complexity – imagine trying to count the number of species, let alone the number of individual plants, in a square meter of a field. Part of the problem is the sheer intensity of the intermingled relationships of the plants present.

• Change – complexity is not evenly distributed. Walking through a grassland (North American prairie is the best for this) reveals a constant shift in the distribution of species, or even their presence or absence.

• Coherence – despite the mind-boggling complexity of the plant distribution, there is an overall sense of unity. Standing back so that the whole can be appreciated, the presence of many thousands of individuals is re-

A prairie in flower is a good place to appreciate the patterns of plant distribution. Here several grasses stand out through their form, pale purple *Physostegia virginiana* and cream *Parthenium integrifolium* through their color, and gray *Amorpha canescens* through both color and form. The scattered and intermingled mixing of the species here is very typical of wild plant communities. This is Shoe Factory Road Prairie, Illinois, very near Chicago's O'Hare Airport, in August.
▼

Seedheads of *Echinacea pallida* indicate a loose group of the plant in prairie on a sand and gravel moraine at Glacial Park, Illinois, in September. Such occasional scattering can be dramatic and is easily replicated in cultivation. In the background a colony of *Rhus typhina* can be seen slowly colonizing the grassland – this small tree is used on New York City's High Line, where annual pruning prevents it spreading too much.
▼

solved into something much clearer, the awareness of a ground-mass of greens (or perhaps browns at the end of the year) and a scattering of color (or again at the end of the year, seedhead forms). This simplicity and clarity among complexity gives a sense of coherence. It is perhaps this, more than anything else, which enables us to see real beauty in wild plant communities.

• Distinction – particularly effective at creating a sense of coherence are those species which rise above the mass: not necessarily literally, but in standing out, either through their color, form, height or mass. The European meadow buttercups do this fairly quietly (they achieve their impact through sheer quantity), but other species in different environments may do so more dramatically. The most effective are those which combine color and form/height, such as the magnificent sight of hundreds of spikes of flowers of *Baptisia alba* (white wild indigo) rising above the grasses in an early summer meadow prairie.

MODERNIST MONOCULTURES – PLANTING IN THE TWENTIETH CENTURY

We are all familiar with most cultivated plants being grown in blocks. Arable farming does it on a huge scale, and the sight of a Brueghel painting of medieval peasants harvesting wheat reveals that it has always been so, only the size of the field varying with time and place. A great deal of the landscape planting with which we are familiar is composed of blocks, usually of shrubs, while much of the conventional advice about gardens of the average suburban size was to plant in groups of odd numbers. This convention of monocultural block planting is very much a creation of the twentieth century.

The dominance of the monocultural block as the basic unit of planting in public landscapes and to a lesser (and, needless to say, smaller) extent in private gardens can possibly be seen as a way of simplifying the cost of labor. Much nineteenth-century planting was very

This garden in western Ireland (2006) uses block planting. However, plant groups are repeated so there is a strong sense of rhythm and unity; here, in July, these include *Veronicastrum virginicum* (center), *Sedum* 'Red Cauli' (right foreground), *Molinia* 'Moorhexe' (center foreground) and *Helenium* 'Moerheim Beauty' (right). In addition, clumps of the very tall grass *Stipa gigantea* stand above the rest of the planting and help tie it together.

Repeated single-species blocks of grass *Deschampsia cespitosa* 'Goldtau' create great impact on the large scale at Berne Park, Bottrop, Germany (2010). In the foreground, mixes give more interest; here are grass *Sesleria autumnalis* and *Sedum* 'Matrona'. This is August.

complex, requiring considerable time and skill to design and maintain. More informal planting styles which were developed by designers such as the English Gertrude Jekyll (1843–1932) used drifts – elongated blocks which were soft at the edges and allowed plant partnerships to be seen and appreciated from a variety of angles. Informality and simplification can be seen as the two dominant but linked trends throughout the twentieth century. Organically shaped blocks of perennials in post-war German public planting and much larger blocks with a clear link to mid-century abstract painting in the work of the Brazilian Roberto Burle Marx (1909–1994) illustrate the influence of modernism. Landscape shrubs in blocks in public places were widely used in the Netherlands in the 1960s, a trend in the landscape profession which proved very influential.

Modernism offered a rationale for the simplification and informality of much twentieth-century planting design. It failed to convince everybody, however. From the 1970s onwards, more ecologically focussed gardeners began to promote the use of native plant species and the idea of the garden as a biodiversity preserve – a Dutch group dedicated to these aims took the name *Oase* (oasis). This same period saw the maturing of a movement in Germany dedicated to creating plantings in public spaces through the development of a naturalistic and wildlife-friendly style. This German style, which has come to be known as *Lebensbereich* (habitat), is most chiefly associated with Professor Richard Hansen of Weihenstephan, a complex of trial gardens, research institutes and a university north of Munich; its roots lie in a plant ecology science strongly focussed on the study of plant communities. The most recent developments in this perennial-based planting style are on the creation of randomized planting mixes, which are discussed later in this book.

One plant, one place – advantages and disadvantages of the monocultural block

The single-species block may be dated, but it should not be written off. It has an undeniably simple graphic quality which may often be regarded as valuable, particularly by professionals working in public environments. In private gardens and other intimate settings, its simplicity may be an advantage as a counterpoint to complex perennial-based planting schemes. In fact, its real value

may lie as a counterpoint to the very focus of this book: intermingled plantings may not always be strong on structure, or they may lack structure at certain times of year; the use of firm monocultural blocks may create an exciting creative tension.

In situations where maintenance is limited by lack of time or skill, the advantage of monocultural blocks is very clear, as anything which looks different can be weeded out. This is particularly useful in the case of grasses. Many of us who have been busily promoting naturalistic planting and grasses over the years have been brought up short by situations where carefully chosen specimens are dug out or sprayed with herbicide because inexperienced or badly briefed staff have mistaken them for weed grasses. The unfortunate fact is that, early in the year, even many gardeners who are familiar with grasses can sometimes find it difficult to know which is a desired and which a weed grass. However, by putting grasses into monocultural blocks, it is much easier to avoid such tragedies.

For the most part, however, unless there are clear design, practical or functional reasons for block planting, we would strongly urge gardeners and designers to do their best to move away from this outdated and unimaginative style. In private gardens it simply acts as a deterrent to developing more creative planting schemes, while in the public realm it is little more than a crutch for those in the landscape profession who have for far too long treated plants as green cement. The exception might be the dramatically big block planting, which can have real design impact, but that is another story.

There are more important and more objective arguments against block planting than that it is boring and out of date, however. One is that, like a great actor drunk in the bar after a performance, a whole mass of one plant can look very dreary when it has finished performing. The fact that only a relatively limited number of perennials in the short to medium height range look at all respectable after flowering has meant that a few species tend to be seen again and again. One of the great advantages of Gertrude Jekyll's drifts was that it made it much easier to hold on to a form of block, but by stretching them out she made it easier to hide plants with a 'past the sell-by date' look.

◄◄ (pages 30–31)

The advantage of intermingling plants over block planting is that random close juxtapositions of species are created. As autumn blurs into winter, these will revolve around the silhouettes, textures and forms of plants. Here, in a dry prairie planting at Hermannshof in Germany, grasses (with *Nassella tenuissima* prominent) combine with perennial seedheads (the dark heads are *Echinacea pallida* and *E. paradoxa*). The grayish seedheads to the right are subshrub *Amorpha canescens*.

►

Chance, or serendipity, should always be allowed to play a part in garden design, and even perhaps in the public landscape too. Here, an unexpected 'meadow' has sprouted over the years in between the paving blocks of a terrace on the south side of the Oudolf family house. Grass *Nassella tenuissima*, a short-lived but strongly seeding species, has germinated alongside purple-blue and pink seedling forms of *Salvia pratensis*, while the questing roots of *Euphorbia cyparissias* have sent up shoots between the pavers.

GETTING THE BLEND RIGHT – THE ADVANTAGES AND DISADVANTAGES OF INTERMINGLING

Moving from planting in blocks to blending, intermingling or mixing – all three words can be used interchangeably – is a major shift in planting design. A working definition would be to say that a 'pure' blend is a complete mixture of individuals of all the species used in a given area. This should not be too much of a challenge for gardeners and designers with good plant knowledge. For some time now, the idea of 'plant combinations' has been an important driver for creativity among both designers and amateur gardeners. A really good combination should have an electric quality about it – two or more plants where a particular complementary relationship of color or form sends the sparks flying. The reality is that these combinations are relatively few. Instead, a great many others are good but not outstanding – particularly useful are those more low-key combinations which look good over a long period. Simply taking a good combination and then repeating it is the

first step in developing an effective intermingled or mixed planting. While two plants together can be dramatic, as a design concept it lacks depth and rarely looks good all year round. Combining four or five plants can create a simple mix, which if chosen well can provide interest for much of the year.

Here, where we discuss intermingled plantings, it is important to emphasize that there are two very different approaches. One is to carefully research a blend and then use it over large areas, either mixing the component plants at random or repeating a designed block, in the way that a mosaicist or tiler laying out a series of small modular units repeats it again and again to create a pattern. There is an analogy with a tea or whisky blender who works intensively on a small quantity of a blend, with an eye to mass production of their eventual choice. Such a planting blend can then be reproduced in two ways, one as literally mass production, with the mix being used anywhere conditions are suitable. Alternatively, it might only be used for one project: a site-specific mix. The other approach is not to randomize or repeat modules but to design in the location of every plant, to intermingle different combinations in different places, so allowing there to be small groups, repetitions at various frequencies and subtle transition effects.

To summarize, there are three approaches to blended planting here:

- randomized mix, planted or sown
- modular repetition
- designed intermingling.

Of course, there are also 'halfway houses' such as blurring the edges of block planting or randomly scattering different species through a block planting.

Any gardener will quickly be able to suggest that sowing a seed mix is one way to achieve an appearance of randomness. Indeed, this is the approach which James Hitchmough of the University of Sheffield uses. The 'Mixed Planting' and 'Integrated Planting' systems developed in Germany and Switzerland aim to achieve a similar effect by using young plants. Modular repetition is technically difficult to achieve but is possible, and could in theory be used to create some highly effective plant juxtapositions.

Blended plantings are undoubtedly very beautiful and highly effective visually. This alone is an important reason for using them. They also have the advantage that it is possible to easily mix together species which flower or perform at different seasons. They are also forgiving of weed infiltration. As a general rule, the more ordered a planting is, the more problematic weeds are – one weed in a highly geometric bed of summer annuals stands out like a beacon. In wilder, more naturalistic planting styles, occasional weeds stand out less, while intermingled styles have the greatest capacity to absorb intruders. In fact, it is possible to take a pragmatic view and allow some spontaneously occurring species to survive and spread within the planting.

Finally, the advantage of the cost of mixed planting styles, or to be more precise randomized or sown plantings, needs to be considered. One of the reasons for the development of the German and Swiss planting mixes was to reduce the costs of large areas of planting for local government, garden shows and other public sites. The idea is that a mix is developed using careful plant selection, with both practical and aesthetic criteria, and so the design cost is all absorbed at the beginning as a one-off. Anyone can then buy the mix for as many hundred square meters as necessary, with seed or plant costs potentially carrying a percentage royalty for the original design team. The decision of the garden or landscape designer is limited to specifying which mix to use. Design costs are therefore minimized.

It is now time to consider the disadvantages of mixed planting styles. The widespread use of a limited number of planting mixes could rapidly turn them into clichés, much as sedum roofs have become. The fact that commercial nurseries are now marketing planting mixes could well result in a situation where a bold innovation, followed by a mass usage, will then become a boring lowest common denominator. The biodiversity value of such plantings could be good, but to earn popularity with the human element of the landscape – who, after all, select and pay for them – they must also offer visual quality. It is to be hoped that randomized plantings will be an area of continuous research and development, so that new combinations will constantly offer change and novelty. Commercially developed randomized planting mixes may be tailored to particular habitats, but these can only ever be crude approximations to the existing conditions where they are used. They are in no sense 'site-specific'.

There is one other possible problem with randomized mixes, particularly those that are planted rather than sown. This is to do with long-term development and the distribution of species. In nature, plant communities are never random. Certain plant species will colonize an area first, followed by others, so the process of community development is cumulative over time rather than the entire community starting off at once – which is what happens if one is planted. Over time, slight differences in soil and microclimate conditions will cause species to select out, so that there are greater and lesser numbers of different species in different areas. Think about how wildflowers are scattered in a meadow or prairie; part of the visual pleasure is not just the scattering and mingling over a wide area, but the subtle ebb and flow of particular species over space in ever-changing combinations. If species are introduced by sowing, the slight differences in microhabitat will be registered very soon by the developing seedlings, so the mix will grow to fit its landscape. The result will be different trajectories of development in different places, leading to a good ecological fit to the conditions and visual diversity. The danger with randomized planting is that this will

Perennial growth by itself can create an effect of intermingling, either through the way in which species with fine branching and spreading stems can knit together or because of seeding.
Here, in August at Hummelo in the Netherlands (left), a variety of perennials in small groups are beginning to mesh together, an effect heightened by the similar color palette of many of them. Pale *Lythrum virgatum* occupies the center, with deeper *Stachys officinalis* to the right. Behind and in front are the narrow spikes of *Liatris spicata*. Paler pink spikes belong to *Sanguisorba menziesii*. To the rear are the pale pink flowers of *Sidalcea oregana*.

At Pensthorpe Gardens in Norfolk, England (right) two species are beginning to blend to form a meadow effect, several years after being planted in separate blocks: *Scabiosa japonica* var. *alpina* and deep pink *Dianthus carthusianorum* both have fine stems which in nature wend their way through grasses; they can also be effective at seeding themselves.

not happen, and in particular that species with a strong tendency to dominance will tend to dominate everywhere, and conversely less dominant species may be forced out everywhere. Just such problems have been observed in randomized tree plantings.

Modular repetition or designed intermingling of plants is a way of getting around this problem. Piet Oudolf's work is undoubtedly a strongly designed intermingling; a mathematical analysis of his planting combinations would surely indicate an almost infinite number of potential species juxtapositions and combinations. Because of this, the long-term development of an Oudolf planting may be more akin to a naturally occurring plant community than a randomized planting. In addition, the number of species he uses is considerably greater than the 15 to 20 in most randomized mixes. Another aspect of Piet's work is that his mixtures for larger areas are often of mingled groups of plants, of 5 to 11 individuals of each species (depending on the overall scale), so that the blend is in fact a blend of small groups.

Designers of the future will no doubt find ways of introducing greater visual richness and possibilities of future development into mixed plantings. In particular, decisions have to be made: whether to randomize, or to design mixes of small groups, or to go for small groups and individuals. Different decisions will be made for different plants and for different situations. Gardeners and designers are only at the very beginning of a whole new and immensely rich seam in planting design. Meanwhile we suggest that the thinking outlined in this book will help with this process.

ORDER AND SPONTANEITY

CREATIVE TENSIONS – BALANCING ORDER AND DISORDER

For the vast majority of garden history, gardening and landscape management have been about exerting order over nature. This was understandable in a world where nature was seen as all-powerful and not necessarily benevolent. Now, the feeling is that nature is very much in retreat in the face of an aggressive humanity – exerting order is no longer seen as always appropriate. Previous generations tended to be highly anthropocentric: to see humanity as central to the world, and therefore the imposition of what we see as beautiful or useful on to the natural world as entirely right. Now, we have come to realize that we are only a recently evolved species on an insignificant planet, and a scientific understanding of our surroundings has largely knocked us off our pedestal. While we still want our planted landscapes and gardens to conform to our ideas of beauty, we are far more prepared to accept what occurs naturally as visually pleasing. Indeed, earlier forms of imposing aesthetic order on nature are seen by some as unattractive; so highly rated now is natural as a virtue that simply describing them as unnatural implies they are undesirable.

The further away from a natural situation a planting is, the more work is required to maintain it – hence the need to clip hedges and topiary every year, and in the case of fast-growing plants, two or even three times a year. It is no surprise that so much gardening in the past was about clipping – it was, and still is, a way of showing that you were able to afford to pay people to do this work for you. It is also about control – we want to control nature and the garden is a place where we show it. The cost of maintaining plantings which emphasize human order, and a growing relaxation in our relationship with nature, are additional reasons for the greater tendency over time to appreciate the beauty of nature's apparent disorderliness.

The growth of interest in natural looking plantings has gone through several phases. Each of these has left a legacy of ideas about what is appropriate to call natural or not – sometimes these are contradictory. For example, the eighteenth-century English landscape garden introduced the idea (revolutionary at the time) that the straight line was not only unnecessary but undesirable. There is still strong resistance to straight lines among many who favor natural style gardening, yet an ecologist will point out that a bird does not mind if the tree in which it makes a nest is growing in a row of others or an informal cluster, and many designers will wax lyrical about how straight lines can add a sense of order and intention to otherwise wild-looking plantings.

In Britain, the Arts and Crafts garden tradition exemplified by Lawrence Johnstone's Hidcote (1907 onwards) and Harold Nicolson and Vita Sackville-West's Sissinghurst (1930 onwards) resolved a central contradiction for British gardeners, balancing their love of informal planting (mostly herbaceous perennials) with a continued hankering after formal garden features, now restricted to hedges, occasional topiary and garden structures. In the Netherlands, Mien Ruys (1904–1999) did something to achieve a modernist version of the same resolution of the conflict between formality and naturalism. For contemporary garden makers there is now a well-developed and richly nuanced range of possibilities for balancing the wildness of nature and the order of culture.

APPARENT DISORDER – THE PARADOX OF DESIGNING SPONTANEITY

The English landlords and their advisors who laid out landscapes with sinuous clumps of trees in the eighteenth century, and indeed all those who followed them, were trying to convince potential viewers, and almost certainly themselves, that what they were achieving looked natural. It is, of course, nothing of the sort, as nature would not tolerate the clear edges between woodland clumps and open grassland for very long, and would seek to clutter and blur them with seedling trees, shrubs and climbers, and eventually to reassert the wood over the grass. In addition, the clumps and their attendant lakes and fields were laid out to fit certain artistically derived ideas. Naturalism is so often a conceit.

Another naturalistic conceit, but on a different level, is the often spectacular plantings developed for garden shows in Germany from the 1980s onwards. These were laid out for one-off events but left behind quality planting for permanent public use. The designers were trying to create plantings which looked natural. They were in no sense pretending that they were imitating nature, but instead were seeking to group plants in such a way that the results had a natural look about them, and would no doubt convince many onlookers they were looking at something very much like the real thing. In the final analysis, though, decisions about which plants to group together, in what combinations and numbers, are aesthetic ones. The creators of what have come to be known as cottage gardens have achieved similar results, but through a completely different route. Margery Fish (1888–1969) and all those who have followed her in this genre had no illusions that they were creating anything 'natural' or indeed pseudo-natural. Their model was another conceit: that they were making something akin to what humble cottagers (rural laborers and their families) would make. Both traditions end up creating an apparently artless combination of plants which have proved highly popular. The spontaneity is, however, apparent rather than real.

The truth is that while much of humanity loves nature, people do not want it untrammeled in their gardens, parks or urban spaces. The stylized natures offered by the various cultures of planting design developed during the twentieth century are the most realistic ways out of this conundrum.

STATIC AND DYNAMIC PLANTINGS – MANAGING SPONTANEITY AND CHANGE

As combinations of living things, gardens will constantly change as they age. The traditional concept of the garden tended to be static – many of the planted features were clipped into shapes that recalled the masonry of the great houses of which they formed the surroundings; trees came and went on a cycle of several human generations – while ephemeral annuals and bulbs filled rigid parterres for a few months at a time. So for many gardens there were two extremes: an almost permanent architecture and short-lived seasonal planting, both requiring high levels of maintenance. Twentieth-century gardens reduced maintenance and formality by relying more on shrubs and perennials, which allowed for

greater leeway in maintenance. They could often almost be ignored for a few years, brought back to order with a blitz of pruning, weeding and dividing, refreshed with a few new plants, and then receive a few more years of relatively unimaginative maintenance. The result was often functional but rather lackluster gardens of slightly unmanaged looking shrubs and ever-expanding clumps of a few robust perennials.

Over time, plantings based largely on perennials will age. There are two main aspects to this: some species will die out, whereas others will spread, some by simply creeping out from their original planting space, others by self-seeding. Less-skilled maintenance often only removes weeds, and does not seriously address either of these issues. In addition, slow spread can creep up on garden owners, and before they know it, the goldenrod (in old gardens derivatives of *Solidago canadensis*) and Japanese anemones (*Anemone ×hybrida*) have taken over. The result is chiefly a loss of diversity. The issues of vegetative spread, self-seeding and plant death are looked at later on.

Perennials, and to some extent shrubs, have their own life cycles of growth and replacement and spontaneously self-seed between different parts of the garden. This dynamism has been played with cautiously for much of the twentieth century, but now with a better understanding of plant ecology gardeners and designers are in a stronger position to work with spontaneity rather than resist it as 'disorder' in the way our gardening ancestors did. A key problem remains, though, the tendency to lose species over time and so lose visual diversity.

How much is lost over time from a planting depends very much on what was planted originally, in particular whether long-lived and robust species were chosen or not. During the early years of the twentieth century, the selection of perennials was dominated by short-lived species or those which were not very persistent. In the latter part of the century these were replaced with more robust and naturally long-lived or persistent species, often less intensively hybridized. At the time of writing, older parts of the Oudolf garden at Hummelo have hardly had any replanting done since they were laid out 20–25 years ago.

How long do perennial plantings last? And – what should be done when they need restoration? Two types

It is not entirely true that species diversity in plantings declines over time. Sometimes, attractive and not-too-aggressive wild species may appear and add themselves to borders. One such is the early spring flowering *Cardamine pratensis* (shown here in close-up), especially on damp soils.
▼

Upright *Verbascum leichtlinii* is one of several species of a large genus of plants in a family (*Scrophulariaceae*) where a great many are either biennials or short-lived perennials. Survival is through scattering their plentiful seed to the wind from sturdy seedheads. Their advantage to gardeners is the spontaneity and naturalness of the way that they move themselves around the garden. Here, at Hummelo, in early June they flower alongside *Knautia macedonica* (deep red, foreground, a short-lived perennial). The combination of clipped yew hedge and self-seeding plants makes for a great expression of creative tension.
▼

of management can be envisaged: a low-key, relatively passive one, and a more active one, but which works very much with the naturally dynamic nature of the planting. A passive approach involves:
• weeding
• removal of the most vigorously self-seeding species
• annual cutting back of dead growth
• bringing the dominant plants back into the right proportion.

Even the best planned perennial-based planting will experience a decline in species diversity – highly persistent and the most vigorously self-seeding species will be the survivors. Cutting back annually and leaving the shredded debris as mulch or taking it away, composting it and returning it as mulch will keep nutrients recycled. Even if material is taken away and not returned, causing nutrients to decline slowly, growth will often continue to be very good for many years on many soils, as long-lived, persistent perennials do not have a great hunger for nutrients.

A more active involvement with the planting recognizes natural processes of death and rebirth: ecological processes, in other words. James Hitchmough and Nigel Dunnett at the University of Sheffield's innovative Department of Landscape refer to this as a 'dynamic planting'. Change and spontaneity are embraced. However, the planting will not look after itself. Engaging with a dynamic planting involves controlling and editing the

In the new perennial meadow in the Oudolf family garden at Hummelo in the Netherlands, perennials arise out of wild grasses and spontaneous flora, such as the wild chamomile (white flowers, foreground). Other species here are *Agastache nepetoides* (seedheads, left), *Aster* 'Little Carlow' (center), *Aster novae-angliae* 'Violetta' (right), and pink-red *Eupatorium maculatum* 'Riesenschirm' in the foreground, right.

Avenues are a traditional way of setting out landscape plants. A row of trees makes an effective backdrop to the apparent chaos of a late autumn border of grasses and perennials at Westerkade, Rotterdam.

outcomes of natural processes, steering the planting in a way which maintains or even enhances its appeal. We will look in more detail at how this can be done later. Key to managing a dynamic planting is understanding that perennials have a variety of life cycles.

However, even with the most skilled management, a point is reached when some sort of restoration becomes necessary. This is very difficult to predict, both because of the complexity of plant–environment interactions and because the perception of the planting is inevitably subjective. Ten years might be a good time if expectations and demands are high. What happens now? 'Restoring' is still favored by many, but this assumes a turning back: recreating how it was when first made. In the (for the sake of argument, ten years) since the planting was made, the following will have happened:

• It will have become obvious which species are problematic.
• New species and cultivars will become commercially available.
• Ideas about planting design will have changed.

Exact restoration will almost certainly be inappropriate, and will often seem undesirable. Renovation might be a better word. New cultivars and ideas need to be taken on board, so that the original plants live on alongside newcomers, and the planting reflects the passage of time.

THE CONTEXT FOR PLANTING

THE HUMAN AND DESIGN CONTEXT

Planting has to please people – as has been said before, people are part of the ecology too. The point has been made by others that in order for natural environments to be valued by humans they have to be liked – simply functional plantings which satisfy technical criteria for sustainability or biodiversity but do not satisfy human users are in the long run doomed, because nobody will care for them enough to campaign for them when they are threatened by other potential users on this over-crowded planet or simply through lack of care.

The role of the gardener or designer is clear, and arguably more important than ever: planting which serves a purpose has to look good too. As practitioners use plant combinations more and more to perform environmental services, it will become increasingly important that they look intentional and attractive.

Tidiness and presence are important issues, although often read very subjectively. In corporate or memorial plantings, even occasional seasonal scruffiness is un-acceptable. If there is no guarantee of labor to keep up standards, planting will have to be limited to species which can be kept acceptably tidy, although it is possible to include species which look unattractive post-flowering in large areas of mixed planting where there is enough structure to maintain the look of the whole. There is more scope for using less tidy-looking plants in more relaxed surroundings. This is an important point, as some of the most popular, easily propagated and re-silient perennials do look bad after flowering. Keeping such plants to no more than an absolute maximum of 30 percent is a good rule, but even so, for some situations where such plants may grow very well and flower for long periods, gardeners and designers may feel they want to use more. Some such plants, certain *Geranium* species in particular being a good example, are also very long-lived and effective ground cover and can be tempting to use in large quantities in low-maintenance situations. The addition of just a few distinctive structure plants, or others with a different (usually later) flowering time, can do much to lift such a planting beyond a

◄ and ►► (pages 42–43)
Bright colors are popular, and can be entirely compatible with naturalistic or functional planting. This is *Astilbe chinensis* var. *tacquetii* 'Purpurlanze' in July, a robust and long-lived perennial eminently suitable for drainage swales and other sustainable drainage plant-ings. Its winter seedheads (overleaf) have great value.

◄◄ (pages 44–45)
During 2011 the Serpentine Gallery, a venue for
contemporary art in London, hosted a Piet Oudolf
planting in a courtyard. For the majority of the
species used, the location would not have been
suitable in the long term, but a summer-long show
garden-type display was perfectly feasible. As with
flower-show gardens, plants were used at higher
densities than would be normal for a permanent
planting, but one advantage (as show garden
designers know only too well) is that the visual
experience is more intense than in the real garden –
this is, of course, useful in a venue such as this
where onlookers are at very close quarters to the
plants.

▶

Temporary plantings do not have to be composed
of garish annuals. Here, at the 2010 Venice Biennale,
is a rarity – an Oudolf annual composition of
Hordeum jubatum (wild barley) and dahlias.
It playfully evokes the spontaneous plant
communities of waste ground.

flat monoculture. Other possibilities are partial conceal-
ment by using them in drifts around more strongly
structural plants or placing them where they can be en-
joyed when they perform but do not detract from key
vistas. These plants can often be managed more intensively for a higher quality look in smaller spaces, and of
course in private gardens, where there is more possibility of managing them through seasonal cutting back.

CONTROL OVER NATURE? – FORMALITY AND MASS PLANTING

Formal planting – the use of geometry or clipping to
create unnatural forms – is widely seen as traditional.
There are, however, many possibilities for a more
contemporary approach. Novel forms of formality (such
as non-symmetric clipped woody plants or blocks of
ornamental grasses) are nowadays more likely to be
seen as appropriate in larger and grander contexts than
traditional, clipped and symmetric formality. Larger scale

settings or those which need to look imposing require
simple graphic qualities, which can be expressed
through some kind of monocultural planting. Traditional
materials like yew or beech can be given new life with
modernist-inspired geometries. Ornamental grasses are
the other great material for monocultural blocks, because
of their relatively long season of interest, adaptability,
longevity (for most species) and simplicity of form. An
added advantage is that they take less maintenance than
clipped foliage. Their disadvantage, vis-à-vis clipped
woody plants, is that they do not have the same level of
presence all through the year.

One of the great uses of any kind of mass planting
like this is that it can contrast so effectively with highly
complex and diverse plantings of perennials, giving
architecture and backbone to what would otherwise be
too visually soft-textured for some environments. It is
worth considering here the global success of the English
Arts and Crafts garden style. Fundamental to it is a balance between order and apparent disorder. Rather than

Molinia caerulea 'Dauerstrahl' in blocks. This is a native plant of acid soils across northern Europe, so its presence here in the Netherlands can be described as a novel use of a formal planting principle with a plant which actually relates to its landscape, much as previous generations might have had clipped hedges of native trees. This kind of simple, calm, ordered planting can be a good point of relaxation after an exuberant perennial-filled border – like the sorbet course in a gourmet meal.

relying on the old vocabulary of clipped woody plants, contemporary gardeners and designers should perhaps be looking at grass blocks to provide the structural part of the equation.

In corporate or monumental landscapes, simple blocks of woody plants with grasses may be all that is needed to create the atmosphere of calm, control and order. Where the general public is concerned, however, these words are more likely to have negative connotations, as many people have an expectation of planting providing life, vitality and color. Where the scale is large, as in public parks, it can be difficult for colorful and diverse planting to actually make much of an impact – or to rephrase this, there is rarely enough funding for plantings that really make an impact. The creators of randomized planting mixes and seed-sown perennial mixes (such as prairies) claim that their combinations can be maintained extensively – all plants attended to at once, mainly through mowing. This may well be the case, at least in some climate zones, but the concept is still too new for a long-term picture of their maintenance needs to be clearly understood. If maintenance can be kept low enough, then these plantings do genuinely offer an option for large-scale situations.

NATURE OVER CONTROL – MAKING WILD-LOOKING PLANTINGS

Those who wish the plantings they make or commission to look tidy and ordered – ebullient nature controlled and organized for the human eye – stand in the majority tradition of garden history. The more recent tradition, which I see Piet Oudolf and myself as part of, is about the opposite – how to create the sensation of nature, often in urban or suburban areas. As we know all too well, this does not mean letting things go by allowing natural processes to take over. When people say they want some nature, what they usually mean is a particular vision of nature, one that looks nice, fitting in to a distinctly human-centered idea of what nature is or

Graphic simplicity is given an added boost through autumn color. Here, *Rhus typhina*, a suckering shrub which can be restricted through coppicing, grows alongside *Calamagrostis* 'Karl Foerster', a grass which is extremely useful for minimalist or 'neo-formal' plantings because of its long season (early summer to late winter) and its weatherproof, upright habit.

A distinct feature of the garden at Hummelo is the big clump of the grass *Miscanthus sinensis* 'Malepartus' in a slightly raised position, seen here through a haze of the seedheads of another grass, *Molinia* 'Transparent'. The miscanthus block acts like a weight, a center of gravity for the garden as a whole, especially since it is more or less midway between two distinct areas of the garden, both dominated by looser perennial borders.

Wild and woolly, the High Line is dominated from late summer on by the seedheads of grasses – anything tidier here would look out of place next to the still scruffy areas of the urban jungle. The flash of orange-red is *Iris fulva*.

should look like. Biodiversity is important too (but not mosquitoes or snakes, of course!), and often locally native plants. 'Nature Lite' in other words. We must not be too cynical – not too long ago any idea of 'nature in the city' would have been anathema or at least incomprehensible to most people. The task for the gardener or designer is to create an enhanced nature (a term coined by Nigel Dunnett and James Hitchmough), one that supports an acceptable level of biodiversity and looks just a little bit wild. How can this be achieved?

• Use plant species which are recognizably native locally – even if in some cases they may be commercially selected cultivars.

• Use a far denser and more intermingled style of vegetation than has been conventional up to now – in particular, layered vegetation, open habitats dominated by grasses blended with perennials, woodland underplanting with a mix of species.

• Use plants which recognizably belong to a particular habitat – for example, grasses in expansive open spaces, ferns and evergreen ground-cover species on woodland floor. Note that these do not have to be locally native species.

• Create plant combinations which evoke wild habitats – such as water bodies edged with lush reedy and leafy vegetation, small shrubs and climbers occupying a mixed zone between woodland planting and open habitat.

• Allow an element of spontaneity – self-seeding and a sense that it is partly the plants that are in control.

• Have a wild or semi-natural background – the viewer can then be persuaded that there is a seamless link between the planting and the existing natural vegetation.

In a public setting much of the above is about getting people to read something subconsciously, and the people concerned will for the most part have very little real knowledge or experience of natural plant communities. What matters to them, what will convince them and enable them to read the designed planting as some kind of 'nature', is that it evokes the country park or nature reserve or state forest or wherever it is that urban and suburban people in a particular place experience nature. The New York High Line is a good recent example of this kind of planting. The world's oldest established and most extensive examples are the parks of Amstelveen in the Netherlands, dating back to the 1930s, where the planting is almost entirely native but is highly managed for a relatively neat appearance.

For homeowners who are only trying to convince themselves and their family and guests, the hardest task is probably to convince themselves that they have built and planted a microcosm of nature. Gardeners or others who are interested in nature and know their wildflowers may be hard to convince. Most who do succeed often mix natives with garden plants, and have cultivated the art of knowing how much to let go.

SIGNATURE PLANTING – DEVELOPING AN IDENTITY

The idea of signature is a strong one in the art world, the distinctive stamp of an artist or maker. Good garden designers have all developed a very strong signature, so that the knowledgeable could probably recognize one of their gardens if they were parachuted into one they had not seen before. Gardens too can develop a signature in the minds of those who visit them, because of some distinctive feature, or the use of a strong theme plant which is scattered throughout the garden.

While private gardeners who develop a theme for their garden which is endlessly admired and photographed by all who visit can sit back and pat themselves on the back, the problem for designers who develop a successful signature for a particular garden is that it becomes very difficult to reproduce elsewhere. The other problem is that everyone else copies you, and usually less successfully, perhaps even turning an innovation into a cliché.

Signature plantings are about making something that is site-specific and gives the garden or landscape a distinct personality which helps to make it memorable. This is clearly important for public landscapes, but home gardeners can try it too. One plant spread throughout a garden can make a real impact in the here-and-now but also in the memory of visitors. I have an immensely tall and narrow clone of *Eupatorium fistulo-*

sum, which grows to 3.4 meters high every year; visitors to the garden in the late summer to winter period inevitably remark on it, and even American visitors are impressed (it is a US native). Over the years it has become the most commented on plant in my garden, and I am sure the most remembered.

Signature plantings may be derived from several sources:

• Historical. Certain plants may be associated with a particular site or period associated with the site, or simply be historical plants in gardens, although usually these are woody plants, such as trees or species used in traditional hedging or topiary; *Liriope* and *Ophiopogon* species in the Far East are a herbaceous example. Radical new uses of these traditional (even clichéd) plants can make a strong impression.

• Locally native. There may be a desire to use certain species or plant communities which are part of the local scenery, so celebrating what is special to the region.

• Ecologically appropriate. Using quantities of a distinctive species which can be clearly linked to the site ecology. Examples include swathes of the very distinctive grass species which dominate many stressful environments, such as *Molinia caerulea* (poor acidic soils) or *Sporobolus heterolepis* (extreme Continental climates).

• Daring to innovate. New plants or familiar plants used in a new way. A new umbellifer in the show garden at the Chelsea Flower Show in London in 2010 designed by leading British designer Tom Stuart-Smith got everyone talking (*Cenolophium denudatum*). It was not in fact very different to many other members of the family currently used in gardens; the fact that it ran through the show garden and was used with great confidence made it a perfect signature plant.

The following Piet Oudolf projects exemplify what have become recognized as strong signatures in the garden and landscape press, or otherwise stand out for me as signature plantings.

Bury Court, Hampshire, UK, 1996

This stylized meadow originally used *Deschampsia cespitosa* interspersed with a small number of contrasting perennials. Widely agreed to be a good idea at the time, it was copied by several other designers, generally unsuccessfully. One problem is that the species can die prematurely on fertile soils, and some cultivars are

◄◄ (pages 52–53)
Piet's use of a grass matrix in plantings started
with what became a well-known new feature, the
Deschampsia meadow at Bury Court (1996).
The latest manifestation is a new planting on the
former nursery site at Hummelo. Created through
both planting and sowing, the species mix will
change from year to year. Tall grass *Calamagrostis*
'Karl Foerster' and the scarlet cultivar of *Helenium*
will be more or less permanent, but many other
shorter-lived species, such as the two color
forms of *Verbena hastata* and Dutch native daisy
Leucanthemum vulgare, will be dependent on
self-sowing for their continued existence here.

►

The double border at the RHS Garden, Wisley
(2001), where bands of intermingled perennials
create interesting combinations at all scales of
observation, from near to far. In mid- to late
summer *Perovskia atriplicifolia* dominates (right
above), counterposed with pink *Gaura lindheimeri*
'Siskiyou Pink' and the seedheads of *Phlomis tuberosa*
'Amazone', while in another band (right below)
gray-white *Eryngium yuccifolium* contrasts with
scarlet *Helenium* 'Rubinzwerg' and *Echinacea
purpurea*; some seedheads of *Allium hollandicum*
survive from an earlier phase of flower.

►

susceptible to fungal diseases and can suffer extensive dieback. *Deschampsia* has now been replaced by cultivars of *Molinia caerulea*, which, although also a plant of infertile soils, is longer lived across a wider range of habitats. This concept makes an impact in design terms and makes sense in management, and it can be emulated by using other grass species and therefore work in many different climate zones.

Conclusion – a signature might be a very good concept, but needs to be adaptable to be effective long term.

Royal Horticultural Society Garden, Wisley, Surrey, UK, 2001

Thirty-three bands of intermingled perennials and grasses, each of equal size, line either side of a straight grass walkway. Looking very formal and rigid on paper, it is anything but in practice. A good example of a simple design concept which underlies an entire scheme, but largely succeeds in hiding itself so that perhaps comparatively few people have really understood it.

Conclusion – strong signatures are sometimes almost invisible, operating on the level of the subconcious.

Dream Park, Enköping, Sweden, 1996 and 2003

The Salvia River is a band of three violet-blue cultivars of European origin. The public loved it – it had impact and the photogenic 'wow' factor that commissioners of such projects always want. Something so simple and dramatic is very hard to repeat, but Piet did so in the Lurie Garden in Chicago; as he describes it, 'It was one of the few times that I really copied myself, it had to do with the graphical quality of the concept, it had to be seen from the surrounding skyscrapers.' No one else has yet copied it or tried to achieve it using other species. One of the problems in doing so is that most colorful perennials in a low to medium height range have poor structure post-flowering (the salvias just look a bit dull, and can be cut back to repeat flower later).

Conclusion – there is always a danger that very strong signatures will be copied, but it is a risk worth taking.

County Cork garden, Ireland, 2006

Stipa gigantea is a tall and expansive but at the same time very light and transparent grass. Piet used it in gardens back in the 1980s and early 1990s, but when everyone started using it, he gave up on it. Here, however, just a few are used to spectacular effect; at a latitude of 51 degrees north, early morning and late afternoon sunlight striking this grass illuminates it to dramatic effect in this open site.

Conclusion – clichés *can* be challenged.

Oudolf garden, Hummelo, the Netherlands, 1982 onwards

The multiple curtains of yew at the rear of the main garden area at Piet and Anja's own garden became, in that much overused word, iconic. In the end, though, they succumbed to the forces of nature in the form of flooding which led to phytophthora disease and dieback, so early in 2011 they were removed and fed dramatically into a chipper. Piet phlegmatically accepted that it was in danger of becoming a cliché.

Conclusion – icons sometimes need iconoclasts.

The High Line, New York City, USA, 2009 onwards

It is perhaps the grasses on the High Line which make it so distinctive. Originally (that is, as an abandoned freight rail line), grasses were part of a rich species mix, so using them was part of the design intent to keep a strong sense of the original spontaneous planting. They certainly make the High Line the most naturalistic Oudolf planting so far, and add hugely to its character. Part of the appeal of the High Line is that it is so successfully brings nature into the city – the grasses are crucial for this.

Conclusion – signature plants can be very useful for evoking atmosphere, so long as the vast majority of viewers can read them.

Scampston Hall, Yorkshire, UK, 1999

A relatively low-growing combination of plants makes the most of a poor soil, in a place which can get cold winters and is on the drier side of England. It is the kind of planting, like Beth Chatto's in Essex, which fits plants to habitat. Colorful and rich in textures, it makes the best of its lean look. A dramatic use of waves of a *Molinia* grass variety is another play with a simple modernist-formal feature.

Conclusion – poor soil and less than perfect conditions can be reflected in planting in a positive way which helps to create a sense of identity.

◄◄ (pages 56–57)
Bands of *Molinia caerulea* 'Poul Petersen' at
Scampston Hall in Yorkshire, northern England,
were designed in 1999 but retain their freshness
as a design feature, powerfully emphasizing the
potential of grasses as material for contemporary
formal structure.

►

The rear hedges of yew (*Taxus baccata*) at Hummelo
(above right) became one of its best-known
features. A classical material and idiom, their
asymmetric cut and modernist flair deservedly
made them a contemporary garden design icon.
After their removal (below right), the garden is
defined by a mix of hedging – a clipped but informal
version of a traditional mixed farm hedge (on the
left here) and more formally clipped beech hedging
at the rear (only just visible).

►

Part of the Salvia River in Chicago's Lurie Garden, where a mix of early summer flowering *Salvia* cultivars are used to dramatic effect: *S.* ×*sylvestris* 'Mainacht' ('May Night'), 'Blauhügel' ('Blue Hill') and 'Rügen', and *S. nemorosa* 'Wesuwe'. The grasses are mostly *Sporobolus heterolepis*.

▶▶ (pages 60–61)
Stipa gigantea needs to be positioned right to be fully appreciated, even more than other grasses. Arguably, it is more successful at higher latitudes where side or back lighting illuminates it more effectively – this garden is in western Ireland. The deep blue to the left is *Agastache* 'Blue Fortune'.

FROM NEAR TO FAR – COMPLEXITY AND SCALE

Intermingled planting styles offer complexity and diversity. But how easily is this read by the viewer? Is there not a danger that it just looks like a chaotic mush? Much must depend on the plants used in it. There is a clear need for structural plants, as relying on color alone risks the planting dissolving into amorphousness once the flowers die. More fundamentally, though, what does the eye see at different scales? It is important to stress here that there is a difference between random complexity and designed complexity.

On a large scale, there is the phenomenon of seeing the wood not the trees: viewing a mixed planting as a vegetation, as a community, not the individual plants in it – one reads only the patterns. What in fact is a highly complex mixture becomes resolved into a unified whole that is greater than the sum of the parts. Within this whole, individual placing does not matter, and randomization works as well as anything else. If it can be seen to work in the long term, this tendency suggests that the mixed planting style has a great future for use in large spaces. In smaller or more intimate spaces, the very randomness of the mix lets it down. As the scale gets reduced, so the importance of limited key spaces within sight becomes greater. What occupies those spaces is too important to be left to chance. Blending and intermingling varieties is possible, but they need to be much more precisely placed. As far as individual plant placement is concerned, control over exact location becomes more important the smaller the planting. At this level, layering becomes of greater importance than at larger scales. If there are plants at different heights within the planting with varying habits – upright, clump-forming, ground-hugging, sprawling – plenty of scope exists for creating rich visual interest.

The distance from which we view a planting makes all the difference in our perception of its scale. Have you ever seen a wildflower meadow from the air? No. Because at that height the flowers blur into the grass and it becomes a green whole. In the garden, some plants sink into insignificance at certain distances, not just because they are small, but because they lack outstanding color or form. Others can make an impact at a distance, but only if grouped, whereas some stand out as individuals.

PLANTING AND SUSTAINABILITY

Sustainability has become a key concept but also a much-abused one, partly because it has become heavily politicized on the one hand and reduced almost to a cliché on the other. It is generally understood as meaning reducing inputs of non-renewable resources and harmful outputs. Like so much else, it is best seen as part of a gradient. Passive sustainability can be understood as not doing actual harm through causing pollution or CO_2 emissions and over-exploitation of resources.

Active sustainability can be thought of as to do with not just minimizing harm to the wider environment, but actively managing and improving it through some of the methods discussed in the Introduction: green roofs, rain gardens, biofiltration. These fields are all quite specialist, but can use the kind of diverse herbaceous vegetation highlighted here very effectively. The input of gardeners and designers into such active systems is to provide the aesthetic dimension. Plant selection has fundamentally to serve certain functions, based on a knowledge of plant physiology, best understood by ap-

propriate specialists. However, leaving plant selection entirely with technicians rarely achieves the most aesthetically pleasing results, and gardeners and designers have a role to play in working with plant lists provided by the specialists.

BIODIVERSITY AND THE NEEDS OF NATURE

Whereas once the needs of wildlife were not recognized, contemporary expectations are that planting should support some part of the web of nature. The good news is that providing for biodiversity is not difficult – in fact, many gardeners were doing this long before the word was even invented. To summarize some of the scientific work on the issue, the most important aspects of planting design for animal diversity are a range of habitats, such as is provided by a combination of trees, shrubs, perennials and ground-cover vegetation, and – crucially – connections between habitats.

Wilderness in the city – this is an area of the High Line in October. A variety of seedheads provides food for birds and small mammals. A high percentage of native species will help support those specialist invertebrates which will only eat specific plants. The brown grass on the right is *Chasmanthium latifolium*, a relatively shade-tolerant North American species.

Promoting diverse perennial vegetation which stands over a long season is a good start, with woody plants and tree cover also having an important part to play. The use of regionally native plants may help but is not absolutely vital.

Nature thrives on diversity, and so it should come as no surprise that the intermingled planting approach has enormous potential for supporting biodiversity. It is not that conventional block planting is necessarily deleterious, but the possibilities for improving resources for biodiversity are greatly improved with more diverse intermingled plantings.

SECOND GUESSING THE FUTURE – CLIMATE CHANGE AND DIVERSITY

We live at a time when the impact of possible climate change hangs over us like a threatening thunder cloud. The garden and landscape world has, with agriculture, a part to play not only in reacting to climate change but also in its mitigation.

Climate change is often mistakenly described as 'global warming'. A two-decade run of mild winters in north-west Europe led to much complacent planting of warmer climate species during this period: there was almost a sense of some gardeners even relishing a new warmer climate and the ability to pick their own olives and pomegranates. At the time of writing this region has experienced a run of cold winters, and climate experts now say that climate change may lead to colder winters here. The gardens of the English Midlands are full of dead *Eucalyptus, Cordyline* and *Phormium*. The one certainty about climate change seems to be greater uncertainty – the prospect of more extreme weather. We need resilient plants.

Fortunately, there are a great many resilient plants, and we already garden with quite a few. There is more scope for not only making new introductions from the wild but introducing a wider genepool of the species already in cultivation. Many of the plants relied on are descended from one single introduction, and may be quite unrepresentative of the species as a whole. We could be missing out on forms which are not only distinct in visual terms but able to cope with different or more extreme environmental stresses. *Astrantia major* is a species common in central Europe; new seed collections and therefore new genetic material for cultivation can be made by driving into a layby in Austria and leaning out of the car window – not surprisingly, there is a considerable range of color and vigor of the species in cultivation. *Phlomis russeliana* is another perennial which in cultivation shows almost no variation whatever, despite being an extremely useful plant, particularly for plantings requiring very low levels of maintenance. Introducing new genetic material from the wild would require more planning and more effort, and traveling further away from the localities where the plant would most likely be used. It may well come about that up and-coming growers in *Phlomis's* native Turkey will eventually make these collections. We need to create plantings resilient to changing weather patterns by making far more effective use of nature's bounty of diversity.

There is one further aspect to the importance of genetic diversity among cultivated plants – diversity can increase resilience in plant populations which are dynamic and self-replicating through self-seeding. Currently, professional planting design assumes that the plants used will be permanent. Private gardeners recognize that the seeding of short-lived perennials or biennials can play an important part in the appeal of their plantings. The acceptance of a dynamic element in larger or public plantings implies self-sowing and a natural process of plant replacement. This is particularly likely to be seen as desirable in randomly mixed plantings. A planting where self-seeding is happening involves a reshuffling of genes and so the appearance of seedlings ever so slightly different to their parents. Some of the seedlings will be better able to cope with the extremes of weather than their parents, and so, through being dynamic, the planting will be able to adapt over time in the way that a natural plant community does. In theory! In practice, most elements will be so long-lived that any change will happen on a time scale far too long to be meaningful. However, this process of adaptation over time (which, incidentally, beautifully illustrates Darwin's theory of evolution) can make a real impact for shorter lived species or those which readily self-seed.

A good example of the potential for Darwinian natural selection to make a meaningful impact on gardens is provided by the South African genus *Dierama*, a member of the Iris family (*Iridaceae*) of great beauty, which commonly thrives and enthusiastically self-sows in gardens

Preparing for climate change should arguably be about selecting plants which survive multiple stresses. A good reference habitat is the steppe of eastern Europe and central Asia with its cold winters and dry summers – analagous to short-grass prairie and sagebrush country. An advantage of many steppe and other drought-tolerant species is attractive silver-gray foliage, such as *Artemisia pontica* here. The yellow is *Euphorbia seguieriana* subsp. *niciciana*. The yellow-green grass foliage is *Sesleria autumnalis*, the pale grass spikes *Melica ciliata*, and the very long silvery grass heads are a form of *Stipa pulcherrima* – this magical effect is unfortunately short-lived. This is early summer.

65

on north-west Europe's Atlantic rim. The plants are variably hardy, but naturally grow in dry-winter climates, adding to the complexity of their response to cold weather. A run of cold winters can have a real winnowing effect on a plant population, with survivors flourishing and reproducing, non-survivors (and their genes) making their way to the compost heap. The result within a garden can be a reliably hardy and resilient population of a beautiful and elegant plant.

Much planting design practice to date has relied on genetically identical plants – cultivars. Cultivars are favored by gardeners and designers because of their consistency, yet they have disadvantages. That clones or extensively grown varieties with narrow genepools are susceptible to the spread of disease is well established in agriculture, especially after the USA nearly lost most of its corn crop in 1968. In addition, some cultivars will not self-seed because of a natural tendency for many perennials to 'out-breed': they will not self-seed unless there is genetic difference between the prospective parents. Even if they do produce viable seed, the genepool of a population of seedlings from a cultivar will be restricted. A more 'natural' varied population will have within it a much wider range of genes, with all this implies for a greater adaptability. Again, *Dierama* offers a good example, as several species are in cultivation and they crossbreed very easily; the result is a range of genetic diversity from which cold winters can select a strain which will survive long term.

THINKING THROUGH RESOURCES – SUSTAINABILITY QUESTIONS

Another major issue raised by sustainability is that of resource use – essentially a complex of issues comprising the exploitation of non-renewable resources, including those for energy production, and the generation of CO_2 and other pollutants through transport and other energy-consuming activities connected with garden and landscape construction and maintenance. Perennial planting almost by definition looks to the long term, and is therefore less resource hungry than traditional seasonal bedding. Little auditing has been carried out, but it is likely that the continual use of mowing machinery for keeping turf grass short involves greater resource consumption and CO_2 output than the maintenance of

perennial plantings. The creation of perennial plantings can involve considerable resources, and this is the main area where we all need to look closely at sustainability issues. Consideration of these issues needs to be carried out objectively and on the basis of evidence; sustainability and other environmental issues are notoriously political, and much decision-making by both private individuals and institutions is carried out in an atmosphere clouded by emotive and ideological considerations – the British debate over the use of peat in potting composts is a good example of this.

The horticulture industry used to be notably insensitive to resource use. Plastic pots and other containers that cannot be recycled, energy for heating and lighting propagation facilities, and compost all gobble up resources and require physical materials and energy for their production and crucially their transport. Over recent years great strides have been made: reusable or recyclable containers, the widespread use of composted green waste for potting and soil improvement and of slow-release fertilizers which reduce the wastage of nutrients, and much more. However, there is one tendency which still needs questioning – the size of plants in new projects. It is accepted that small plants usually establish better and more quickly than large ones. Yet, so many new planting schemes, both private and public, involve the purchase of container-grown plants far larger than would have been traditionally used. Moreover, these plants often travel long distances from nursery to site. So, two issues have come together which massively increase the embodied energy of many commercially grown plants. Every perennial in a two-liter pot as opposed to a half-liter one weighs four times as much and takes up about four times the space in a delivery truck; delivery from a nursery 400 kilometers away uses four times as much fuel as from one 100 kilometers away. Do the math!

The case for using small plants is easily made for perennials, which tend to grow quickly, but is less easily made for woody plants. Many design professionals are under pressure from clients for quick results (those spending public money are often worse than private), and it can be difficult to resist. What can clinch the argument is pointing out that small woody plants often catch up with larger ones in a few years, such is their superior ability to adapt and make the best of new

On the High Line, regionally native plants make an impact. Fine, blue-gray grass at the centre *Schizachyrium scoparium* 'The Blues' with *Bouteloua curtipendula* (the grass with fine, one-sided seedheads), yellow *Rudbeckia subtomentosa* and in the background *Vernonia noveboracensis*. All of these are now well established in cultivation.

The days of automatically cutting down dead perennial growth in the autumn are long gone. Most gardeners and those involved in plant management are now familiar with the idea that seedheads feed birds and may harbor a variety of invertebrates too. The idea that the city can be a habitat is widely accepted in the industrialized world. It is also worth pointing out the value of misty weather adding a sense of drama to combinations of tall perennials, such as this *Angelica gigas* on the Westerkade in Rotterdam.

Early autumn at Hummelo with the lush perennials and grasses which create so much of the distinctive character of this time of year. Grass *Molinia caerulea* 'Transparent' with pink *Eupatorium maculatum* 'Riesenschirm', the tiny red heads of *Sanguisorba* 'Bury Court', white *Persicaria amplexicaulis* 'Alba' and yellow *Solidago ×luteus* 'Lemore'.

◄◄ (pages 70–71)
Regionally native plants bring nature and a hint of the wilderness to the High Line in early autumn. *Rhus typhina* is already changing color, as the flower-heads of *Eupatorium hyssopifolium* repeat down the line. *Aster oblongifolius* 'Raydon's Favorite' is just visible – an example of an increasing trend in naming cultivars of native plants.

Plants in designed landscapes may even play a role in conservation. The graphic qualities of the royal fern (*Osmunda regalis*) are used here in a private garden (Dyffryn Fernant, Pembrokeshire, Wales), creating visual weight amongst a mass of finer foliage. This species is now very rare in the wild but extremely long-lived, making it a good landscape plant.

▼

circumstances. It is also worth remembering that large (and therefore expensive) plants are high risk – they are more prone to wind damage and drying out, and so large initial investments are more likely to be lost than small ones. Small plants are not only more sustainable, but a safer investment too!

NATIVES AND EXOTICS – THE DEBATE CONTINUES

The long standing debate over the role of native and exotic (introduced) species continues, with an unfortunate tendency toward adopting entrenched positions in some countries (such as the USA) or arousing little interest in others (Japan). The key issue is the role of plants in gardens and designed landscapes to contribute to biodiversity by supporting food webs of insects, birds and other wild animals. It is worth noting the positions adopted by leading practitioners working in planting design. There does seem to be a consensus that using only native species is entirely appropriate in certain environments – chiefly rural ones or where the conservation of local and indigenous biodiversity is a priority. In many other situations, planting in the past would have used mostly or entirely non-native species, but now involves a larger proportion of natives.

The strictly nativist lobby, which believes in the exclusive use of regional natives, is not one which has arisen from within the garden and landscape communities, but rather has been imported from outside, from the world of environmentalist politics, where ecology is a word which can often weave dangerously between the evidence-based and scientific and the emotive and ideological. Unfortunately, the native plant lobby has on occasion acquired sufficient political support in some communities that the use of native plants has been mandated for landscaping projects, compromising their visual effectiveness and therefore the public support they receive.

Piet Oudolf's work at the Lurie Garden in Chicago and the New York High Line provides an example of synthesis which many in the profession would agree with. He chooses plants because they perform a function and meet certain visual criteria. In these two projects over half the plants used are natives of their region. One of the criteria for both commissions was that the planting should reflect something of the regional natural environment: in the case of the High Line, this being the plant community which had established on the elevated rail line prior to restoration. A large proportion of natives was therefore essential. Crucially, though, the plants selected highlight just how good in design terms many of the plants in these regional floras are – a great number of species with garden and landscape potential have been largely ignored up until now. This is perhaps the most crucial point here – that prior to the current wave of interest in native plants, the nursery industry produced and sold what was beginning to look like a global flora of easy to use, easy to propagate plants. In the case of plants used by the landscape industry, they may have been different from one climate to another, but the effect was the same – too often both architecture and planting could be anywhere. The use of a proportion of locally native plants can do much to add a distinct signature to projects.

The native/exotic debate is complex, and here we will consider a range of points, some of which are more relevant to some localities than others.

• The issues are different from place to place, often very different. Take two island groups: the British Isles and New Zealand. The former has a very limited flora, with whatever managed to get across after the last ice age before the land bridge with the mainland was flooded by rising sea levels; the plant-eating invertebrate fauna at the base of the food web is largely generalist, and relatively few are totally dependent on native plant species. The local grass flora has a tendency to dominate – hugely reducing the ability of introduced species to spread. New Zealand also has a limited flora and fauna but one which has evolved in isolation and is extremely vulnerable to introduced plants, many of which have become invasive (the native flora possibly lacking its own vigorous pioneer species).

• Native plants are often a hugely underexploited design resource. The globalized garden and landscape flora alluded to above offers limited options. A walk in any natural habitat will reveal plants with ornamental or amenity potential, but they need to be brought into cultivation and evaluated for their visual and commercial potential, which takes time and effort. Increasingly, gardeners, nurseries and designers are realizing this, and undertaking this 'close to home' plant hunting. Even in

A meadow of the US native grass *Sporobolus heterolepis* in a garden on Nantucket Island, Massachusetts, includes *Echinacea purpurea*, a species which has become something of a poster boy for promoting native plants. It is important that planting schemes for biodiversity combine species which really support wildlife effectively as well as those which simply look good and tick the 'native' box.

Britain, with its restricted flora and long garden history, we are still learning to exploit the ornamental potential of our wildflowers – look at *Stachys officinalis*, almost unknown as an ornamental twenty years ago.

• Native plants enhance a sense of regional distinctiveness. Cultures sometimes want to emphasize their superiority by using 'civilized' plants. Hence the scandal when, in one of the rare iconic single actions in garden and landscape history, Roberto Burle Marx planted local plants in a public square in Recife, Brazil, in 1945. Nowadays the zeitgeist has moved toward celebration of the local and the regionally distinctive, about what sets a place apart and gives it its identity in the world. Locally native plants clearly have an important role to play here.

• The idea that exotic equals potentially invasive has no factual basis. What makes a plant an invasive alien is a question which ecologists continue to argue about. The reality is that of all the plants introduced into one country from another, only a few go feral and spread. The more dogmatic plant-nativists tend to tar all exotics with the same brush. Having said this, the nursery trade does have a responsibility to assess new plants for their ability to spread.

• Some native plants play a crucial role in local biodiversity webs, but this does not mean that exotic plants do not have any wildlife value. The food web which supports larger animals (mostly birds) is founded on invertebrates, chiefly insects. In many regions these are predominantly specialists – their larvae will *only* eat particular plants; a garden of introduced species will therefore support very few of them and thus greatly impoverish the food web. However, most other animals are more generalist: nectar-drinking insects such as bees are not tied to native species in this way, and neither are berry-eating birds. Adding species to a locality through planting may actually improve the richness of the food web by providing nectar sources for bees at a time when the native flora has little to offer.

• Planting design is at least as important in supporting biodiversity as the species chosen. Research work undertaken in Britain at the BUGS project (Biodiversity in Urban Gardens) has shown that the most important factors in improving biodiversity are not the species used but the diversity of habitat. Trees, some shrubs, perennials, ground cover, and connectivity between different plant layers are what matter. And, a diversity of species.

• Planting design is, fundamentally, for people. In urban areas, planting in private gardens or public spaces is about providing a habitat for people. Anything which fails to interest or please them will lose support, as local governments that have created untidy 'wildlife areas' in parks have found out to their cost. In regions where poisonous spiders and snakes are common, there may be good reasons to actually fear such places! Areas for nature have to be seen to be attractive or in some way valued by people; only then will they gain political support. Using introduced species to provide interest for human users of landscape is one way to do this; very often non-gardening users of public spaces will find it easier to 'read' a planting if some familiar cultivated plants are included.

• There is plenty of room for both natives and exotics. Gardens, parks and areas of land around offices, malls, airports and road systems take up a lot of space on our crowded planet. Add up all the space which is currently mown, and which does not actually need to be 20 millimeter high grass, and the total will be huge. Globally it would probably be the equivalent of a modest-sized European country. There is plenty of space for both natives *and* exotics.

TWO

GROUPING PLANTS

How plants are grouped plays a major role in how they are seen and appreciated.

It makes sense to start with what happens in nature, and then look at how plants have

been grouped historically in gardens. Finally, we will consider the plant grouping systems

which Piet Oudolf has used in his work since the mid-2000s.

NATURAL ENVIRONMENTS

When we look at a natural environment it is a snapshot in time. Come back ten years later and it could be very different. Despite the timeless feel to many natural environments, they are all in a state of constant change and flux – ecological science now tells us that there is no balance of nature, but only a constant ebb and flow of species. This is particularly true of the many environments we are familiar with which are not really natural but semi-natural, such as meadows, where an annual cut for hay prevents trees and shrubs from growing, or even prairies, many of which were historically maintained by the burning practiced by Native Americans. Such environments are inherently unstable, and only constant human input maintains their particular range of plant life.

A good place to start is with an observation experiment. Look at a meadow (or indeed grassland managed for pasture) or prairie, and then compare it with a garden planting of perennials. What are the differences?

◄ A public park, Potters Fields in London.

GARDEN PLANTING	MEADOW OR PRAIRIE
Usually fewer than ten plants per square meter	Hundreds of plants per square meter
Usually one to five species per square meter	Up to 50 species per square meter
Individuals of a species often in groups	Individuals of species present, usually intensely intermingled
Almost all plant varieties present chosen for distinct aesthetic value	Plant community usually composed of dominant species (usually grasses or grass-like plants) – these species act as a matrix, together with smaller numbers of other species
Bare earth or ground-covering mulch often visible	Bare earth almost never present

We should point out here that meadows and prairies are maintained extensively – everything has to be treated as one, and there is no possibility of maintaining individual plants – whereas in a conventional garden or landscape planting, individuals are often treated differently. Thinking about these differences purely in design terms, what are the implications?

• A meadow or prairie lacks order, and plants often appear to be randomly distributed.

• A meadow lacks much graphic quality or structure, but instead appears fine-textured and diffuse, although a few prairie and dry meadow habitats contain species with a strong long-term structure as individuals.

• A meadow can look untidy after flowering, as it is almost impossible to maintain individual plants.

• A garden planting can only fit in so much to a unit area, which can make continual seasonal interest difficult.

• A garden planting can seem a restricted canvas, with little scope for repetition.

Clearly, there are advantages and disadvantages to the look of the meadow/prairie. Traditionally, garden design has largely disregarded the meadow as a garden feature, but more recent thinking has made many of us more aware of some of its aesthetic advantages. It is these which have encouraged a new generation of gardeners and designers to reconsider the more diffuse beauty of the meadow and other grasslands.

Meadows and prairies are among many types of habitat where one species – or more usually one category – dominates, often grasses or grass-like plants, but with a large number of other species present in much smaller numbers. The whole forms a rich community, but in looking at it most of us tend to notice the highly visual minority element (the flowering perennials and occasional shrubs) rather than the dominant matrix of grasses which appear as a background. These type of habitats are actually very complex, with many species distributed through space with a high level of intermingling.

Thinking of other natural environments, what other types of plant grouping are there? At the opposite extreme to the meadow look are environments where one species appears to almost completely dominate. A good example is marshland colonized by reed (*Phalaris arundinacea*) or reedmace (cattails in North America, *Typha latifolia*), which are almost as much a monoculture as a field of maize or wheat. Between them are situations where plants form distinct patches, often intermingled with smaller species, for example in heathland with species of heather such as *Calluna vulgaris* and bilberry (*Vaccinium myrtillus*).

Astilbe 'Visions in Pink' is part of an intermingled plant mix on New York City's High Line. Repetition in a matrix of other plants evokes the repetition of plants in wild habitats.

PLANT GROUPING IN GARDEN HISTORY

During the nineteenth century summer bedding plants were grown in complex, often geometric and regular, patterns. At the turn of the nineteenth and twentieth centuries this style began to be applied to perennials as well, with the development of a style where plants were grown intermingled in strips, with each strip being repeated at regular intervals. Nowadays this is very rarely seen done with perennials, although it has been revived in France and Germany for temporary summer plantings dominated by annuals.

Planting in groups of a mass of individuals of the same species or cultivar dominated planting in the twentieth century – we shall refer to this as block planting. The British designer Gertrude Jekyll promoted the use of elongated blocks, called drifts, which had the effect of changing the way plants were seen as the viewer walked along. The Brazilian Roberto Burle Marx, an artist by training, 'painted' with plants on a vast and dramatic scale, juxtaposing large blocks of strongly contrasting plants. Somewhat influenced by him have been the American partnership of James van Sweden and Wolfgang Oehme, who have also made effective use of large single-species blocks. For much of the century, however, block planting of a rather unquestioning and often lacklustre kind held sway, with countless landscape projects setting out plants, both perennials and small shrubs, in similar-sized blocks. Even in private gardens, block planting – at least where space allowed – held sway.

With the rise in interest in naturalistic planting, two developments have arisen which aim at a more thorough detailing of plant groupings. One is the randomization approach, which is derived from the almost-random effect of sowing a wildflower meadow from seed.

The other is the work of the German researchers Richard Hansen and Friedrich Stahl, who from the 1960s onwards developed a highly structured approach which aimed at a stylized representation of natural plant communities. Hansen and Stahl recognized five categories based on structural interest and level of grouping: theme plants, companion plants, solitary plants, ground-cover plants and scatter plants.

The selection of plants for Piet Oudolf's planting style has similarities to the Hansen and Stahl style. In particular, both he and they recommend that plantings comprise about 70 percent structural plants (those which maintain distinct visual structure for most of the growing season) and 30 percent filler plants (often rather formless, grown mostly for early season color).

The Hansen and Stahl approach is extremely useful, but is in danger of becoming formulaic. What is distinctive about the Oudolf design style is its constant evolution, at the core of which is now the intermingling of plant varieties.

A reaction against single-species block planting began around the end of the twentieth century. The movement toward planting for biodiversity was expressed through a growing interest in sowing wildflower mixes and in ecology more generally. In the UK, Netherlands and Germany more sophisticated and naturalistic approaches to putting perennials together were established. When we talk about breaking the rules, the rule that individuals of each variety have to be clumped together in blocks is the first one to be broken.

WOODY PLANTS

Conventional planting has relied very heavily on woody plants – not surprisingly, since they make a major impact on the landscape and the majority are very long-lived. In conjunction with perennials, they will inevitably change the growing conditions beneath them, making the ground layer suitable only for shade-tolerant species. The mixed border, beloved by British amateur gardeners, is a small-scale example of the possibilities for combining shrubs and perennials (and indeed also annuals, bulbs and climbers), but given its scale, and the

fact that these borders are often against a backdrop, it does often rather mean that the shrubs dominate – visually and ecologically. Larger scale and visually more innovative combinations of shrubs or small trees and perennials may allow more space for perennials.

One simple innovation which can make a great impact on many different scales is the shaping of hedges. Instead of cutting hedges straight, the individual plants in them can be given curves, so that each one stands out as an individual. This works particularly well with

---

ABILITY TO REGENERATE

NON-EXISTENT → LIMITED → INCREASINGLY PROLIFIC → SUCKERING

| *Picea* spruce | *Quercus* oak | *Salix* willow | *Corylus avellana* hazel | *Aesculus parviflora* bottlebrush buckeye | *Rhus* sumac |

The ability of woody plants to regenerate from cutting lies on a gradient, at one end of which there is no ability to regenerate from cutting back to the base, and at the other a strong tendency to produce suckers without any cutting back of the main trunk.

Large shrubs can be kept to a reasonable size by occasional cutting back to the base (coppicing). Frequent cutting back stimulates suckering, which can create an interesting effect. This technique can be applied to some familiar plants such as *Cotinus coggygria* (shown here) and the staghorn sumac (*Rhus typhina*) to limit their height and encourage suckers. It is, however, easy to pull out and keep the forest down to a small colony of variously sized individuals. It is used on the High Line, and since this plant is so familiar to semi-natural woodland-edge habitats, including North American highway verges, its appearance can be a very effective way of saying 'natural', even two stories up in New York City.

mixed hedges, where the individuality given to the plant by its own cut is reinforced by its size relative to the others and its characteristic foliage color and texture. Hedges cut like this help to merge it, and the garden it contains, into wider rural landscapes, or indeed any landscape where trees are part of the wider view.

REGENERATION CUTTING

Trees and shrubs vary widely in their ability to regenerate, which has implications for their management and their design use. Cutting a tree down, for example, may not be the end of the tree; this will kill nearly all conifers, but most deciduous trees will grow back with multiple shoots, a technique which is made use of in the traditional woodland management technique of coppicing. Many shrubs regenerate themselves constantly from the

base – as old stems become senescent and deteriorate, vigorous young shoots emerge, growing straight up and eventually replacing the previous generations. The result is often a formless and tangled mass, but cutting back to base will result in a cleaner, more upright shape developing.

Some woody plants can spread through underground runners like many perennials, an example being the North American bottlebrush buckeye (*Aesculus parviflora*), forming large clumps. Species of *Rhus* are notorious among gardeners for suckering, but only after a period of existing as a deceptively tame-looking single-trunk tree. By cutting back every year or every other year, *Rhus* can be kept relatively small, sending up odd suckering shoots and creating the impression of a woodland-edge habitat with young trees merging with perennials and ground-covering plants.

A HIERARCHY OF PLANTING:
PRIMARY PLANTS, MATRIX PLANTS AND SCATTER PLANTS

Take a quick look at a wild plant community such as a meadow, and you soon realize that you are not really seeing the plants. Our eyes tend first of all to be drawn to brightly colored flowers, and then to strong structures. The longer we look the more we see: more subtle colors, interesting shapes, juxtapositions and combinations. Repetition of key elements makes a big impact, with low-key features more likely to break through into our consciousness if they are extensively repeated – who notices a single white daisy in a field? But if it is repeated 100,000 times, then it will dominate all else. There is a good case for recognizing the importance of 'immediate impact' species in a planting – those which stand out and make the most impact.

Still looking at our wild plant community in early to mid-summer, if we try to disregard the most obvious plants, what else is there? There are quietly colored species, often with cream or buff flowers, and of course plants which do not have either strong colors or distinct structures, such as grasses. Finally, there is the inevitable fact that the vast majority of what we are looking at is foliage: green, undistinguished, background.

Compare a natural plant community with a garden planting. The latter is almost inevitably going to have more concentrated visual impact. But how much more? And how is this visual impact distributed, and what relationship does it have to its background? On looking at the design of gardens down the ages (excluding parks or wider landscapes), it would appear that there has been a long-term trend from high visual intensity to lower intensity, but also a more graduated range of impact on the eye. Modern recreations of Victorian bedding schemes can leave some onlookers with a headache: so many colors, so much going on, everything there for impact, with a consequent rapid onset of visual exhaustion. The perennial borders which followed them in the early twentieth century were also packed with intense colors and striking juxtapositions. As the century progressed, some gardeners began to try to promote plants which were more subtle: in Germany Karl Foerster (1874–1940) began to use grasses and ferns, while in England the artist Cedric Morris (1889–1982) surprised visitors to his garden with his wide range of 'unconventional' plants. One of Morris's circle was the young Beth Chatto (born 1923), who in the 1960s puzzled some in the gardening establishment and inspired others with her choice of plants, chosen for form and line and natural elegance rather than eye-grabbing color: creamy astrantias, green euphorbias and broad-leaved brunneras.

Contemporary tastes in planting owe much to pioneers such as Chatto, but also to those who have promoted the creation of natural or semi-natural habitats as beautiful and worthwhile garden features: wildflower meadows, prairies and informal country hedgerows. Now, very much under the influence of the wildflower enthusiasts, gardeners and designers are more open to plantings where higher impact plants are set in a matrix of lower impact ones – just as the wildflowers in a meadow are only a small proportion of what is actually dominant: the grass matrix.

It is useful to think about a hierarchy of plants in terms of impact.

Primary plants are those which have the bulk of the impact – in conventional plantings all the plants can be considered as primary plants, although among them there will also be a clear hierarchy of impact. In a traditional English-style border, for example, there will be high-impact plants chosen for strong colors or structure being played off against lower impact ones such as pale lime-green *Alchemilla mollis*. For those new style plantings where higher impact plants are contrasted against a backdrop of lower impact ones, we will use the term 'matrix plants' for these quieter elements.

Matrix planting is where one or a limited number of plant species is used *en masse*, within which are embedded individuals or small to medium size groups of other, usually more visually prominent species.

A good analogy for the primary plant/matrix plant relationship is with a fruitcake, where nuts and fruit are scattered through a dough matrix. Having primary plants distributed through a matrix of others with lesser visual impact creates a more naturalistic and less obviously deliberate effect. It recalls, even if only psychologically, the visual feel of wild habitats, where a large mass of low-impact plants are studded with stronger impact clumps or individuals.

Scatter plants are often most effectively added to a planting by literally randomly scattering them, for their role is primarily that of adding a sense of naturalness and spontaneity, and by being scattered throughout the whole, a sense of visual unity.

So, now we will look in more detail at what role plants in these categories might play in planting design and what kind of plants might be used. Unless specified, all schemes are Piet Oudolf's.

PRIMARY PLANTS – GROUPS

For many years, planting design on any scale larger than that of a domestic border involved putting plants in groups. These might be as small as three or involve blocks of hundreds of plants – the key point being that the group is a monoculture of one species or cultivar. There are some advantages to using single-variety groups of perennials, but these only really apply to larger public plantings and not to private gardens. One is that it simplifies maintenance where staff are unskilled

and cannot be adequately supervised. Another is that it allows the clear expression of leaf textures which can get lost in more diffuse plantings.

In public spaces there is also an educational reason for block planting; there is no doubting the role of parks and public gardens with a wide variety of perennials in inspiring the public to be more adventurous in using them in their own gardens, particularly in regions where there is little history of using perennials. In order to inspire people, they need to be shown how plants look, which is most easily achieved with single-variety groups. The impact of the plant's color and form can be seen right away, without viewers having to work out which flower belongs to which bit of foliage or how it relates to the ground beneath it. The character of a plant, that indefinable sum of habit, foliage form and flower color, can often only be really appreciated when it is grown in a single-species block – though if it is rangy or has unattractively sprawling stems when it looks at its best, then perhaps it would do better intertwined more naturalistically with its neighbors. Educational – but disadvantageous for the overall effect – can be the untidy or unattractive appearance of certain plants after

◄
Here, in August at Pensthorpe Nature Reserve in Norfolk (1996), the impact is created by groups of plants where multiple individuals of a variety are clumped. The red is *Helenium* 'Rubinzwerg'. Several pale pink *Persiciaria amplexicaulis* 'Rosea' also make an impact.

►► (pages 84–85)
Taken when part of the Oudolf garden in the Netherlands was run as a nursery, this photograph illustrates very clearly two approaches to structural planting. One is the formal arrangement of geometric clipped shapes – in this case *Pyrus salicifolia* 'Pendula' (silver pear) – and the other is the scattering of grass *Calamagrostis* 'Karl Foerster'. The grass with its long season of interest can be distributed in plantings in many different ways, all to great effect. Here it can be regarded as a random scatter element. The small tree in the foreground is *Rhus typhina*, which is coppiced every few years to limit its size.

Small clumps of purple *Stachys officinalis* 'Hummelo' make a dramatic splash against pale green *Sesleria autumnalis*, which is here used as a matrix plant on the High Line in New York in July. Note how the stachys is repeated.

flowering, or when under stress or pest or disease attack. Group planting can throw a harsh spotlight on to a plant's character and point to its shortcomings.

Group-based planting can be made a lot more interesting in several ways:
• Different sized groups can be used.
• Key groups can be repeated to develop a sense of rhythm.
• Different shapes of group can be used – as in the concept of the drift.
• Large groups can be interspersed with scattered repeating plants – either individuals or small groups.
• Groups can be made up of two or more different species, using various percentages of plants that combine well together or including a small percentage that flower earlier or later than the majority of the group.
The last method is the most radical as it challenges the dogma of the monocultural block, and is the first, albeit cautious, step toward the idea of mixed plantings.

Just as in all but the smallest domestic gardens repetition provides a sense of rhythm and unity, in large-scale plantings which use more or less equal-sized groups there is also a need for clear repetition. Without repetition, group-based plantings lack a sense of unity. Just as a domestic garden with one of everything becomes a botanical collection – or 'plantsman's garden' in the polite terminology of British guides to gardens open to the public – so does a larger planting offering nothing but chunks of disparate plants. Repeated groups work best if made up of species with very good structure over a long time, or a long flowering season combined with a reasonably good appearance when no longer in flower. Taking the Trentham planting as an example (see opposite), there would appear to be a bewildering number of varieties – there are around 120 – but since many of these are very closely related, the number of truly distinctive plants is more like 70.

The eleven most frequently used plants in the 'Floral Labyrinth' at Trentham (see the table opposite) illustrate the value of repeating species with a long season of interest, and the importance of looking beyond flowering as the only or even main source of interest.

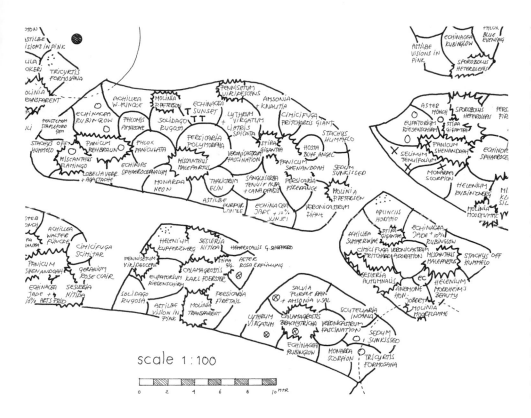

scale 1 : 100

The 'Floral Labyrinth' at Trentham, Staffordshire (2004–7). This planting, in the grounds of what was a major country house garden and is now a visitor destination in the English Midlands, occupies an area around 120 meters long and 50 meters wide, including wide grass paths and two central grass areas. It has an interesting place in the development of the Oudolf planting style, as it is based overwhelmingly on the equal-sized groups which he used in previous large projects, such as Pensthorpe Nature Reserve in Norfolk (1996) and Dream Park in Enköping, Sweden (2003), but includes some hints of the levels of added complexity which he started to develop in projects which came later.

The overwhelming preponderance of grouped perennials is broken up a little by a few groups being mixtures, such as *Lythrum virgatum* with *Liatris spicata* (both deep pink narrow spikes) – shown on this plan section. Not visible on this comparatively small excerpt are also some small groups of repeating plants scattered through, such as *Baptisia* 'Purple Smoke' (very good bushy structure from May to October) and *Astrantia major* 'Roma' (long season of pink flowers).

Seasonal Interest of the 'Floral Labyrinth' at Trentham

	Early summer	Mid-summer	Late summer	Early autumn	Late autumn	Winter
Astrantia 'Roma'	▓			▓		
Baptisia 'Purple Smoke'		▓	▓	▓		
Echinacea 'Rubinglow'		▓	▓	▓	▓	▓
Eupatorium 'Riesenschirm'			▓	▓	▓	
Lythrum virgatum		▓	▓	▓	▓	
Molinia 'Transparent'			▓	▓	▓	▓
Persicaria 'Firedance'		▓	▓	▓	or first frost	
Phlomis 'Amazone'	▓	▓	▓	▓	▓	▓
Sesleria nitida	▓	▓	▓	▓	▓	▓
Stipa gigantea	▓	▓	▓		▓	▓
Veronicastrum 'Fascination'	▓	▓	▓	▓	▓	▓

Flowering

Foliage interest

Structural interest: seedheads, stems, grass flowers

Block planting at Trentham in the context of a historic landscape (the Cedar of Lebanon, *Cedrus libani*, would date to the eighteenth or early nineteenth century). Now, in September, the definition of grouped plants is partly lost and the area takes on a wilder look. The orange is *Helenium* 'Rubinzwerg', while the grass on the right is *Molinea* 'Transparent'. The odd dark 'dreadlocked' seedheads in the right foreground are *Veronicastrum virginicum* 'Fascination'.

Repetition in block plantings

A large park such as Trentham planted in a very informal way with blocks of perennials in large beds among which it is possible to meander has a very definite similarity to what can be used on a smaller scale in the domestic garden with single plants or small groups. The principles are exactly the same. There should be a feeling of fluency so that as you walk through you are presented with not only variety (lots of different plants) but also the sense of familiarity which builds up when plants are repeated. Repetition can be regular, but in very informal plantings this has little meaning, so aiming for the random look is often better. Random repetition often works subliminally, so that as you walk around, the same species is seen again and again, not so often as to be obvious but often enough for it to work its way into the subconscious.

Repetition, of either individuals or blocks, works very differently as the year progresses. Early on, in spring or early summer when hardly any perennials are above half a meter high, repetition effects are obvious because everything is seen at once, and indeed are vital if the garden is not to seem disparate and messy. Later on at the height of summer and beyond, as perennial growth gets taller, the clarity of repetition becomes much less obvious. If growth is so high that the exploration of a planting becomes a journey *through* rather than a look *over*, with vision restricted to what is growing immediately around, the experience becomes very different. Repetition will be appreciated by seeing the same plant or perhaps the same combination – in other words, it is appreciated as a function of repetition in *time* not repetition in *space*, and is more likely to be perceived subconsciously.

PRIMARY PLANTS – DRIFTS

Favored by Gertrude Jekyll, the drift is an easy way out of the dangers of the monotony which overreliance on block planting risks. Drifts are long and thin, and can be winding and snaking, so bringing different plants into close proximity. Often, given the tendency of many perennials to sprawl, trail and weave, there will be an impression of intermingling. More basically, however, the shape of the drift inevitably means that groups of plants will be seen differently from head-on to side-on, so there will be a sense of development as the viewer walks by. Jekyll's drifts were designed for the wide rectangular borders favored by early twentieth-century British garden architects.

At Trentham, two cultivars of grass *Molinia caerulea* are used to create what is essentially a matrix, into which are embedded perennials and some small shrubs. The grasses very much dominate, however, so the overall effect is that of a stylized meadow. What is important to stress here is that the two *Molinia* cultivars used ('Heidebraut' and 'Edith Dudszus') are both planted in monocultural blocks, but in the form of complex drifts. If the two varieties had simply been mixed together the effect would have been a blur, as they are too similar to be easily distinguished. Planted as separate drifts, the distinction between the two can be appreciated, but the drift effect melds and intertwines them in a way which evokes the subtle patterns of grasses in natural grasslands.

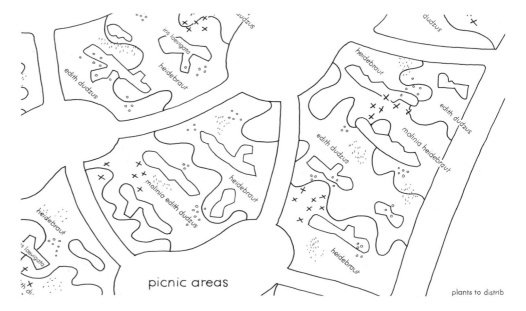

picnic areas

plants to distrib

▲

Drifts of *Molinia caerulea* cultivars at Trentham in September.

▶

The rivers of grass at Trentham in early June with cultivars of *Iris sibirica* in flower among *Molinia caerulea* 'Heidebraut' and *M. c.* subsp. *caerulea* 'Edith Dudszus'. Some yellow *Trollius europaeus* and pale pink *Persicaria historta* are also visible – all are tolerant of the occasional flooding which affects this area.

◀

Rectangular drift planting at the Royal Horticultural Society garden at Wisley in Surrey (2001) uses strips of plant combinations of between four and six varieties seen long end on to viewers as they walk down a central grass aisle. The geometry of the plan is invisible beneath vigorous, intermingled plant growth. Here deep blue spikes of *Agastache* 'Blue Fortune' are intermingled with white *Eryngium yuccifolium*; in the background purple *Veronicastrum virginicum* 'Fascination' is visible in another strip. The shrub to the right is *Cotinus coggygria* with its distinctive seedheads.

A detail from the plan for Potters Fields Park, London (2007), where jagged drifts are an effective way of creating simple mixed planting combinations.

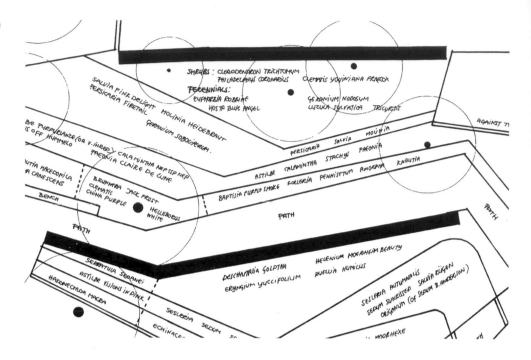

▲

At Potters Fields Park, London (2007), drifts of grass and perennial combinations create an orderly but dynamic effect. In the foreground is a mix of *Echinacea purpurea* and white-flowered, sprawling *Calamintha nepeta* subsp. *nepeta*. The grass in the background is *Deschampsia cespitosa* 'Goldtau'.

▲

A drift of *Sesleria autumnalis* in the foreground with red *Helenium* 'Moerheim Beauty' and *Deschampsia* behind. Other perennials are also included in each drift, but are not visible here. The use of drifts in this park creates a strong sense of movement and maximizes the trade-off between relatively simple, easy-to-maintain planting and visual complexity.

An advancement on drifts is the use of simple combinations of up to five or six varieties in a large drift. This was used extensively in the double borders at the RHS Wisley garden in Surrey in 2001, where each drift was exactly the same size and rigidly geometric. The reality on the ground is that plant foliage spills over the straight edges, and given that each drift is a mixture, there is no sense of regimentation.

Drifts offer a good midway format for gardeners and designers who want to break away from traditional block plantings but feel that they do not have the experience to attempt more complex mixed plantings. Drifts can create an illusion of intermingling, and they have certain advantages for ongoing management above mixed plantings. If there are plants which need a mid-season tidy-up or pruning, it is easier to gain access to them as well as to carry out additional planting – for example of bulbs, which are notoriously difficult to add to existing perennial plantings. Perhaps most importantly, by keeping the complexity low and relatively predictable, it is easier for maintenance staff with low plant knowledge to weed and manage the planting.

REPEATING PLANTS

Repeating plants can be used individually or in small groups at – very generally – regular intervals to add rhythm and variation to block plantings and to generally break up their chunkiness. Fundamentally they are about creating a sense of unity; whether in a private garden or a large public space, the repetition of a few distinct long-season plants creates a feeling that 'this is one place, with one design and one vision'. They can be used to lead the eye and so direct the viewer.

On a smaller scale, one particular area can be given a sense of unity with repeating plants, and in this case it will be more about stamping a distinct personality on that area with respect to the rest of the garden. An example of both these uses of repeating plants can be seen in the plans for Leuvehoofd (see pages 107–109).

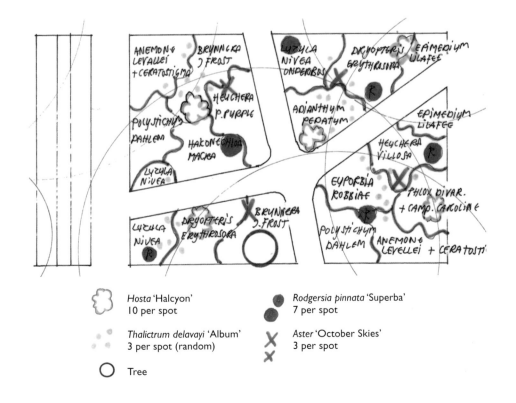

A shaded area from the van Veggel garden, Netherlands (2011), the large pencil arcs representing tree canopies. This excerpt from a much larger plan illustrates group planting of shade-tolerant plants interspersed with repeating plants. The key below (left) is for the repeating plants. Numbers for the repeating plants are given for each mark, with an additional annotation for *Thalictrum delavayi* 'Album' that they be scattered. All the repeating plants used are quite solid clump-formers, with the *Thalictrum* being an exception. Its tall stems and fluffy flower-heads are relatively insubstantial, and so small groups of it need to be repeated in order to make much of an impact. Note the wavy edges to the blocks – this blurs the boundaries between plant groups.

Hosta 'Halcyon'
10 per spot

Thalictrum delavayi 'Album'
3 per spot (random)

Tree

Rodgersia pinnata 'Superba'
7 per spot

Aster 'October Skies'
3 per spot

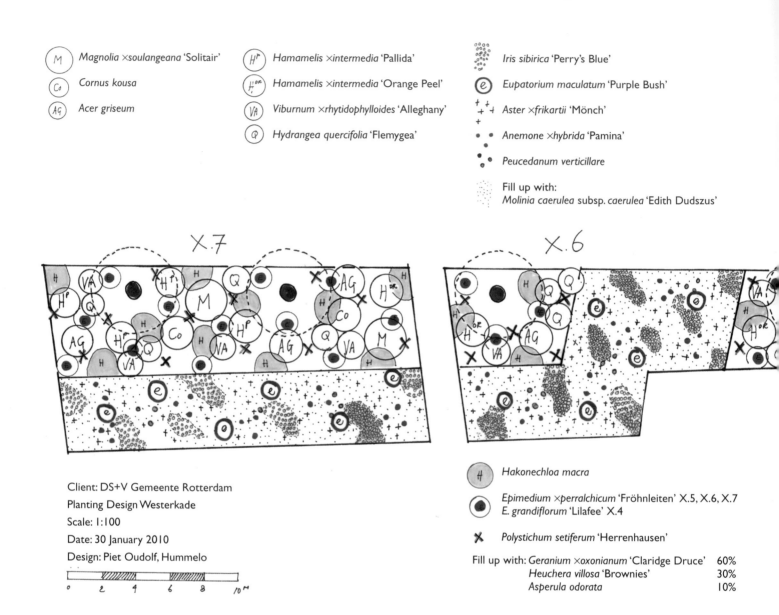

M — Magnolia ×soulangeana 'Solitair'

Co — Cornus kousa

AG — Acer griseum

H^P — Hamamelis ×intermedia 'Pallida'

H^{OR} — Hamamelis ×intermedia 'Orange Peel'

VA — Viburnum ×rhytidophylloides 'Alleghany'

Q — Hydrangea quercifolia 'Flemygea'

Iris sibirica 'Perry's Blue'

e — Eupatorium maculatum 'Purple Bush'

Aster ×frikartii 'Mönch'

Anemone ×hybrida 'Pamina'

Peucedanum verticillare

Fill up with:
Molinia caerulea subsp. caerulea 'Edith Dudszus'

X.7

X.6

Client: DS+V Gemeente Rotterdam
Planting Design Westerkade
Scale: 1:100
Date: 30 January 2010
Design: Piet Oudolf, Hummelo

0   2   4   6   8   10 M

H — Hakonechloa macra

Epimedium ×perralchicum 'Fröhnleiten' X.5, X.6, X.7
E. grandiflorum 'Lilafee' X.4

X — Polystichum setiferum 'Herrenhausen'

Fill up with: Geranium ×oxonianum 'Claridge Druce' 60%
             Heuchera villosa 'Brownies'   30%
             Asperula odorata   10%

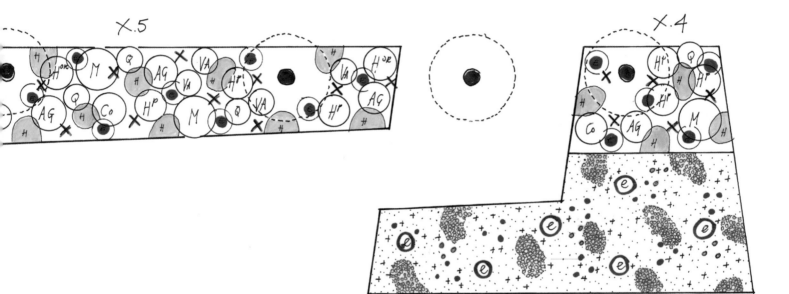

A public planting for the Westerkade – the old quayside of the river Maas in Rotterdam, where beds of varying size run for several hundred meters. There are two planting combinations. One is around the canopy of some existing elm trees and uses small ornamental trees and shrubs such as varieties of viburnum and hydrangea and perennial underplanting for foliage interest. The other is for the more open areas and uses a matrix of a molinia grass and a limited range of perennials. Of these, the tall, self-seeding umbellifer *Peucedanum verticillare*, was intended to provide an element of the unpredictable as well as an imposing winter sight. There were, however, not enough *Peucedanum* so some of the smaller, dark-flowered *Angelica gigas* were also used.

AR — Aruncus 'Horatio'

Molinia 'Transparent'

S — Sanguisorba tenuifolia 'Alba'

TH — Thalictrum rochebrunianum

IN — Inula magnifica 'Sonnenstrahl'

CH — Eupatorium altissima 'Chocolate'

Aster tataricus 'Jindai'

Panicum 'Shenandoah'

Per — Persicaria amplexicaulis 'Orange Field'

SES NIT — Sesleria nitida

GER.PS. — Geranium psilostemon

VERONIC. ERIKA — Veronicastrum virginicum 'Erica'

AC — Aconitum 'Spark's Variety'

scale 1:100

Excerpt from a plan for the Maximilianpark in Hamm, Germany (2009–10).

Good repeating plants need to have a distinct personality and a long season of interest, or at least disappear tidily or die back discretely, as seen in the plan from the van Veggel garden in the Netherlands on the previous pages:

- *Hosta* (Tardiana Group) 'Halcyon' – looks good from spring to autumn.
- *Aster oblongifolius* 'October Skies' – tidy mounds, late flowers.
- *Polystichum setiferum* 'Herrenhausen' – looks good from spring to autumn.

- *Polygonatum ×hybridum* 'Weihenstephan' – flower and structure in spring, can go into early dormancy but does so tidily.
- *Tricyrtis formosana* – relatively inconspicuous until late flowering,
- *Salvia pratensis* 'Pink Delight' – combines color and structure and looks tidy after flowering,
- *Thalictrum delavayi* 'Album' – relatively inconspicuous before and after flowering. Its transparency takes the eye away from the stiffness and solidity of any surrounding groups.

At the Maximilianpark in Germany, groups of roughly similar size are interspersed with repeating plants, chosen for long-season color or structure interest or else late interest often preceded by attractive foliage. An exception might be *Geranium psilostemon*, which like all geraniums has poor structure and can look untidy after flowering, although it disappears among taller planting later in the season. It is, however, valuable for its vibrantly colored flowers in early summer, which have a great capacity to seize the attention and so stamp a unifying personality on a planting. It is interesting to look at the numbers of the repeating plant species in the plan. There are twice as many groups of the species which are used the most – that is, certain plants are used to visually dominate. These include two grasses (*Molinia* 'Transparent' and *Panicum* 'Shenandoah') – structural but at the same time relatively low-key – and *Aster tartaricus* 'Jindai', a late, bright variety with an upright and unusually neat structure for an aster. Among the repeating plants with the lowest level of appearance are a number (such as *Persicaria amplexicaulis* 'Orange Field' and *Inula magnifica* 'Sonnestrahl') which are physically large and bulky – not many are needed to make an impact.

The numbers of the repeating plants used are as follows (see the table below):
- Three per circle for *Eupatorium* 'Chocolate', *Geranium psilostemon*, *Inula magnifica* 'Sonnestrahl', *Molinia* 'Transparent', *Panicum* 'Shenandoah' and *Sanguisorba tenuifolia* 'Alba'.
- Three to five per circle for *Aruncus* 'Horatio', *Persicaria amplexicaulis* 'Orange Field' and *Veronicastrum virginicum* 'Album'.
- Seven to nine per circle for *Aconitum* 'Spark's Variety', *Aster tataricus* 'Jindai' and *Thalictrum rochebrunianum*.

Seasonal Interest at the Maximilianpark, Germany

	Early summer	Mid-summer	Late summer	Early autumn	Late autumn	Winter
Aconitum 'Spark's Variety'		■	■			
Aruncus 'Horatio'	■	■	■	■	■	■
Aster tataricus 'Jindai'				■	■	
Eupatorium 'Chocolate'		■	■			
Geranium psilostemon	■	■				
Inula magnifica 'Sonnestrahl'		■	■			
Molinia 'Transparent'			■	■	■	
Panicum 'Shenandoah'		■	■	■	■	
Persicaria amplexicaulis 'Orange Field'		■	■	■		
Sanguisorba tenuifolia 'Alba'		■	■	■		
Thalictrum rochebrunianum	■	■	■	■	■	■
Veronicastrum virginicum 'Album'	■	■	■	■	■	■

Flowering

Foliage interest

Structural interest: seedheads, stems, grass flowers

Yellow *Rudbeckia subtomentosa* is repeated along a stretch of the High Line, set in a matrix of grasses, mostly *Sporobolus heterolepis* and *Panicum* 'Shenandoah', in August. This effect is remarkably similar to the grass-dominated and perennial flower-studded semi-natural habitat to be seen alongside many American highways and in prairie remnants.

MATRIX PLANTING

The concept of matrix planting is one which has been around for some time, but like many terms in planting design it has had the unfortunate history of being used by different people to mean different things – in part because of a misunderstanding over the meaning of the word. 'Matrix' is defined in the *American Heritage Dictionary of the English Language* as 'a surrounding substance within which something else originates, develops, or is contained', and it is with this in mind that we will use the term – we have already suggested the analogy of a fruitcake for describing a matrix.

The matrix evokes the situation in many natural habitats where a small number of species form the vast majority of the biomass, studded with a larger number of species present in much smaller numbers but which are a visually important element. Consequently, good matrix plants are visually quiet, with soft colors and without striking form. They also need to be effective in physically filling space – part of their function is to be a ground cover (or at least to hide the soil surface), so they need to mesh together well. It is vital that they always look good or at least acceptably tidy, so that even when they have finished their main season of interest they have good structure, do not flop over or look sad and bedraggled.

Grasses are the obvious plants to use for matrix planting, especially tussock-forming or bunch grasses (that is, cespitose species), or the denser and slower growing clump-forming species. For a variety of reasons to do with their physiological efficiency, grasses dominate most open temperate zone habitats. Researchers and practitioners like James Hitchmough and Cassian Schmidt have suggested that using cespitose grasses might be a good way to create low-maintenance plantings. Many such grasses are very long-lived and stable, with 'closed nutrient cycles': that is, they recycle nutrients from their old leaves as they fall down and rot around them. The environment they create is potentially a competitive one, which would have the desirable effect of reducing weed growth. Yet because they do not form runners and so create a complete canopy in the way that turf grasses or slowly spreading ones like *Miscanthus* or *Calamagrostis* 'Karl Foerster' do, they will not compete so strongly with flowering perennials that they risk eliminating them. Long-lived perennials or other species which have a similar form of growth may be considered as stable companions in the long term. Early Oudolf matrix-type plantings used *Deschampsia cespitosa* as the dominant grass; in cultivation on fertile soils it is relatively short-lived, but it can also self-sow strongly, so the chances of the long term development being either no-*Deschampsia* or too-much-*Deschampsia* are all too likely. The good thing is that *Deschampsia* does appear to be compatible with a great many other plants – it does not totally out-compete them. Varieties of *Molinia caerulea*, a long-lived species, also offer the hope of greater stability, although the tight clumps of many cultivars of these plants leave a lot of bare soil between them and so are best in combination with low spreading or sprawling perennials such as varieties of *Calamintha*. *Sporobolus heterolepis* has great potential as it has the fuzzy charm of *Deschampsia cespitosa* and is an important natural matrix plant; in its native dry prairie it is known to live for decades; it is, however, slow to establish in cooler European climates.

The potential of *Carex* (sedges) and other plants which can substitute for grasses both ecologically (in that they naturally dominate) and visually (they have long narrow leaves) to act as matrix plants is enormous; there is a feeling that the surface has hardly been scratched with these long-lived, often evergreen, stress-tolerant and resilient plants. Other plant genera which offer similar evergreen possibilities include *Luzula* in cool, moist climates and *Liriope* and *Ophiopogon* in climates with warm, humid summers – the latter are commonly used in the south-east USA, much of eastern China and Japan. Behavior varies from the strongly spreading to the tight clump, so huge opportunities for gardeners and landscape designers exist here. All these plants together are commonly known as 'grass-like plants' – it is important to understand that although they may look like grasses, they are not; grasses have a different physiology and tend to be greedier for light and nutrients.

Other potential matrix plants include clump-forming species grown chiefly for their foliage, like varieties of *Heuchera, Tellima, Epimedium* or woodland species

A simple matrix planting at Bury Court, Hampshire, with *Molinia caerulea* forming a meadow-like mass in which *Digitalis ferruginea*, a short-lived but self-seeding foxglove, and *Allium sphaerocephalon* are flowering in July.

of *Saxifraga*. Plants such as these, or with similar semi-evergreen leaves and a spreading habit, often form a major component of the ground flora in woodland. *Iris sibirica* is possible as a lesser component in matrix planting – its flowering season is so short that its strap-like leaves make it function almost as a grass, it always looks tidy, is very long-lived and has good seedheads; a habit of crushing competitors with a dense thatch of slow-to-rot leaves does, however, mean that it can only be combined with equally robust plants or that a maintenance program specifies their removal.

Finally, there is the potential of certain late flowering perennials as minor components in a matrix. *Limonium platyphyllum*, those varieties of *Sedum* descended from *S. spectabile* or *S. telephium*, and several species of *Eryngium* (for example, *E. bourgatii*) are very long-lived, stress-tolerant – particularly of drought – and never look untidy. In Chicago's Lurie Garden, the broad heads of *Limonium platyphyllum*, composed of thousands of tiny flowers, form a soft haze that other flowers blend and blur into, showing the potential of the visual aspect of the matrix.

One thing which needs to be borne in mind about the limited range of plants used in matrix-based plantings is that they are relatively stable in the sense that they continue to occupy the same space over long periods of time. This is true of many cespitose grasses, but also of flowering perennials like *Sedum telephium* varieties and *Limonium platyphyllum*. *Iris sibirica* and the low clump formers like *Tellima* do spread slowly, but they have a proven ability – in suitable conditions, of course – to dominate and hold space over long periods.

While the use of cespitose grasses, and sedges as well, is clearly an application of what is often seen in nature, the use of non-grass clump formers also has a natural model in that some woodland-floor habitats are dominated by these plants, at least where light and other conditions allow. Among clump-forming perennials, though, there is considerable variation in medium- to long-term performance, *even between cultivars within the same genus*. This is emphasized because of the importance of selecting plants which will do the functional ground-covering work demanded of them. In the case of *Heuchera*, for example, some cultivars do this well and others do not, becoming gappy after only a few years and frequently dying altogether.

Other possibilities for matrix planting are those lower growing species which run, and so make effective ground covers and fillers of space. Generally these are more suited to shaded or partially shaded habitats where grass growth is weak. Examples would be *Phlox stolonifera* and some lower growing and spreading ferns like *Adiantum pedatum*. A few species for open habitats, such as *Euphorbia cyparissias*, occur in nature as occasional shoots among a mass of grasses and other meadow components. In cultivation it rapidly fills in gaps between other plants which form denser clumps, but is readily out-competed by larger plants. However, recent research in Slovakia suggests that some species of *Euphorbia* and certain other plants may be allelopathic: they release toxic compounds which reduce the growth of other species around them.

Many gardeners and designers will be happy with keeping the matrix concept simple, so that there is only one limited plant combination which is randomized over a large area, to which other plants in smaller quantities are added. In a private garden or small space, this idea of the matrix as something which is uniform is probably important to keep to, as part of the concept of the matrix is its simplicity. However, nature is not like this! Walking through a botanically rich grassland habitat such as American prairie or central European meadow makes the observer aware of just how complex these places are; what appears at first to be a mass of uniform grass and perennials resolves itself into complicated patterns and constant change. The minor elements, the decorative perennials in particular, vary enormously in their distribution – this is obvious. But the majority (usually grass) components also often vary. Typically, a walk through a natural habitat reveals greater concentrations of one species in one area, transitioning to another area where another species assumes more importance.

In more extensive landscape plantings, greater interest and greater naturalistic effect might be achieved by *not* having an identical matrix spread over large areas.

▲
Sesleria autumnalis forms a matrix for *Agastache* 'Blue Fortune', *Echinacea purpurea* cultivars and, in the background, *Veronicastrum virginicum*. *Sesleria* grasses have the advantage of forming a weed-excluding mat but are not aggressive spreaders, while this particular species has a color which acts as a very effective foreground for flower colors. This is a garden in West Cork, Ireland, in July.

▲
In late September on New York's High Line, grass *Calamagrostis brachytricha* forms a matrix, while the seedheads of *Achillea filipendulina* 'Parker's Variety' and the yellow flowers of *Coreopsis verticillata* add touches of color and definition.

Nature's tendency to grade one species into another can be imitated with transition effects. Also, large blocks can be planted up with different matrix species – what will be perceived here is one pattern overlaying another. The underlying matrix will be changing, but the perennials scattered across it, either as small clumps or individuals, will have another pattern linking across the underlying matrix groups.

MATRIX AND REPEATING PLANTS

A design based on a matrix is essentially a two-stage planting: one is the larger areas of less visually dominating plants and the other is more the visually dominant elements, what we have so far been calling primary plants. The more visually dominant elements are most effective if they too are repeated. A matrix is a filler, a backdrop, which – whatever visual merit it may have on its own – is about throwing the primary plants into a higher relief and emphasizing their special values. I might argue, too, that making a clear distinction between the primary plants and matrix plants creates more diversity of visual interest than having a purely random distribution of all the elements, as might be seen in meadows or plantings which seek to imitate them. To continue with the fruitcake analogy, part of the pleasure of eating fruitcake relies on the distinction between the fruit and the surrounding cake.

The purest and most natural form of matrix planting is simply to create a grass meadow and repeat a limited number of perennials across it. By using cespitose grasses, the planting at least has the chance of achieving a compromise between long-term survival (most likely because of the presence of the grasses) and ornamental effect (the flowering perennials).

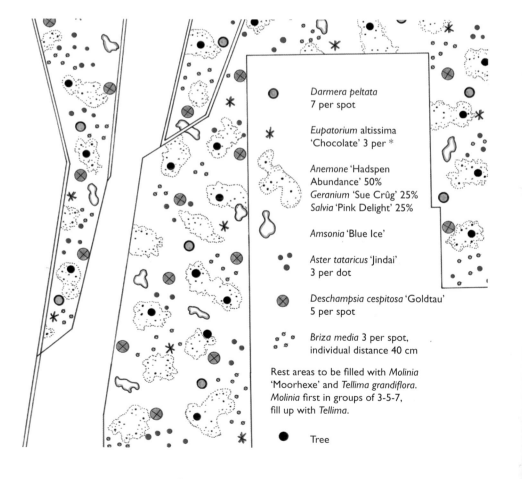

Extract of a plan for Ichtushof, a project for Rotterdam City Council in the Netherlands (2011). This is a site where office buildings create a northerly aspect. Young multistem specimens of the river birch *Betula nigra* 'Heritage' are indicated by black dots. As young trees they will exert little root pressure on surrounding perennial planting, and in any case they cast relatively light shade. However, in time it is envisaged that some perennial species will be lost. Note that shade and tree-root tolerant plants are intermingled in groups around tree bases. The planting takes the form of a clearly functional, but not very natural, matrix of *Molinia* 'Moorhexe' and *Tellima grandiflora* 'Purpurea' with small groups of repeating primary plants. Species used are indicated in the table opposite.

Darmera peltata
7 per spot

Eupatorium altissima
'Chocolate' 3 per *

Anemone 'Hadspen Abundance' 50%
Geranium 'Sue Crûg' 25%
Salvia 'Pink Delight' 25%

Amsonia 'Blue Ice'

Aster tataricus 'Jindai'
3 per dot

Deschampsia cespitosa 'Goldtau'
5 per spot

Briza media 3 per spot,
individual distance 40 cm

Rest areas to be filled with *Molinia* 'Moorhexe' and *Tellima grandiflora*. *Molinia* first in groups of 3-5-7, fill up with *Tellima*.

● Tree

The table below shows the distribution of interest throughout the year for matrix and primary plants for the area of the Ichtushof planting. It is worth noting that *Darmera* and *Amsonia* have good autumn foliage color – relatively unusual among perennials.

In the Ichtushof planting shown, the matrix is made up of grass *Molinia caerulea* 'Moorhexe' and perennial *Tellima grandiflora* 'Purpurea', laid out in the following ratio per square meter:

- *Molinia:* 5–7 plants
- *Tellima:* 5–9 plants

Tellima is a low, clump-forming, semi-evergreen perennial which acts as an infill between the upright *Molinia* foliage to minimize the amount of bare soil. The primary plants are, for the most part, in small groups, repeated at relatively regular intervals over the site. This planting also illustrates the importance of the order in which plants are placed:

- Plants around the birches:
    1. *Geranium* and *Salvia*, 7–9 plants per square meter
    2. Fill any gaps with *Anemone* 'Hadspen Abundance'
- Place the following in order:
    1. *Amsonia* 'Blue Ice'
    2. *Eupatorium* 'Chocolate'
    3. *Darmera peltata*
    4. *Deschampsia* 'Goldtau'
    5. *Aster tataricus* 'Jindai'
    6. *Briza media*
- Distribute *Molinia* in groups of 3, 5 and 7 over the rest of the space.
- Finally, fill in with *Tellima*.

Seasonal Interest of the Ichtushof planting

	Spring	Early summer	Mid-summer	Late summer	Early autumn	Late autumn	Winter
Primary (repeating) plants							
Darmera peltata	■	■	■	■	■	■	
Eupatorium 'Chocolate'		■	■	■	■	■	■
Anemone 'Hadspen Abundance'				■	■	■	■
Geranium 'Sue Crûg'		■	■	■	■		
Salvia 'Pink Delight'		■	■	■			
Amsonia 'Blue Ice'		■			■	■	
Aster tataricus 'Jindai'					■	■	■
Deschampsia 'Goldtau'			■	■			
Briza media		■					
Matrix plants							
Molinia 'Moorhexe'				■	■	■	
Tellima grandiflora 'Purpurea'	■					■	

Flowering

Foliage interest

Structural interest: seedheads, stems, grass flowers

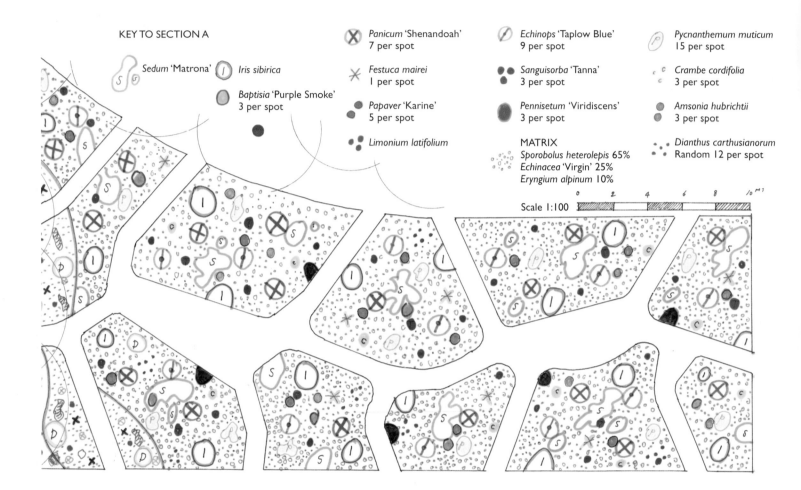

KEY TO SECTION A

Sedum 'Matrona' / *Iris sibirica*

Baptisia 'Purple Smoke'
3 per spot

Panicum 'Shenandoah'
7 per spot

Festuca mairei
1 per spot

Papaver 'Karine'
5 per spot

Limonium latifolium

Echinops 'Taplow Blue'
9 per spot

Sanguisorba 'Tanna'
3 per spot

Pennisetum 'Viridiscens'
3 per spot

MATRIX
Sporobolus heterolepis 65%
Echinacea 'Virgin' 25%
Eryngium alpinum 10%

Pycnanthemum muticum
15 per spot

Crambe cordifolia
3 per spot

Amsonia hubrichtii
3 per spot

Dianthus carthusianorum
Random 12 per spot

Scale 1:100

An extract from a plan for the van Veggel garden
in the Netherlands (2011). A matrix with repeating
primary plants for a sunny situation. The matrix
is made up of *Sporobolus heterolepis* (65 percent),
Echinacea purpurea 'Virgin' (25 percent) and
Eryngium alpinum (10 percent).

Seasonal Interest at the Van Veggel garden

	Spring	Early summer	Mid-summer	Late summer	Early autumn	Late autumn	Winter
Primary (repeating) plants							
Amsonia hubrichtii		Foliage	Foliage	Structural		Foliage	Structural
Baptisia 'Purple Smoke'		Flowering	Flowering	Foliage	Structural	Structural	
Crambe cordifolia		Flowering	Flowering	Structural			
Dianthus carthusianorum			Structural	Structural	Structural	Structural	Structural
Echinops 'Taplow Blue'		Foliage	Foliage	Flowering	Structural	Structural	
Festuca mairei		Foliage	Foliage	Foliage	Foliage	Foliage	Foliage
Iris sibirica		Flowering	Foliage	Foliage	Foliage	Foliage	Foliage
Limonium latifolium			Foliage	Flowering	Structural	Structural	Structural
Panicum 'Shenandoah'			Foliage	Foliage	Structural	Structural	Structural
Papaver 'Karine'		Flowering					
Pennisetum 'Viridescens'			Foliage	Foliage	Flowering	Structural	Structural
Pycnanthemum muticum			Foliage	Foliage	Flowering	Structural	Structural
Sedum 'Matrona'				Foliage	Flowering	Structural	Structural
Matrix plants							
Sporobolus heterolepis			Foliage	Foliage	Flowering	Structural	Structural
Echinacea purpurea 'Virgin'			Foliage	Flowering	Flowering	Structural	Structural
Eryngium alpinum		Foliage	Foliage	Flowering	Structural	Structural	Structural

Flowering

Foliage interest

Structural interest: seedheads, stems, grass flowers

The table above lists the primary and matrix plants used in the area shown in the van Veggel garden.

COMBINING MATRIX AND BLOCK PLANTING

Combining matrix and more conventional block planting effectively contrasts these two different approaches to perennial planting. The discipline needed to restrict the numbers of varieties necessary for matrix mixes to work is perhaps too tight for many locations, where a wide variety of plants are needed to engage the onlooker. There is also the fact that matrix planting, being a kind of mass planting, is particularly dependent for its success on the plants used flourishing and growing on the site chosen. Failures on such a large scale cannot be risked, so there will be an inevitable tendency to rely on tried and tested varieties – arguably this limits innovation and the creation of a sense of novelty. Combining the mass effect of matrix planting with blocks enables a compromise, with plants less well understood by the gardener or designer being used in small groups. Blocks also allow

POSSIBLE MATRIX PLANTS

Perennials

Acaena species and cultivars
Asarum europaeum
Asperula odorata (Galium odoratum)
Calamintha nepeta subsp. nepeta
Campanula glomerata
Coreopsis verticillata
Epimedium species and cultivars
Euphorbia amygdaloides
Euphorbia cyparissias
Geranium nodosum
Geranium sanguineum and cultivars
Geranium soboliferum
Geranium wallichianum
Heuchera species and cultivars

Iris sibirica
Lamium maculatum
Liriope species and related genera such as
    Ophiopogon, Reineckia
Limonium platyphyllum
Origanum species and cultivars
Phlox stolonifera and other procumbent Phlox
Salvia ×superba, S. nemorosa, S. ×sylvestris
Saponaria lempergii 'Max Frei'
Saxifraga, clump-forming woodland species
Sedum 'Bertram Anderson' and other low-
    growing sedums
Stachys byzantina
Tellima grandiflora

Grasses and grass-like plants

Carex bromoides
Carex pensylvanica, many other potential
    Carex
Deschampsia cespitosa
Hakonechloa macra
Luzula species
Molinia caerulea, smaller varieties
Nassella tenuissima (syn. Stipa tenuissima)
Schizachyrium scoparium
Sesleria species
Sporobolus heterolepis

Ferns

Adiantum pedatum

A plan for a meadow of *Sporobolus heterolepis* in a garden on Nantucket, Massachusetts (2007 onwards), with loosely grouped repeating plants: the *Allium christophii* for late spring/early summer and the others for mid-summer interest. As plants of sandy and dry prairie soils, the *Dalea purpurea* and the *Asclepias tuberosa* would be natural companions for *Sporobolus*.

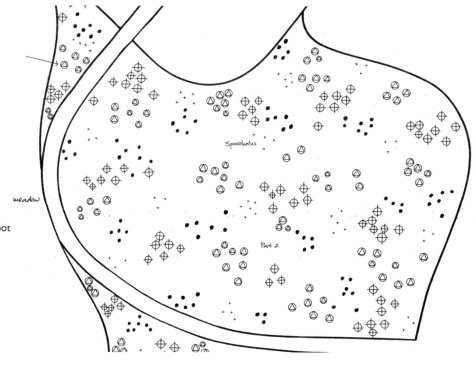

Sporobolus heterolepis

Echinacea purpurea 'Vintage Wine' 3 per spot

Dalea purpurea 3 per spot

Allium christophii 1 per spot

Asclepias tuberosa 1 per spot

for plants which need specific cultural care: it is not very practical to wade into a matrix planting to cut back all the specimens of a particular variety. A group of one variety, however, can be easily dealt with, useful for tidying up those which have a 'bad hair day' after flowering or which benefit from mid-season pruning.

Contrasting blocks with a grass or grass-like matrix is essentially about combining a classic form of planting with a blend of plants which most onlookers would read as a meadow. The old and conventional and the new and naturalistic are brought together, and the contrast can be striking and informative. The design can also be driven by a simple artistic conception of contrasting different plant qualities. Viewers are confronted with the possibility of breaking into new ways of planting and reminded that plants do not naturally grow in orderly blocks. A similar effect can, of course, also be achieved by having borders of grouped plants adjacent to a sown wildflower meadow or prairie.

Leuvehoofd, Rotterdam, Netherlands, is a recent example of public planting (2009) using grouping of perennials, matrix planting and repetition. A central unifying stripe of grass *Deschampsia cespitosa* 'Goldschleier' creates a striking impression. The more complex arrangement of perennials in groups creates sustained interest.

In this example, the *Deschampsia* matrix includes a high proportion of *Sedum telephium* 'Sunkissed' and occasional plants of *Limonium platyphyllum*. There are also some repeating plants for added late season color and dark seedheads (for example, *Helenium* 'Moerheim Beauty') and *Molinia caerulea* (a late season grass, an upright contrast with the mounding of the *Deschampsia*). Crucially, these last two repeating plants are used throughout the rest of the planting, tying the whole together for the time that they are performing. Two other repeating plants are also used here, but they are only in the outer group-planted areas: *Festuca mairei* (a medium-sized and incredibly resilient grass with a long flower/seedhead season) and *Agastache foeniculum* (an upright mid-summer flowering perennial with good seedheads).

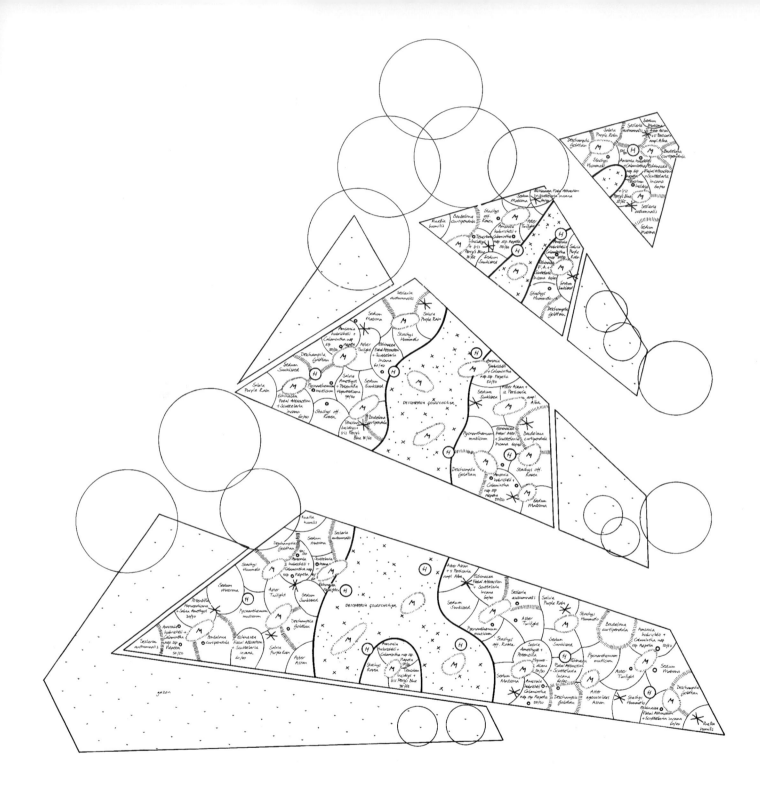

Helenium 'Moerheim Beauty' 7 per spot

Molinia 'Moorhexe'

Festuca mairei 1 per spot

Agastache foeniculum 1 per spot

Limonium latifolium 3 per spot

Sedum 'Sunkissed'

Rest area *Deschampsia cespitosa* 'Goldschleier'

Plan for a planting on the waterfront at Leuvehoofd
(2009), using a combination of matrix and group planting.

The plan shows six beds of a dramatic shape; the
masterplan was developed by the city landscape
architects. Three different planting treatments are used:
• On the right, a long, narrow bed (approximately
55 meters long and a maximum of 10 meters wide) is
planted with a matrix of grass *Calamagrostis brachytricha*
and a number of other perennials and grasses as
repeating plants.
• In the four beds on the left, a central core is made
up of a matrix of grass *Deschampsia cespitosa* 'Goldschleier'
(a maximum of 10 meters wide) with a limited number of
other perennials and grasses as repeating plants.
• On either side of the *Deschampsia* core are strips of
planting based on groups with repeating plants (to a
maximum of 20 meters wide).

Iris sibirica 'Perry's Blue'
Panicum 'Shenandoah'
Perovskia atriplicifolia 'Little Spire' 1 per spot
Persicaria amplexicaulis 'Orange Field'
Rest areas *Calamagrostis brachytricha*
Lawn

Client: City of Rotterdam
Planting design Waterfront Leuvehoofd
Scale 1:100
Date: September 2009
Design: Piet Oudolf, Hummelo

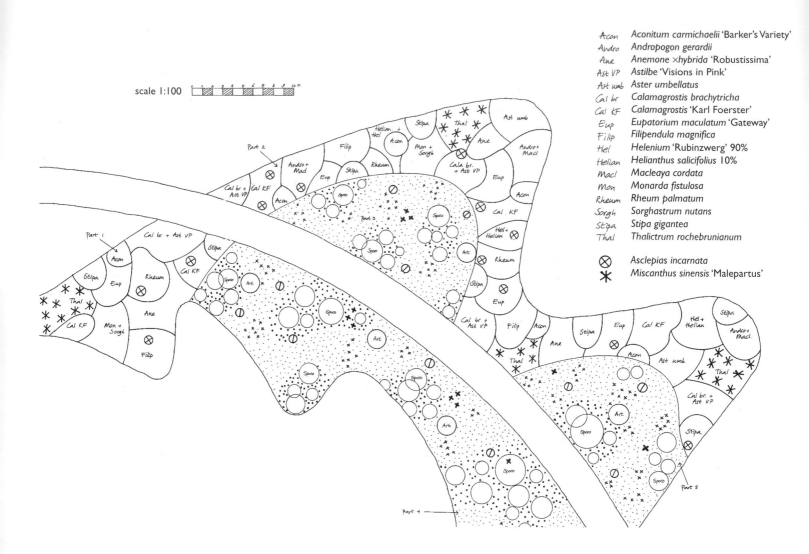

scale 1:100

Acon — Aconitum carmichaelii 'Barker's Variety'
Andro — Andropogon gerardii
Ane — Anemone ×hybrida 'Robustissima'
Ast VP — Astilbe 'Visions in Pink'
Ast umb — Aster umbellatus
Cal br — Calamagrostis brachytricha
Cal KF — Calamagrostis 'Karl Foerster'
Eup — Eupatorium maculatum 'Gateway'
Filip — Filipendula magnifica
Hel — Helenium 'Rubinzwerg' 90%
Helian — Helianthus salicifolius 10%
Macl — Macleaya cordata
Mon — Monarda fistulosa
Rheum — Rheum palmatum
Sorgh — Sorghastrum nutans
Stipa — Stipa gigantea
Thal — Thalictrum rochebrunianum

⊗ — Asclepias incarnata
✳ — Miscanthus sinensis 'Malepartus'

Matrix and group planting plan. Here, in the Nantucket garden, an area of meadow-like matrix in the middle contrasts with plant groups around the edge. The matrix planting is essentially *Eragrostis spectabilis* with *Molinia* 'Moorhexe' and *Anaphalis margaritacea*, and loose groups of a number of other species represented by symbols (right).

x x — Amsonia hubrichtii 1 per spot
(Art) — Artemisia ludoviciana
⊘ — Baptisia leucantha 1 per spot
x ˣ x — Echinacea purpurea 'Rubinstern', *E. p.* 'Fatal Attraction' 90%, 10%
⫶⫶⫶ — Molinia 'Moorhexe', *Eragrostis spectabilis* 50%, 50%
⣿ — Anaphalis margaritacea, *Eragrostis spectabilis* 50%, 50%
(Sporo)(Sporo) — Sporobolus heterolepsis

SCATTER PLANTS

Species which appear more or less at random through a planting can be termed scatter plants. They are added as individuals, not even in loose groups, and create a feeling of spontaneity and naturalness. They can be randomly scattered into groups of other species, including matrix mixes, the key aspect being to repeat them to create a sense of natural rhythm.

This technique is useful for a variety of plant forms which enhance a planting through a seasonal splash of color or a long period of distinct structure – the point is that they must be distinctively different to the rest of the planting. On a large scale, even something as bulky as *Baptisia alba* subsp. *macrophylla* could be a scatter plant. This is actually a good one, as once its white flowers have faded, its foliage texture, shrubby shape and tough, dark seedpods give it character and distinctiveness. On a smaller scale, the best species are often those which are physically slight, so that when they are not in flower are hardly noticeable. A good example for a smaller planting would be *Dianthus carthusianorum*, whose bright pink flowers have a visibility out of all proportion to their size; they are produced at the end of rangy stems best left to trail through the more substantial clumps of other species. When not in flower this plant is virtually invisible.

LAYERING PLANTS – READING NATURE AND WRITING DESIGN

Looking at a natural environment can be a confusing experience. Whereas some plant communities are clear and graphic, or can be at certain times of year, others can appear as a tangled web – a mass of plants confronts the eye, and it can be difficult to work out what is going on. Understanding a plant community as layered can help a lot. Plants can be thought of occupying a limited number of physical layers within a community. Sometimes these layers are clearly segregated by eye and so visible, but at other times they are not and are more difficult to distinguish. In some cases the word 'layer' is more of a metaphor, but nevertheless it can be possible to read the confusion of leaves and stems in front of you.

Having understood the concept of layering in wild or semi-natural plant communities, it is possible to transfer it to designed plantings, both as a way of helping the gardener and designer structure space but also as a way of simplifying the planning, visualization and implementation of a planting.

Mature temperate zone forest is very clearly layered. Mature trees form a dense canopy, beneath which are understory trees and shrubs, usually much less dense. In North America and Asia, small trees or large shrubs such as *Acer* (maple), *Cornus* (dogwood) and *Rhododendron* occupy this zone, although their growth is often very thin and open compared with how they appear in cultivation. In Europe, examples which fill this layer are species of *Ilex* (holly) and *Corylus* (hazel). Below this is a ground layer, composed of herbaceous perennials, ferns and sometimes small-growing suckering shrubs, often evergreens such as *Mahonia* or *Vaccinium*. Below this are smaller perennials, mosses and fungi. Climbers – plants which root into the ground and use other plants for support – can be thought of as another layer: often a conceptual layer, as their visual role is often to blur and confuse the appearance of layering to the human eye.

In grasslands such as meadow or prairie there are also layers, but they are rarely distinguished as clear physical divisions. Grasses tend to dominate and form one layer; in prairie long-lived upright perennials such as *Baptisia* species form another. Subsidiary herbaceous flowering perennials are a minor but highly visible layer, along with perennials which tend to lean on others for support. European meadows include many in this latter category, such as species of *Geranium* and *Knautia*. Still others are herbaceous climbers such as the vetches, a varied group of plants in the pea family.

For design purposes, such complexities and ambiguities can be, and indeed often must be, swept away. Layering is about segregating plants so that the visual effect

Pink and white cultivars of *Echinacea purpurea* are scattered through a matrix of grasses on the High Line; the scatter plant principle of occasional flashes of pink and white among grass seedheads strongly evokes natural vegetation. The shrub is *Cotinus coggygria*, which is kept coppiced: cut down to base every few years to encourage bushy growth and more striking foliage.

is clear and coherent and about clarifying the design process and simplifying setting out for planting. For planning purposes two or three layers are all that is needed, although these can potentially include several plant categories.

The New York High Line provides an example. One layer is missing here, of course – there are no large trees (otherwise the owners of apartments lining the track would have a lot to complain about). On parts of the High Line, there is a clear distinction between shrubs and a ground layer of grasses/sedges and perennials –

here there are two layers. In other areas the planting is divided into layers which are conceptual rather than physical – a matrix layer and a layer of perennials in clumps or groups. Scattered plants can also be described as a third layer.

It is relatively straightforward to design a planting in layers using tracing paper; each can be looked at individually or all put together to get an overview. For implementation, each layer can be treated separately, which greatly simplifies the process of setting out plants.

Examples of the use of layers in planting. Tracing paper enables the planning of complex plantings to be broken down into several simpler processes.

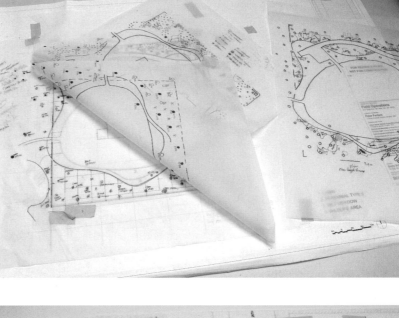

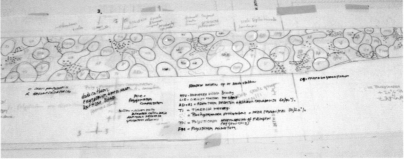

Layer One

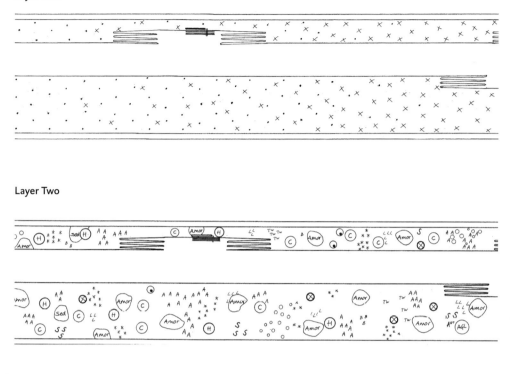

Layer Two

An extract from plans for sections 28–29 of the High Line – this is just downtown of West 28th Street; the central horizontal gap in each one is the walkway. Layer One illustrates a simple and relatively open matrix where a transition is occurring between *Panicum* 'Heiliger Hain' (indicated by dots coming in from the left) and *Calamagrostis brachytricha* (shown by crosses, right) – these grasses are spaced at around 1 to 1.5 meters apart. Layer Two shows a range of perennials present as small clumps, often intermingled with the matrix grasses. About twenty different perennials (mostly late flowering) are included. To achieve the intermingling effect, the planting density of the perennials in the clumps is only 50 percent of normal to allow for the integration of grasses with them. Any space left is filled with grasses *Sporobolus heterolepis* and *Bouteloua curtipendula*, which are lower than the other two grasses. Keeping the density of the taller *Calamagrostis* and *Panicum* low helps to improve the visibility of the perennials. Much of the success of the High Line as a visual experience is the way that the flowering perennials poke out of the grasses.

The mind can easily visualize the layering technique applied to the underplanting of woody plants with a ground-cover layer of perennials, but less easily to grasses and perennials. Each layer tends to deal with the distribution of plants in a different way: one layer may be a simple matrix, another with groups, or another with scatter plants. It is helpful to think about one layer being superimposed on to another, even though in reality there may be no height differences between plants in one layer and those in another.

Generally, the first layer to be designed is the simplest, the one which deals with either a matrix or extensive blocks or groups; the second overlaying this deals with a finer texture of planting – smaller groups or more intricate patterning. Ecologists talk about 'coarse-textured' and 'fine-textured' plant communities: the former consists of large clumps, the latter a dense interweaving. Transferring this concept, one can talk about designing the coarse-textured first, and then overlaying that with the second, fine-textured layer.

Layer One

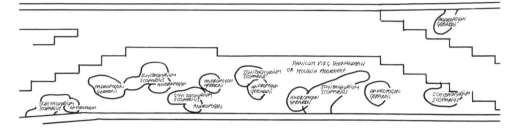

An extract from plans for sections 35–39 of the High Line, between West 18th Street (to the left) and West 19th Street (to the right). In Layer One *Panicum* 'Shenandoah' and *Molinia* 'Moorhexe' are used as a matrix, and scattered among them are blocks of other grasses. In Layer Two a variety of perennials indicated by alphabetic abbreviations are scattered in loose clumps – each abbreviation represents one plant.

Layer Two

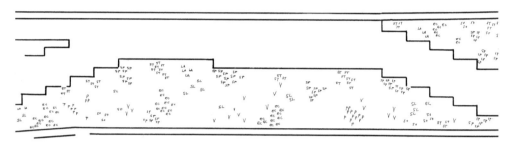

Layer One

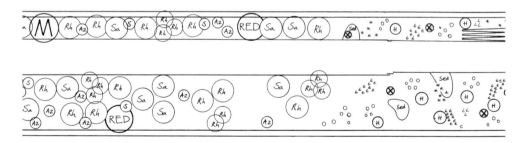

An extract from plans for sections 26–27 of the High Line, just downtown of West 27th Street. This plan illustrates the transition from an open area dominated by perennials and grasses on the right, to a shrubby zone underplanted with woodland species on the left. It shows that a two-layer plan can illustrate two very different kinds of vegetation.

In Layer One, circles on the left illustrate the expected spread of tree and shrub species, while on the right the shapes illustrate perennial clumps. In both cases these will be the main and immediate visual impact. In Layer Two, areas for planting ground-cover and woodland perennials are indicated on the left, while on the right there is a matrix of grass (*Panicum* 'Heiliger Hain'). Any gaps are filled with another grass species. In this latter area, bulbs and spring-flowering perennials are also included as randomized plants.

Layer Two

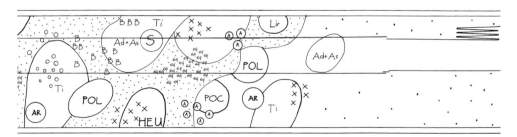

CALCULATING NUMBERS OF PLANTS

Plans are usually done at a scale of 1:100, which works well for perennials, as it allows enough detail to be shown. Large areas involving planting mixtures where it is not crucial or desirable to show individual plants can be done at smaller scales.

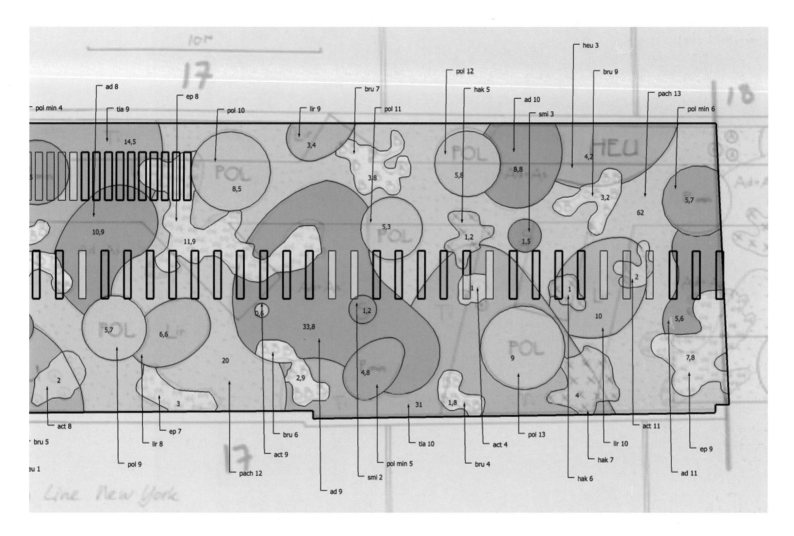

This is an excerpt from a plan for an area of shade-tolerant planting from sections 26–27 on the High Line (page 116 bottom). What is shown is an overlay to the planting plan with each plant group or combination indicated.

- Each group is given a code, which is based on the first letters of the plant (or one of the plants), and a number.
- Using a program such as Google Sketchup, AutoCAD or Indesign, it is possible to work out the area (in square meters) of each clump.
- Each group can then be listed on a spreadsheet.
- A sample of the species used is shown in the accompanying table (page 118). This spreadsheet is a small and adapted excerpt from the one used to calculate plant quantities for three of the plant groups used in the plan.
- Guidance for the numbers of plants to be used per square meter is given in the Plant Directory at the end of the book. However, it should be noted that here a higher density has been used, as a quick effect was necessary.
- Where intermingled plant combinations are used, a percentage of the mix is given.
- Intermingled plants are to be set out in groups of five or seven.
- Where groups of plants are overlain over a matrix layer, the planting density will be reduced.

Sample of woodland floor plants in bed 17 of the High Line

	Code	Square meters	Plants per square meter	Plants per group
Bed 17		974.3		
Rail ties (sleepers), i.e. not planted		97.8		
Woodland-floor plants		876.5		
Pachysandra procumbens + *Phlox stolonifera 80/20%*	pach 1	36	12	432
	pach 2	6	12	72
	pach 3	8.3	12	100
	pach 4	5	12	60
	pach 5	34.8	12	418
	pach 6	0.5	12	6
Adiantum pedatum + *Asarum canadense 60/40%*	ad 1	1.4	10	14
	ad 2	8.5	10	85
	ad 3	57	10	570
	ad 4	8.2	10	82
	ad 5	6	10	60
	ad 6	41.5	10	415
Polystichum setiferum 'Herrenhausen'	pol 1	6.7	9	60
	pol 2	5	9	45
	pol 3	5.5	9	50
	pol 4	6.2	9	56
	pol 5	6.6	9	59
	pol 6	5.4	9	49

Setting plants out:

• Lay out a grid of 2 by 2 meter squares, corresponding to a grid set out on the plan.

• Using the grid as a guide, mark out lines separating planting blocks or the borders between planting mixes; in complex plans, markers with numbers can be used to correspond to the code numbers of each planting block (see the plan on page 117).

• In an adjacent area plants are grouped according to the code number of their block.

• Plants can now be set out in each block.

Now get planting!

— THREE —

COMBINING PLANTS

Combinations are the basic building blocks of planting design. To make effective

combinations, we have to understand the visual character of the plants we work with.

Color has been analyzed many times, but structure is more fundamental as it is

with us over a longer season — so this will be our main focus.

The cool temperate climate of north-west European countries has dominated so much writing, thinking and dreaming about gardens; here it is possible to have a wide range of species in flower for long periods. In harsher climates this is not possible, and so foliage, form and structure have been seen as more important. Given that color is basically about flowers, and since flowers are relatively short-lived, it makes sense for structure to be seen as *the* fundamental aspect of ornamental plants, whatever the climate. Perhaps color is best seen as an added extra, the icing on the cake, a seasonal gift and a psychological bonus. Here we look first, quite analytically, at plant shape, then at broader issues of structure, harmony and contrast, at the seasons and, finally, at some examples of effective combinations.

◄ *Echinacea purpurea* seedheads with *Agastache* 'Blue Wonder'

THE ARCHITECTURE OF PERENNIALS

Perennials vary greatly in shape. An effective planting combines shapes in such a way as to create interest and a reasonably solid canopy of vegetation for as much of the growing season as possible. So far the most consistent way of describing how this can be done has been the system developed in Germany for naturalistic mixed plantings (discussed in chapter five). Structure plants (*Gerüstbilder*) are combined with less clearly structural companion plants (*Begleiter*) and the self-explantory ground-cover plants and filler plants (*Füllpflanzen*) – the last being short-lived species which fill space in the early years. In our first book together (*Designing with Plants*, 1999), Piet and I made a simple division between structural plants and what we have called filler plants. However, there is a need for a more detailed look at plant structure, in particular an attempt to develop a consistent language for this vital topic.

Perennials develop particular shapes (increasingly referred to as plant architecture), which are defined by the relationship between the stem and the leaf. These shapes should be the starting point for any discussion of using structure as a design tool. Our perception of shapes is affected by scale and by other surrounding shapes – what may be a good structure plant in a large border may be a bit overwhelming in a confined courtyard garden. By looking at the fundamentals of what defines a plant's architecture, we can think about its qualities as a building block; some shapes will be better for some purposes in composing a planting than others. Plant architecture may also have implications for the appearance of the plant at different seasons.

A better understanding of just what it is that gives perennials their visual character can help us make better decisions about using them in the garden or landscape. Also, it can help us to better understand plants new to cultivation, which is a particularly important topic for those experimenting with locally native species which have not been grown in gardens or other designed landscapes before. Furthermore, those involved with breeding new cultivars could learn a lot from a deeper understanding of these fundamentals of plant structure.

BASAL LEAVES

Linear basal leaves

Botanists call plants with linear leaves monocotyledons (often shortened to monocots). However, grasses, sedges and other grass-like plants have special qualities and are considered separately. Monocot leaves arise from the base of the plant either in a clump (for example, *Liriope*), as in diagram A, or from a creeping root (*Iris*), as in diagram B.

Apart from a few rather majestic rosette forming plants like some species of *Kniphofia*, hardy perennials

A

B

with this leaf-stem combination are visually quiet and undistinguished, with an advantage that their foliage rarely gets untidy. Flower-head or seedhead shapes can be strong, but the foliage is rarely a structural element in its own right. Linearity, however, is a useful break from the shape of most broad-leaved perennials. Many are slightly tender southern hemisphere plants, and only suitable for milder winter climates.

More examples: *Crocosmia, Dierama, Libertia, Hemerocallis.*

Broad basal leaves

These are plants which are perceived as leaves at ground level, emerging from a tight clump like *Helleborus* (C), directly from a running root or ground-level stem like *Bergenia* (D), or held aloft on stout stalks as in *Rodgersia* (E).

Since the stem is either minimal or at ground level, the visual impact of these plants is entirely due to their leaves and flowers/seedheads. Some may be useful ground covers or fillers in between taller and more structural plants. Many are spring-flowering; many too are woodland species. Some E types are magnificently large-leaved species of very moist habitats (for example, *Astilboides, Darmera, Petasites, Rodgersia*) with a clear visual role. In design terms, though, the lack of a stem limits their usefulness in providing structure at height or during the winter; in spring and early summer their foliage plays a vital role in many plantings.

More examples: *Heuchera, Hosta, Trachystemon, Epimedium.*

Most perennials have leaves attached to a stem, although sometimes this can only be seen if the plant is examined closely. It is perhaps useful to think of a gradient, from those where leaves are very clearly gathered at the base, as in *Verbascum* (F), through lower leaves being predominant, as in *Phlomis tuberosa* (G), through some with leaves in the middle of the stem predominating, as in *Macleaya* (I), to those where strong stems have a large number of small leaves of more or less equal size from top to bottom (J), as with *Eupatorium*. Sometimes, however, the stem is weak, which gives the plant a very different appearance, as in many *Geranium* species (H).

Emergents – lower stem leaves predominant, strong stem

With foliage concentrated toward the base of the plant and flowers on an upright stem, these plants are relatively non-structural when not in flower or seed but can be dramatically so when a flower spike emerges. Often visually graphic anyway, they are particularly useful for planting schemes where low to medium height foliage is wanted, but with flowers/seedheads hovering above; it is the physical separation of the flower/seedhead and the majority of the foliage that makes this group so distinctive. Prairie species of *Silphium* can do this dramatically at heights of around three meters, while species of *Verbascum* (F) and *Digitalis* are distinctive for their rosettes near ground level and strong vertical flower

C

D

E

stems thrusting upwards. Narrow spires of flower/seedhead such as *Verbascum nigrum* and *Digitalis ferruginea* give the gardener and designer a wonderfully vertical element to play with by repeating in loose groups or drifts, especially since these biennials or short-lived perennials have physically strong stems. At a lower level, the multiple heads of *Persicaria bistorta* and *Phlomis tuberosa* (G) can create a similar effect. Plants like *Anemone×hybrida*, *Aquilegia* and *Sanguisorba* can present a haze of flower or seedheads at height too, effective when grouped at a distance but often transparent when seen closer to.

Astrantia illustrates the gray area where this category merges with the next – distinctly shaped and well-presented flower-heads over a plant which can become rather untidy after flowering or lax if grown with strong competition. Indeed, one paradox is that the perennials here tend to have weaker stems than the shorter-lived species (which need to invest more in physically strong stems to ensure seed distribution and therefore survival of their genes). *Inula* species can look magnificent or they can flop terribly – especially if too well fed in a windy site.

We must not forget the leaves of this group. The rosettes of certain *Verbascum* and *Eryngium* can be fine features in their own right earlier in the year, while *Acanthus* and *Cynara* are very good foliage and structure plants for early spring in maritime or Mediterranean climates. The fact that these species concentrate their foliage low down is also very useful for the designer and gardener, as it ensures good coverage of the soil, often important for both the visual effect and weed suppression.

More examples: *Cephalaria*, *Cirsium*, *Echinops*, *Geranium sylvaticum*, many *Thalictrum*.

Leafy mounds – lower stem leaves predominant, weak stem

With a leaf-stem arrangement not dissimilar to those in diagram G or I, but with the stem tending to be lax or arching or even procumbent, it is the leafiness of these plants which makes a strong impression when they are not in full flower – see diagram H, where a single stem only is shown. They are overwhelmingly plants of meadow or woodland-edge habitats where competition is intense. In the wild or when growing in high-density naturalistic plantings, the growth of these plants can be seen to be amazingly plastic, with immensely long leaf-stems insinuating themselves among surrounding plants, often relying on them for support – the leaf blade finally emerging in light some tens of centimeters from the base of the stem; *Geranium* and sometimes even *Astrantia* can be particularly striking in this regard. These are plants which can be said to be almost formless, as they shape themselves into the environment created by their neighbors and competitors.

In the garden, with little competition, most form a neat mound, but they often deteriorate after flowering, which is why professional designers of larger landscapes tend to avoid them. Very often it is the lower leaves on the stem which visually dominate, as they tend to be

F

G

very much larger than those higher up. These are classic filler plants. Designers can use them as a small part of a planting, making use of their flower color or interesting foliage but not expecting them to contribute to the overall structure. They are ideal plants for amateur gardeners who have the time to manage them through individual cutting-back after flowering. The fact that many of these are meadow or grassland plants, used to being intensely intermingled with grasses, suggests that they have great potential for low-maintenance, grass-based plantings.

More examples: *Alchemilla*, *Brunnera macrophylla*, *Geranium* – many species and cultivars including *asphodeloides*, *endressii*, *phaeum*, *renardii*, *sanguineum*, ×*oxonianum* and most blue-violet cultivars – *Papaver orientale*, *Pulmonaria*, *Symphytum*.

There are a very large number of perennial species in cultivation with strongly upright stems with a large number of more or less equally spaced leaves from top to bottom. A small number have fewer leaves, getting larger towards the middle of the stem, but not enough to be worthy of consideration separately – the majestic gray-leaved *Macleaya* is one of these few (I). There appears to be a gradient from ramrod-straight stems (as in J) through arching to procumbent.

Uprights – erect stem with multiple stem leaves

A brief look at a late summer or autumn perennial planting reveals that a lot of late flowering species stand tall and erect. Most have large numbers of relatively small leaves up their stems, but often only the upper ones are alive by the time the plants are flowering. These upright plants have several great advantages, but a serious weakness. Their advantage is that by flowering relatively late, they look good for all the growing season, and their stems ensure a real sense of structure, often enough to carry it off for the winter too. Many have a strong presence, which gardeners and designers can make great use of. However, the lower stems can look bare and unattractive, which is reason enough to combine them with lower growing and more compact filler plants.

Many of the species used are North American in origin, often from prairie habitats, and many of them belong to the aster/daisy family (*Asteraceae*), such as species of *Aster* and *Eupatorium* (J). Many are from an intensely competitive environment with fertile soils, where height means survival. In Eurasia there is the so-called 'tall-herb flora', which is also an environment rich in moisture and nutrients, with similarly tall plants, such as *Aconitum* and *Filipendula* species.

More examples: *Amsonia*, *Artemesia lactiflora*, *Campanula latifolia*, *Eupatorium*, *Euphorbia* – many species, for example, *schillingii* – *Helianthus*, *Leucanthemella serotina*, *Lysimachia*, *Monarda*, *Phlox paniculata* and related species, *Solidago*, *Vernonia*.

H

I

J

STEM MOUNDS – ARCHING OR PROCUMBENT, MULTIPLE STEMS WITH STEM LEAVES

A great many garden perennials have multiple stems with large numbers of leaves scattered up them, but what we tend to see is only the overall shape – or perhaps if the leaves are distinctive, our eyes register a mass of good-looking foliage. These plants rarely have real drama on their own, but they may do so in groups. They are usually more physically resilient than those classified as 'leafy mounds' because of their stems, so they have a longer season as clear design components.

A good example are the meadow sages, a whole complex of *Salvia* species: *nemorosa, pratensis, ×sylvestris, ×superba*, important plants for drought-tolerant plantings. Aside from their color, their multiple flower spikes give them a distinct character, and their mound shape is always neat. The well-known group of *Sedum* cultivars descended from *S. spectabile* and *S. telephium* are similar in size and habitat tolerance but with umbel flower-heads (K) – they too need little or no maintenance in the growing season to keep them tidy.

Some members of this group are so large that they can be mistaken for shrubs, such as *Aconogonon* 'Johanniswolke' and varieties of *Aruncus*; what is useful about them is precisely this shrubiness and sense of solidity, which derives from their multiple stems radiating out from a tight basal clump and even leaf distribution. At the other end of the scale, the stems of some are weak and without the support of neighbours tend to sprawl in all directions, such as *Knautia macedonica*. Many species actually branch, so producing multiple flower-heads (including *Aconogonon* and *Knautia*), and so we grade into the next section.

More examples: *Aster amellus, Calamintha, Centaurea, Euphorbia* – many species including *palustris* and *polychroma* – *Origanum, Tanacetum macrophyllum*.

BRANCHING – DIVIDED STEMS

Some perennials have stems which branch, or sometimes an upright stem produces side-stems ending in a flower; other species, however, have a continually multiplying habit – at the point at which a flower is produced, a stem divides in two, and when they flower, they divide again. The result produces a bushy or branching shape, quite unlike that of other perennials (L).

When the thrust of the stems is upright, the result can be a sturdy shape which combines a sense of the vertical with enough bulk to give it real presence, as with *Lythrum* species. When branching reaches out horizontally as well as vertically, the result can be the wide shrubby shape shown by *Baptisia australis*, which, with its neat, nearly gray leaves, makes it an almost uniquely valuable foliage perennial.

The species mentioned so far all have very strong stems and so stand winter well. Others have notably weak stems, but their habit makes them useful low-level filler or ground-cover material, such as *Euphorbia*

K   L

cyparrisias and many species of *Nepeta*. Finally, there is *Persicaria amplexicaulis*, whose combination of a long season of summer color and a rare ability to look good from all angles – a result of its branching habit – makes it such a useful plant, but which it ruins by collapsing into dark brown mush with the first hard frost! Perhaps there are no perfect plants?

GRASSES

The architecture of grasses and various other plants used in similar ways – sedges (*Carex*), wood-rushes (*Luzula*) and the *Liriope, Ophiopogon, Reineckia* group – can be described through a simple gradient:

Turf grasses (1) form turf (sod in the USA) where sideways running stems or roots rapidly form an interlocking mat composed of many individuals, ideal for making lawns but not good as ornamentals, as they tend to smother other plants.

Mat grasses (2) spread steadily, but often slowly, to form a dense mat, largely through a few starter individuals. Species of *Carex* which do this are increasingly popular as ground cover or lawn substitutes. *Sesleria* also does this. Larger species which we read as 'clumps', such as *Calamagrostis* 'Karl Foerster' and *Miscanthus*, also form mats on a very different scale, but may take many years to do so. The growth pattern is similar

Cespitose grasses (3) are those often described as 'bunch grasses' in the USA. They form very tight clumps, which tend not to increase once they have reached a certain size, although the living shoots of the plant often move upwards, forming a tussock. They have a distinct shape: narrow at the base with leaves arching out, which makes them useful in design terms. Examples are *Molinia caerulea* and *Sporobolus heterolepis*.

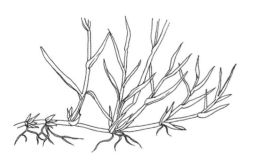  

Turf (1)...Mat (2)...Cespitose (3)

CREATING COMBINATIONS

Any planting is crucially dependent on combinations. A combination can be described as at least two plant varieties which can be seen together – usually adjacent. The oft-repeated design dictum 'less is more' points to a fundamental factor (some might say truth) in any field of design – that simplicity often has a greater emotional impact than complexity and variety. There is a tendency, however, for us to tire of such simplicity quite quickly – we need some complexity to keep us interested. Needless to say, everyone adopts a different position on this gradient of simplicity to complexity. All positions on questions of aesthetics are very personal and subjective, and have a cultural component too: the Mexican love of putting bright pink next to bright yellow, for example, is not shared by many Europeans.

We all have likes and dislikes, even if we cannot consciously express them. Anyone who gardens or who works with plants tends to build up a personal flora of varieties they like to put together. They often then find themselves drawn to unfamiliar species similar in some ways to ones on their list of favorites. In other words, almost subconsciously, we are selecting plants according to a set of criteria. Anyone who wants to design with plants needs to be aware of this; if they try to analyze their list of favorites they should be able to see what these criteria are. This is the first step to making effective design decisions about combinations.

Having understood their personal design criteria, it becomes easier for the gardener or designer to work out how to make visually exciting plantings. Repeating plants is one simple step forward, as this creates a sense of rhythm and unity. Repeating combinations will reinforce this. Repeating plants which flower, or in some other way perform, in a particularly striking way for defined seasonal periods is a very effective way of creating a powerful impression; Heiner Luz's 'seasonal theme planting' principle, described more fully in Chapter 5, exploits this idea.

◄◄ (page 128–129)
Plants here at Pensthorpe Nature Reserve in Norfolk in September are combined to bring together a range of colors as well as different forms. In the foreground the delicate pink spikes of *Persicaria amplexicaulis* flutter in contrast to the solidity of *Helenium* 'Moerheim Beauty' behind. An important part of the scene here is the big block of *Deschampsia cespitosa* in the background. This links to the wider rural landscape as well as providing a foil of simplicity to the relative complexity of the perennial planting.

►
The blue of *Scutellaria incana* is unusual and very special. Flowering in mid- to late summer, it creates a classic harmony with pinks, such as the *Anemone ×hybrida* 'Pamina' behind. More striking is the combination with *Sanguisorba* 'Tanna' to the left – although early morning sun is giving these flowers an especially strong glow.

COLOR

Color tends to dominate discussion of planting design, particularly where perennials are concerned. Many books have been written, some of them very good indeed. All the more reason not to discuss it in detail here!

We, Piet in particular, wish to downplay the importance of paying too much attention to color. Color should be seen as part of the whole; it is, Piet says, a 'layer on top of the structure . . . an element of emotion . . . not something separate'. Some rules have a basis in scientific evidence, and the well-known color wheel illustrated in most of the books on color in the garden does indeed show why certain color combinations are effective. Color, though, is particularly subjective. It is also very dependent on weather and light conditions: what may look good at one time of day may be almost drab at another.

At certain times of year, there may not actually be a great deal of choice. Spring and autumn in temperate zone climates tend to be dominated by yellow and purple-blue, probably for very good reasons to do with insect perception of light wavelengths. Gardeners may be best advised to exploit nature's suggestions for the season.

Using color to develop plant combinations is arguably less important now than it once was. The gardening which dominated the latter half of the nineteenth and much of the twentieth centuries relied heavily on hybrids or selections of plants bred for large and colorful flowers. Juxtapositions of these could create striking effects which drew strong reactions from those who saw them – of love or hate! In reaction to this, others worked with creating strongly harmonious color combinations. Current trends, however, tend to downplay color. Gardeners are now more aware of structure and texture, so include more plants with good foliage or form, many of which may not be strongly colored. Such aspects of plants may be difficult to define, but as Piet says, 'You know that you see a plant as being distinctive without being able to describe why, just like when you meet someone you like, you can't usually say why.'

Naturalistic planting promotes the use of wild species or cultivars very similar to the wild species,

A classic autumn or early winter trick involves putting together a hard, dark, defined shape (such as the globes of *Echinops bannaticus* here) with soft, pale, wispy grasses (*Deschampsia cespitosa* here, with another *Deschampsia* and *Miscanthus* to the rear). It can last for months, and can be made to work with a wide range of species. Unlike many late season effects, it does not depend on sunlight either.

where the size of the flower relative to the rest of the plant is not so large. All in all, compared to previous planting styles, this type of planting involves more green, more soft fawn-brown shades, more neutral creamy whites. Such colors not only make for a softer overall effect but break up the impact of strong colors by separating them more effectively.

<h2 style="text-align:center">STRUCTURE</h2>

Whereas designing with perennials has historically tended to focus on color, the use of woody plants in both garden and landscape design has dealt much more with, first, size and form – essential for functional reasons – and, second, structure and visual texture. By emphasizing color, designers with perennials have perhaps contributed to a perception that these plants are only for private or other relatively intensely managed gardens, while in public gardens this has led to a failure to fully exploit the value of perennials. This situation is now changing, partly because of a growing appreciation of the potential of perennials for winter and other out of season interest, where structure/texture is far more important than color.

It might be interesting to make a comparison with food. Most people's aesthetic experience of food – how much they enjoy it beyond the merely functional desire not to feel hungry – is based very heavily on flavor. But not if you are Chinese. One of the world's most complex and sophisticated cuisines puts surprisingly little emphasis on flavor; instead, an appreciation of texture, and the tactile experience of eating, is more important. Cuisines which focus so heavily on flavor are arguably missing a trick here. Might we make an analogy with planting design and an overemphasis on color?

The emphasis on color is actually very much a feature of a garden tradition centered on north-west Europe with its gray skies and relatively cool weather. This reflects perhaps the historical role of the British garden in inspiring garden-making across the world, and of the role of the Dutch nursery industry in supplying many of the plants to make it possible (with French, Belgian and German gardeners and nurseries contributing). With a long growing season and soft light, northern Europeans have opportunities to use color in the garden for months on end and to appreciate great subtleties; in addition, cool conditions mean flowers last for much longer than in hot climates. Such opportunities are much more limited for gardeners who have to cope with long cold seasons or long dry ones. Other climate zones also have floras which may offer far more structure and texture interest than color interest.

Designing with structure and texture is less amenable to rules – there is no color wheel to kick off the discussion or provide a first step for the beginner. The basics of a structural approach to designing with perennials was outlined in our first book, *Designing with Perennials* (1999), while other aspects of this subject have been dealt with elsewhere. Here we simply outline some basic principles and observations.

The 70 percent rule
There are few general rules in planting design, but this is one of them, and it gains credibility from the fact that several practitioners working independently have reached it. As discussed, perennials can be divided into those which have clear structural interest and those which do not – referred to as filler plants. Plantings work best if these two are used in a ratio of approximately seven structure plants to every three fillers.
• Structure plants: clear visual interest, other than being reliant on flower or foliage color, until autumn at least.
• Filler plants: only used for flower or foliage color; structural interest early in the season, but becoming formless or even untidy after mid-summer.

In the Plant Directory at the end of the book Piet indicates how effective certain plants are for structure.

Being led by the flora
A gardener or designer never has an infinite range of possibilities to work with. This ideal position is most likely reached by those working in balmy west coast climates where mixing and matching of plants from a wide range of climate zones is possible: such lucky people live and garden on the north-west Atlantic-facing fringes of Europe, and the area around San Francisco Bay where the temperature is more or less the same all year round.

Each different environment suggests particular plants, and those plants which thrive in a given environment are highly likely to share certain structural and textural (and indeed foliage color) characteristics. Anyone wanting to put together a planting for a site needs to

◄
Geranium 'Dilys' sums up what filler plants are good at. This particularly sprawly mid-summer-flowering geranium fills space between more clearly defined structural plants almost like a liquid. Left to itself, it is more or less amorphous.

►► (pages 134–135)
It is September in the Oudolf garden at Hummelo in the Netherlands, and although these plants are beginning to look a bit untidy, they all have a defined structure which keeps them interesting. The orange *Helenium* 'Moerheim Beauty' and the purple *Aster novae-angliae* 'Violetta' are upright growers, while *Sanguisorba* 'Thunderstorm' scatters its dark red flower clusters around at many different angles on long multiply branched stems. Behind, the grass *Molinia* 'Transparent' forms a mass of stems which is somehow simultaneously both solid and hazy.

◄
Grasses play a very important role in many natural environments and often act as signature plants for particular habitats. This role can be picked up in gardens or parks to create links to the surrounding landscape while at the same time be combined with more striking plants. Here, in the Hummelo garden, purple *Veronica* 'Eveline' emerges from *Deschampsia cespitosa*, along with the plumes of *Filipendula rubra*.

A quick look at the color wheel shows that blue/violet and yellow are complementary colors. They look striking together, perhaps too striking to repeat too often in a planting. Here, in August, *Solidago* 'Goldenmosa' grows alongside *Aster* 'Twilight'. From the current position to the right is pink *Lythrum virgatum*, which forms a harmony with the aster; move around to the left and it would be viewed from behind but would be rather strident if next to the yellow solidago – which tends to be an unpopular combination. Block planting like this emphasizes the juxtaposition of color combinations, but how they are seen is very dependent on the viewpoint.

Cream *Eryngium yuccifolium* alongside purple-blue *Lobelia* 'Vedrariensis' and pink *Monarda* 'Scorpion' form a harmonious mix for late summer. That they are all a similar height creates possibilities for blending or mixing.

▼

become aware of their particular environment and the visual themes it suggests – and then run with it. Very often climatic and other environmental factors constrain the potential range of plants, which may well eliminate whole suites of particular structural types: for example, windy situations rule out large, soft foliage. If using locally native plants is emphasized, this may well dictate certain levels of structural interest; think of the wide range of plants with clear rosettes to be found in the southern hemisphere. Habitats tend to feature distinctive plant shapes and textures for very good reasons of evolutionary adaptation, such as the hummocky shapes of fine-textured foliage so typical of environments where desiccation is a major issue, be it the winds of exposed sites in northern Europe or the relentless summer sun of the continent's south.

A self-consciously naturalistic aesthetic also dictates certain structures. In particular, the fact that grasses and grass-like plants dominate much open habitat in temperate regions means that any attempt at naturalism is going to have to involve them. This becomes especially clear in a project such as the New York High Line, where grasses are such an important part of the mix.

Harmony versus contrast

This is a fundamental tension in planting design – but tension can often be creative! Some designers and gardeners veer toward the expression of contrast, others toward the creation of harmony. This divergence is usually expressed in talking about color, but structure can also illustrate both principles.

With temperate Eurasian and North American species it is difficult to have 'too much' structure, as the palette of plant shape tends toward a great similarity of form; shrubs tend to have a rather amorphous shape and a very large number of both woody plants and perennials have small leaves, creating a diffuse and unemphatic appearance. Other climates often include a greater range of form, such as the rosettes and spiky shapes which appear in seasonally dry North American climates and many temperate zone southern hemisphere habitats. Tropical and near-tropical climates offer a whole order of magnitude more options in plant form and foliage form and size – indeed, warm climate planting design inevitably starts with structure, pushing color into second place. There has always been a thirst among temperate zone gardeners and designers to try to jazz up their plantings by adding exotic-looking instruments to the orchestra. To do so can play a risky game with hardiness, while in places with climates that encourage such experimentation inevitably gardeners work with a considerably larger array of plant structure combinations. The downside can sometimes be plantings which are exhausting to the eye with their wide variety of shapes, especially if lots of jagged, spiky or upright forms are used.

The range of structure illustrated by temperate zone grasses is wide, but with shapes that are rarely emphatic; they can be safely used to create interest among shrubs and flowering perennials with little fear of 'over-egging the pudding'. Indeed, it is ornamental grasses that have allowed temperate zone gardeners in Europe and North America to really explore structure as an alternative to color as the core aspect in planting design with perennials; imagine working without them to realize just how limited the structural options were before their widespread use. Other than grasses, the most important structural element is the single vertically thrusting stem. The repetition of identical strong verticals can be a very powerful device for stamping unity on a planting, especially since many of these have good temporal continuity with strong seedheads following on from their flowers.

With a variety of plant forms, it is easy to appreciate that it is possible to express a greater or lesser variety of contrast with them. Expressing harmony requires a little more imagination. Repetition of forms is perhaps the key here, especially grasses. There is something soothing and restful about grasses dotted through a garden or landscape, either the resonance of repeating soft shapes or the sense of unity created by the heads of those, like *Miscanthus*, which all face the same way in the lee of the prevailing breeze. Harmony can also be powerfully expressed by hummock-forming subshrubs such as species of *Lavandula*, *Hebe* or *Artemisia*.

LIGHT

Contemporary plantings have hugely opened up the possibilities for playing with light. Traditional borders were largely front-lit, which emphasized the role of flat blocks of color. Plants which needed backlighting to look their best, especially medium to tall grasses, were seriously disadvantaged.

The quality of light depends very much on latitude and time of year. Certain places are famous for the quality of their light, which is often a difficult to analyze combination of local geographic and climatic conditions. It is sometimes impossible to talk about light without being quite specific about place.

A particular light can be seen after dawn or before dusk in summer in Scotland and Scandinavia and, of course, other places at similar latitudes. It is almost hallucinogenic in its intensity, transforming everything with a golden glow. This is because of the low angle of the sunlight reaching the earth, which concentrates warmer toned wavelengths. Something of this can be seen in winter, too, at mid- to late afternoon throughout northern Europe. For a time of year when days are short and often oppressively gray, bursts of sunshine which create these effects are magical – but only if the right plants are around in the right places to catch the light and make the most of it. Summer light in higher latitudes is soft, and in maritime climate zones where skies are often gray, it can be very subdued indeed – perfect for the expression of an endlessly subtle range of color variations.

Further south or at lower latitudes, stronger sunlight creates very different effects. Summer light is particularly harsh; although during early morning and evening it can be rosily soft, it is not around for long. With clear

Rosy early morning or evening light in late summer brings out the best in red tones, such as *Persicaria amplexicaulis*, but also picks out a range of subtle colors in grasses, particularly *Miscanthus sinensis* cultivars, which present a huge array of color variations.

skies, winter light can be remarkably strong. In North America winter landscapes after snow, which browns the grass, can look utterly bleached of color – beneath an intense blue sky only fawns and browns are visible, with even conifer foliage looking so stressed that it hardly registers as green. At similar latitudes, Mediterranean climates often have a clear winter light too, but here there is often more green, and unlike the harsh light of summer, flower colors can seem luminous and the subtle variations in green and gray foliage appreciated. Summer light at these latitudes can be so strong in full sun that flower colors lack intensity; shade or overcast conditions provide a better opportunity to appreciate plant life. Plant structure, however, is more easily appreciated in these harsh light conditions – a powerful argument for relying on it.

Fog and mist are often seen negatively, but cloudy conditions at ground level can offer wonderfully evocative visual effects. Sometimes this is recognized, as in Hangzhou in coastal central China where the mists over and around the Western Lake have been praised by poets and painters for over a thousand years – perfect for woods and woodland flora. Swirling mists can add mystery and drama to a garden, with taller plants in particular looming in and out of sight. Weak sun penetrating the mist can add to the spectacle, and when it finally lifts, the mass of tiny water droplets left behind on leaves and stems can catch the light and sparkle until they too evaporate.

PLANTS FOR ALL SEASONS

SPRING INTO LIFE –
BULBS AND ALTERNATIVES

Spring in the garden is for many people fundamentally about color, which they yearn for after the months of cold and the bleached landscape that winter often brings. However, very little color is actually needed to make an impact, and many other aspects of plants such as structure and texture can contribute, albeit a more subtle one. There is an incredible sense of dynamism about this time of year: a border can change almost from day to day. Capturing this dynamism and energy is the key to enjoying and making the most of spring: unfurling foliage, the noses of perennials like hostas and peonies as they emerge from the ground, the fresh tones of young leaves, the neat shapes of expanding perennial clumps. Everything is palpable energy, and the task of the gardener or designer is to capture this.

The international trade in plants has resulted in spring in the garden being a remarkably similar event around the world. What is so different from place to place is its length. In maritime climates, spring can last for months, coming and going as cold and warm weather systems alternate back and forth. In Continental climates, it may only be a matter of a few weeks before high temperatures bring spring flowering to a rapid end, to be followed by a quick succession of early summer bulbs and perennials. Juxtapositions and combinations unknown to others, such as daffodils flowering with peonies, may occur as spring and early summer concertina together.

Woody plants can be an important source of life-affirming color, but of course they take up more space than perennials and bulbs. While trees can be underplanted, frequent maintenance is required to keep lower shrub branches from occupying the space which can potentially be used for underplanting.

Spring planting almost inevitably means bulbs, or – to use a more technical term covering them as well as other forms of discrete 'easy to sell in a packet' plants

Narcissus 'Lemon Drops' in the Lurie Garden, Chicago, in April, illustrating how bulbs can make a show when perennials are still hardly out of hibernation. Notice the scattering of the plants – they are not planted in groups as is often done, because (1) leaves of groups of daffodils make a big and fairly unattractive impact for several weeks after they have finished flowering, and (2) they will slowly form groups anyway.

such corms and tubers – geophytes. Bulbs are so easy, so instant and so cheap that they are almost too good to be true. As a result, they are in a danger of obscuring other possibilities for spring interest.

Most of the bulbs sold for gardeners are plants of woodland or meadow habitats from temperate or Mediterranean climate zones. These generally repeat flower well from year to year. The exceptions are primarily the tulips, whose ancestry lies in harsher climate zones further east; they need hot summers in order to initiate the formation of next year's buds and high nutrients during the brief period of their active growth.

Most bulbs can be distributed more or less at random with good results. In other cases more care needs to be taken over their distribution, either to reduce the risk of disturbing them in gardening operations later in the year, or to minimize the competition which they can sometimes face from perennials. Another reason to take care over distribution concerns daffodils and camassias, and the many weeks of increasingly untidy foliage which the plants show to the world after their flowering season, and which all good gardeners know must not be cut back for fear of losing next year's flowers. Tatty daffodil leaves are easily hidden behind vigorously growing perennial clumps in late spring and early summer, but careful planning is needed. Another way of minimizing this problem is not to group the bulbs as is often done, but to scatter them so that their foliage is then distributed rather than being a prominent clump.

The ease with which many bulbs can be added and grown among other plants and the fact that they are dying back by the time perennials are beginning to perform make it possible to think about the spring planting as being quite different in design conception to the summer planting. Having two plans – one a transparent layer for bulbs, the other for perennials – is one way of appreciating this as well as it making it possible to ensure that bulbs with leafy foliage such as daffodils and camassias do not overshadow emerging perennials. It is also important to ensure that young perennials do not cover the foliage of alliums, which need to grow early (their leaves die around flowering time).

Smaller bulbs – species of *Chionodoxa*, *Crocus*, *Galanthus*, *Scilla* and many more – are especially easy to combine with perennials because their period of active growth (and so their need for light, nutrients and mois-

ture) is separate to that of perennials, so there is only the most minimal competition. Consequently, they can grow remarkably close to perennials, or even inside perennial clumps.

Other plants can perform a similar trick to bulbs – flowering early and living in close proximity.

Summer dormant perennials

A great many woodland or woodland-edge perennials hug the ground, flowering early and tending to die back early. The extent to which they are summer dormant is often very dependent on climate. The familiar primrose of north-west Europe, *Primula vulgaris*, is quite capable of staying green all summer, but in hot or dry summers it almost entirely dies back; evolution has led it to make most of its growth during the mild winters and springs this region experiences. Plants such as *Pulmonaria* and *Omphalodes* are from more Continental climates in central Europe across to the Caucasus, but they too achieve most of their growth in spring, dying back into dormancy if the summer is too dry. The fine foliage of many *Pulmonaria* varieties appreciated by gardeners in more maritime parts of Europe through the summer should be regarded as a bonus, not necessarily something to be expected.

Species such as these can be grown in close proximity to later perennials, often flowering before many have even woken up. *Mertensia virginica* (and other related species) is a good example of a perennial which is able to fill spaces between other plants, even flourishing in the center of dense clumps of grasses, and glowing blue in spring sunlight among the bare clumps of perennials only just stirring into growth. In prairie habitats the deep pink reflexed flowers of species of *Dodecatheon* can be seen to perform similarly. European woodlander *Anemone nemorosa* is known to be able to occupy clumps of the infamously invasive Japanese knotweed (*Fallopia japonica*), because it can occupy the window of opportunity (February to April) before the knotweed carries on what many see as its mission of world domination. Autumn-flowering *Colchicum* species can also grow among the knotweed – bringing to mind those small birds which pick between the teeth of crocodiles.

A great many perennials could possibly perform this role, but their slow growth and consequent high price lead gardeners to cosset them – species of *Trillium* being

◄

A woodland is not just about trees. On the High Line in New York City, a layer of small trees (mostly birches) is underplanted with sedges, just as might occur in nature, especially on a low-nutrient soil. The tight, fine-leaved clumps are sedge *Carex eburnea*, a tough species native to the North American Midwest; it spreads but very slowly so it keeps its neat tufted structure. The larger clumps in the upper picture are *Carex pensylvanica*, increasingly popular as a lawn substitute in shade, and in the lower the grass *Sesleria autumnalis*, which needs higher light levels.

◄

►► (pages 142–143)
A variety of perennials can flourish beneath shrubs and small trees. Here, from left to right, are *Uvularia grandiflora* and, behind it, a carpet of cream-flowered *Anemone* ×*lipsiensis*; *Helleborus* ×*hybridus*, in front of which is blue *Mertensia virginica*, and in front of that pink *Dicentra formosa*; dusky leaved *Paeonia emodi*; and, just below the tree trunk, a fresh blue-gray, as yet unfurled shoot of *Polygonatum* ×*hybridum* 'Betburg'. Of these, *Uvularia*, *Anemone* and *Mertensia* are summer dormant, and *Dicentra* may sometimes be.

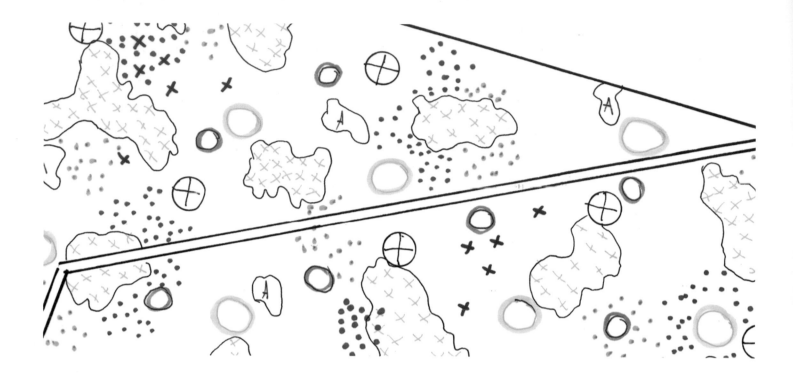

Bulbs and other spring and winter performing plants at Ichtushof in Rotterdam, Netherlands. Bulbs or other spring-performing plants are used in groups, and flower at various stages from early to late spring. *Anemone nemorosa* is planted in among the clumps of perennials *Anemone* 'Hadspen Abundance', *Geranium* 'Sue Crûg' and *Salvia* 'Pink Delight' – the diminutive but tenacious and steadily spreading *Anemone* consorts well with perennials whose main season of growth is after its flowering time. Small bulbs can be effectively placed simply by scattering them in groups, the positioning of the groups being more or less random, as with *Allium moly* and *Crocus speciosus* here.

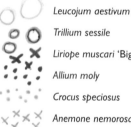

	Leucojum aestivum	25 per spot, every 7-9 meter (random)
	Trillium sessile	20 per spot, every 7 meter (random)
	Liriope muscari 'Big Blue'	3 per spot
	Allium moly	250 per spot scattered
	Crocus speciosus	250 per spot scattered
	Anemone nemorosa	100 per spot
	In between clumps of perennial Anemone/Geranium/Salvia	lightly scattered

a good example. In nature, however, they often grow in close proximity to other plants. In cultivation they may spread or self-sow into these situations, as long as soil disturbance is kept to an absolute minimum. Even *Trillium grandiflorum* has been known to sow itself and spread in garden conditions!

Annuals, biennials and short-lived spring-flowering perennials

Not many cultivated plants are in this category, but perhaps we should be more aware of it in the opening of our gardens to the flora of other lands. Woodland and woodland-edge habitats, especially those of maritime or Mediterranean climates – where winters are too mild to kill seedlings – contain a certain number of annuals and biennials which germinate in autumn and flower in spring or early summer. The well-known honesty (*Lunaria annua*) of cottage gardens with its intense mauve flowers and silvery seedheads is an example from traditional garden practice, the yellow-green *Smyrnium perfoliatum* another. Short-lived perennials such as the common European wildflower *Silene dioica* perform similarly, making most of their growth in autumn and spring, dying back in summer if necessary. Many species of *Viola* do likewise; this genus seems to have adapted particularly well to suddenly appearing in spring at the feet of other plants across a wide range of habitats and climate zones, seeding themselves and then disappearing.

The secret of the success of these plants is their seeding ability. They can scatter themselves about, perform and reseed without competing with later developing and longer lived perennials. We would do well to pay them more attention.

▲
Anemone nemorosa is a typical example of the growth pattern of true woodland plants; slow to establish and only rarely seeding, it forms large colonies when well established. Such species may find it difficult to survive in woodland-edge or heavily managed forest environments where changing light levels and frequent disturbance will reduce its growth (and the same in gardens); it needs full shade and to be left alone.

▲
Pink-flowered *Tiarella wherryi* emerges among gray-leaved *Dicentra formosa* and glossy *Asarum europaeum*. All three are woodland plants capable of forming extensive mats when established, *Asarum* being particularly useful for its ground-cover capabilities.

Ajuga reptans is a low-growing plant of damp places in northern Europe. It introduced itself to the Oudolfs' Hummelo garden some years ago – a good example of a spontaneous welcome arrival. It slowly spreads among the emerging shoots of later perennials, flowering in spring, with long-lasting bronzy leaves.

▼

Uvularia perfoliata is one of many woodland species, mostly of East Asian or North American origin, which are slow to establish and really only flourish in humus-rich soils, so have a reputation for being rather special. In fact, once established in good conditions, they can be very long-lived and persistent. Most actively grow in spring, dying down in summer if drought induced by tree roots becomes a problem.

▼

Evergreen perennials

Some shade-tolerant woodland plants invest in tough leaves which are either truly evergreen, lasting for several years, such as species of *Liriope*, or which last for a whole year, replacing each other in spring, such as species of *Helleborus*, *Carex* and *Luzula*. Either way, they always have a photosynthetic surface to make the most of light during the winter and early spring. Some of these plants are used in extensive ground-cover plantings, but are perhaps more creatively used in combination with other truly herbaceous perennials. Species of *Carex*, *Luzula*, *Liriope* and *Ophiopogon* are sufficiently grass-like to form an effective ground cover too. Indeed, in the Far East *Liriope* and *Ophiopogon* have been used extensively this way for centuries, and also in other areas with a similar climate, such as the eastern states of the USA. Many of them have a remarkable ability to survive intense competition with larger herbaceous perennials, so can be used as a low-level layer, almost invisible during the summer, but visible again as soon as the herbaceous species are cut back. While their growth rate is much slower in Europe, *Liriope* and *Ophiopogon* can do the same here. *Carex* and *Luzula* will grow at a faster rate – these two genera have enormous potential, with considerable variation between and within species in size and growth rate – and there is still much to learn.

EARLY SUMMER – BREAKING THE STRANGLEHOLD OF THE ROSE

As a general rule, structural interest among perennials in the garden increases as the season progresses. Early summer is very much dominated by neat hummocks of foliage spattered with flowers. Plants which later in the year are rather nondescript or even untidy may be the center of attention. Such 'filler plants' offer a great deal at this time, and given how so many gardeners' attention span is high at the beginning of the season and low later on, there is a great tendency to plant many of them, and so compromise the structure of the garden for the rest of the year. Some filler plants, such as the innumerable varieties of *Geranium*, can sprawl and spread out so much that they suppress or distort the growth of slower developing late flowering plants. Professional designers can keep a cooler eye, and are less likely to be seduced by a geranium-led explosion of garden color.

More even than the host of geraniums, the priorities of early summer planting design have been distorted by the rose. Central to European garden culture, the first flush of flowers in early summer (for most old varieties, of course, the *only* flowers) has tended to drag so much planting design after them. Once the appalling practice of growing them on their own, surrounded by herbicide-treated bare earth, is abandoned, there arises the question: what shall we plant with them? Underplanting or combining with perennials which do not compete with the roses is the obvious answer, which is perhaps part of the reason for the growth in popularity of genus *Geranium*. Subshrubs such as lavenders work well in combination too, but are unsuitable for colder Continental climates. Tall, late season flowering perennials or grasses do not mix well with roses, so the planting becomes stuck with only limited late season interest.

Roses have poor structure – most are rather formless blobs – and, as Piet pointed out many years ago, 'have low quality foliage'. Other shrubs which flower at this time, for example *Philadelphus* or *Deutzia*, are often worse on both counts – their scent is delicious, but they need careful placing so the foliage does not make too much of an impact. Once their role is restricted somewhat, the early summer planting can become rather flat: a season which waits for the growth of the promising green clumps of later flowering perennials. Some taller perennials with good structure flower now, such as species of *Thalictrum*, but not many; some medium-height plants have good structure, but many of these need moist soil (*Astilbe*, *Rodgersia*). Perhaps it is for this reason, as well as their undeniably unique shape, that the drumstick alliums have come to the rescue. These wonderfully spherical flower-heads are now so popular for early summer that they are in danger of becoming a cliché. There seem few other alternatives – *Eremurus* are superb but need very good drainage. Scope here, then, for more plant introductions.

Gardeners in climates where early summer segues into continual flowering until autumn are lucky. For many it is the end of floral interest in the garden until cooler weather at the end of the year. For those in arid climates, such as many in the American West or western or central Asia, it may be almost the time of the last flowers of the year. Interest has to be sustained with grasses, seedheads and drought-tolerant woody plants.

As spring turns to summer a variety of bulbs flower alongside early perennials. Here purple *Scilla peruviana* flowers in front of blue perennial *Amsonia hubrichtii* with yellow *Smyrnium perfoliatum* behind, and to the left one tall stem of *Allium hollandicum*. Once it has finished flowering, the *Scilla*'s foliage is relatively unobtrusive. *Smyrnium* is an overwintering annual, but often self-sows in light shade.

►► (pages 148-149)
As spring turns to summer New York's High Line is dotted with alliums: deep pink *Allium christophii* and white *A. nigrum*. These bulbs make very good plants for random scattering. Other perennials are just emerging as clumps but growing fast.

MID-SUMMER – ESCAPING THE HEAT

The earlier part of mid-summer can see some good structure: *Amsonia*, *Veronicastrum* and *Baptisia* species are superb and maintain their structure into seedhead-time. In cooler temperate climates, summer now continues apace with flowers and good structure until the late summer and autumn perennial flowering climax. British gardeners used to complain about how little there was in flower at this time: varieties of *Phlox* and *Monarda* and little else. There is little such complaint now with the growing use of *Echinacea* species and hybrids, and of plants not formerly cultivated in gardens, such as *Stachys officinalis*, species of *Asclepias*, *Eryngium* and *Monarda*, and many more.

In areas with very hot summers, growth can slow. In regions at latitudes where summer heat is combined with drought, such as Mediterranean climates, structure has to be the basis for interest if irrigation is to be avoided – this will often mean grasses and seedheads or evergeen shrubs. Even in regions where high temperatures are combined with high rainfall, such as the American South, southern Japan and central-eastern or southern China, plants often cease to grow – it is simply too hot or leaves scorch, and anything which does flower is over in days. In such climates the garden and landscape become like the tropics – a wall of green.

LATE SUMMER AND AUTUMN – THE SECOND SPRING

It is customary in Mediterranean climates to talk about the cooler and often wetter days of early autumn as being a second spring: annual seedlings germinate, some bulbs flower, perennials emerge from dormancy with fresh leaves and sometimes flowers. The same term is used by those in the hot and humid summer climates just described as a host of late season perennials respond to warm (as opposed to hot) temperatures and rainfall. East Asia has a rush of flowers: *Anemone*, *Ligularia*, *Tricyrtis*, *Actaea* and *Chrysanthemum* to name a few. Even more so, the American prairie flora is now at its height – literally and figuratively – with a vast number of species, many of them members of the daisy family (*Asteraceae*). These plants have deservedly become popular in cooler climates for good reason.

From now until the first frosts, gardens in many and varied regions can enjoy a vast range of perennials and grasses, all at their peak of growth, and often at their peak of structural interest. With so much to choose from, it is not surprising that northern European gardeners at the turn of the nineteenth and twentieth centuries developed the 'herbaceous border' as a grand finale for the garden year. The exact plant species we use now may be different (longer lived, lower maintenance) although often related.

This is the time when planting design has to cope with maximum biomass. In addition, many of the species which are at their best now are from environments where height is everything, such as prairie and tall-herb flora; plants will have spent all summer growing as tall as they can in a competitive race for the skies. Fertile and moist soils will support this kind of vegetation, whereas less fertile or dry ones will be suitable for much shorter, and in some ways more manageable, planting. A mass of tall plants may be attractive from afar but not necessarily close to, as many of the lower stems will be bare or covered in dead leaves. Traditional planting of late flowering perennials was built on the dogma of 'tallest at the back and shortest at the front', which resulted in an even slope toward the viewer, but at least this was a sensible strategy for dealing with tall and leggy perennials. More contemporary planting has opened this out, but still needs to articulate plant heights. Contrast and differentiation between taller and lower plants has to be achieved or it becomes a mass of more or less all head-high plants. Shorter grasses have a valuable role, and there is still a space for lower-level filler plants, some of which are either still in active flower or repeat flowering, as with many of the geraniums. Plants of medium height with good structure are at a premium now, and it is mostly grasses which fit this niche.

How to deal with so many tall plants and maximum growth at this time of year? Here are some of the options.

The 'walk-in prairie'
Large numbers of tall (that is, head height) plants may be massed – Piet and I have written before about how awe-inspiring this can be. Set in blocks to be viewed from broad paths is one option. A more exciting but risky option is to have narrow paths which make the viewer

Sporobolus heterolepis is an extremely useful grass: drought tolerant and immensely long-lived. Its flower and seedheads form a transparent haze through which other flowers such as this *Helenium* 'Moerheim Beauty' can be appreciated.

▼

►► (pages 152–153)
Blue-violet-purple and yellow combinations dominate many North American habitats in autumn. Inspired by these places, this combination is used to bring a final flush of color to the prairie area at Hermannshof, Germany. Here, blue *Salvia azurea* and yellow *Heterotheca camporum* var. *glandulissimum* make an impact; the small duller blue on the right is Aster patens. The height of the plants makes for a sense of enclosure.

plunge right in, just as in a real prairie grassland or tall-herb vegetation. Such an experience brings you face to face with the wonder of tall vegetation, but the risks include stems falling over in rain, too many bare stems, a sense of bewilderment: too much like an undesigned natural environment in other words. Such plantings can work best if they are looked down on from a higher vantage point, looked at from afar, or viewed from a boardwalk.

Blocks

Blocks of very tall plants surrounded by shorter ones or used in ways which define them and separate them from other parts of the planting can work, and are particularly effective for species which do not have such good structure. Many of the late flowering tall perennials are little more than stems with leaves and flowers near the top; by themselves they may have distinct form, but grown with others they can just become an amorphous mass.

This dramatically big planting at Hermannshof is designed to show a stylized version of prairie for fertile moist soils using conventional block planting but repeating to develop a sense of rhythm. Hybrids of *Helenium*, *Heliopsis* and *Solidago* provide much of the color. Some annuals are also used. The grasses are predominantly *Panicum virgatum*.

Blue *Aster laevis* and yellow *Rudbeckia triloba* in late summer at Hermannshof. The grass is *Panicum virgatum*.

At Hummelo in the Netherlands the strategy for the all-important late season is to use plants which do not get so tall that they obscure the view through and over, with a few emergents, such as *Veronicastrum virginicum* (now in its seedhead stage) to the right of the path junction or the taller arundinacea types of grass *Molinia caerulea* (for example, 'Transparent', which can be seen highlighted against the rear hedge).

Emergents

Plants which are notably higher and therefore seen separately to their fellows are extremely useful. An effective emergent is at least a third taller than surrounding plants. Natural emergents are those that tower above competitors in their natural environment, such as the three-meter *Silphium laciniatum* of the prairies – impressive but liable to flop. *Rudbeckia maxima* is an example of a shorter species which can be more effective, with most of its leaves at a lower level and flowers held well above on upright stems.

• Grasses. Taller upright grasses like *Calamagrostis* 'Karl Foerster' and many *Miscanthus* varieties stand tall and always look good growing above shorter plants.

• Bulky flowering perennials. Some can carry it off – some species of *Solidago* form graceful arching clumps, but many asters do not have a distinct enough habit to look really good other than as sources of color.

• Transparents. See-through emergents can be highly effective, with a hazy look of sometimes being visible and at other times disappearing into the background.

Transparency

Plants with masses of tiny flowers/seedheads on fine, widely flung stems can be incredibly valuable. It is possible to see through them to other plants or whatever is behind. They stand out against the sky and colored walls, but can disappear against other plants, or just hint at their existence by gently adding a color wash to the view. Transparent plants are most effectively used as a rhythmic element or to lead the eye through a planting. *Verbena bonariensis* adds a violet veil and often dancing butterflies, too, but has become something of a cliché. Many grasses, such as *Stipa gigantea*, do this well, and the increasingly important *Sanguisorba* genus. Transparency is something of a new concept (one I like to think Piet and I introduced) and has caught on. We expect the future to bring many more good see-through plants.

Gone are the days when brown and yellow foliage was seen as compost material to be cleared away as quickly as possible. Modern perennial varieties and, of course, grasses tend to stand better than many traditional varieties, and growing numbers of gardeners and landscape managers have come to accept that seedheads and dead foliage have their own beauty. Furthermore, it is increasingly recognized that some perennials have good autumn color, just as many shrubs and trees do.

It is no longer necessary to bang the drum for the autumn-into-winter look. Doing it well, however, does need some planning. A lot of perennials do not look good at this time, either because they collapse into mush with the first hard frost or they die untidily and get blown about by stormy weather. These may be best cleared away to leave room for those that do look good to show off their finery.

Late autumn and winter seedheads and dead foliage need good light to look their best. At latitudes where clear winter sun provides good illumination, this is not a problem. At higher latitudes hours of daylight are limited, but the effects can be truly magical. Given that sunlight in such situations comes in low and does not last long, getting plants to catch the sunbeams may require precision planting. Putting some plants in pots around the garden before planting them, to make sure the effect works, is a good idea. The planting situation also needs to be visible from a path, a viewpoint or the house in order to be appreciated.

Finally, the role of woody plants in winter cannot be underestimated, particularly clipped foliage shapes – evergreen or deciduous – and willows, dogwoods and others with colored stems or bark. As perennials finally get cut back, they may be all that remains.

Emergents are particularly useful late in the season, when perennial growth is at a maximum. This *Veratrum californicum* at Hummelo is an impressive example. Behind it is *Molinia caerulea* 'Transparent', with an emergent character but also see-through. *Deschampsia cespitosa* is shown left foreground and *Panicum virgatum* varieties are further back. Note the cutting of the hedge, designed to help it fit into the surroundings.

GOOD COMBINATIONS

SPRING

Spring in the perennial border

The ground is still very bare in April, but shows the first signs of growth from perennials and grasses. A number of plants can be seen here: the blue *Mertensia virginica*, one of those plants which is summer dormant and so like a bulb, is able to coexist with summer flowering perennials. The flash of red is *Tulipa wilsonii*. On the left at the foot of the column are two larger perennials, both of them with greater persistence through the summer, a yellow-green *Helleborus foetidus* and a pale lilac *Lunaria rediviva*, both of which tend to seed, a useful mechanism as if they get out-competed by strong-growing perennials they have a chance to survive.

Location: Piet and Anja Oudolf's garden, Hummelo, Netherlands.

For a damp patch

Camassia cusickii is one of several species of these North American bulbous plants which flower on the cusp of spring turning into summer, especially on damp soils. Their spikes of blue flowers are a good accompaniment to the emerging red leaves shown by many shrubs and perennials or, as in this case, the fresh young growth of the fern *Osmunda regalis*. Both the bulb and the fern thrive on moist soils. *Camassia* foliage is a bit like daffodil leaves – plentiful and somewhat untidy. Here it will be at least partially concealed by the extensive arching fronds of the fern, but elsewhere careful positioning may be necessary to hide it behind plants which will grow taller than the bulb after it has finished flowering.

Location: Hummelo.

Complementary colors

The intense blue of *Amsonia tabernaemontana* var. *salicifolia* combines supremely well with the greeny yellow of *Zizia aurea* – a good example of the electricity generated by complementary colors. The darker blue (in the foreground) is *Salvia ×sylvestris* 'Rhapsody in Blue'. The effective color combination is well supported by the contrasts in shapes, such as the prominent upright stems of *Amsonia* and the umbels of *Zizia*. Over time, *Amsonia* will slowly spread to form large clumps. Location: Hummelo.

The uses of height

Peucedanum verticillare is a very tall umbellifer, growing to 2.5 or even 3 meters, with a beautiful bloom on the stems. The seedheads stand firm for months, right through the winter. Its value is not just for the strong statement it makes, but also the fact that up close it creates a sense of looking past narrow pillars to whatever else is behind. Here, fluffy young flower stems of the grass *Deschampsia cespitosa* repeat among a variety of other perennials, with the uprights of pink *Veronicastrum virginicum* prominent on the left, and some scattered *Verbascum lychnitis*. Such uprights are useful at a time of year when most herbaceous vegetation is at a relatively similar height. *Peucedanum* lives for two to three years, dying after flowering but scattering many seedlings. Location: Hummelo.

Harmonies of form and color

The grass *Deschampsia cespitosa* sets the scene here – its misty flower-heads creating an ethereal backdrop and a little of the look of a wildflower meadow. The accompanying *Stachys officinalis* also has a wild look about it, especially when several different color forms blend together like this. With a relatively limited range of colors, the eye subconsciously focuses more on structure, so the uprights of *Veronicastrum virginicum* behind the grass, and the pale *Verbascum lychnitis* (left-hand side of picture) and *Veratrum californicum* (rear of picture) all reinforce each other, with only the balls of *Echinops ritro* 'Veitch's Blue' in the background and *Allium* 'Summer Beauty' in the foreground as a contrast in flower-head shape. The softly harmonious colors of the plants here create an atmosphere of great beauty and serenity. Location: Hummelo.

Form over color?

What is most important here: the colors – soft, pastel, harmonious – or the variety of shapes? The globes of *Allium* 'Summer Beauty' in the foreground are a kind of solid presence in a planting where soft and diffuse shapes dominate. The pale yellow-green of *Sedum telephium* 'Sunkissed' serves to highlight surrounding colors, intensifying them; it does not look particularly structural now, but by the late autumn its strong stems and well-defined seedheads will be making a distinct impression, and will continue to do so into the winter. Grasses here include *Festuca mairei* (left and right) and *Pennisetum* 'Tall Tails'. The height of the latter makes it a particularly effective structure plant. Less clearly visible in the picture but important for the longer term aspects are several perennials with upright flower-heads which form long-lasting seedheads: *Perovskia atriplicifolia*, *Veronicastrum virginicum* and *Phlomis tuberosa*. Location: Garden in Bonn, Germany.

Balls and daisies

Vivid in color and strikingly contrasting in shapes, the spheres of *Echinops bannaticus* and the big chunky daisies of *Echinacea purpurea* are an effective mix. They are highlighted against a number of grasses (including *Deschampsia* and *Molinia* varieties). The spherical heads of *Allium* 'Summer Beauty' echo the *Echinops* (bottom of picture). *Echinops* and *Echinacea* seedheads will have some value later in the year too, but for only a short time, as once the seed drops off they lose impact. A few strands of *Pycnantheum muticum* are also visible; this relative of the more familiar *Monarda* has silver-gray bracts and mixes well with stronger colors.

Echinacea and *Echinops* are two perennial genera whose lifespan can be uncertain. Close examination of the base of the plant reveals a very tight clump with only a limited capacity to spread, although in some gardens, some varieties do seem to seed. Experiences among gardeners vary greatly, but both species can suddenly just disappear.

Location: Hummelo.

Seedhead haze

It is generally grasses whose flowers or seeds form this cloud-like mass. *Limonium platyphyllum*, however, is a perennial with tiny mauve flowers which lead on to persistent seedheads, which are perfect for showing off deeper colored flowers such as this *Origanium* 'Rosenkuppel', although it is possible to imagine many other late performing plants in its place. *Limonium* has a very tight basal clump, making it suitable to combine with many other species at relatively close quarters. Behind this combination is a variety of the grass *Molinia caerulea* and *Stachys officinalis*.
Location: Lurie Garden, Chicago, Illinois.

Misty grasses

The multiplicity of flowers and the maturity of the grasses here create a combination which speaks strongly of the lushness and productivity of summer. The grasses in this photograph appear to dominate, although in fact there are not as many as it appears – at this time of year they tend to spread outwards, often from quite narrow bases, and create a feeling of flowering perennials being immersed in them, much as would happen in natural habitats. *Molinia caerulea* 'Transparent' on the right is an example of a grass which occupies a far larger visual space than might be expected from its narrow base. The central fawn grass is *Deschampsia cespitosa* 'Goldtau'.

The pale colors and soft textures of the grasses effectively highlight the deeper colors and more defined forms of the flowers, especially the tight, dark red button heads of the *Sanguisorba officinalis*. The tall stems of *Peucedanum verticillare* are an effective vertical element but one which takes up very little space. Additional species include *Pycnanthemum muticum* (white, center), *Helenium* 'Die Blonde' (yellow, rear) and *Lobelia syphilitica* hybrids (pink spire, foreground).
Location: Hummelo.

Foliage impact

The great advantage of many shade-tolerant plants is their high quality foliage, which makes up for the comparative lack of summer flowers. Here the bronze-purple leaved *Actaea simplex* 'James Compton' is just about to flower. Its dark foliage contrasts with that of silvery *Brunnera macrophylla* 'Jack Frost', although the different colors of these leaves simply reinforce what are very different leaf shapes. *Brunnera* and hazy *Deschampsia cespitosa* 'Goldtau' (left) are very effective repetition plants on this scale. *Tricyrtis formosana* is coming into flower (just visible, foreground) – with time

these plants can spread to form clumps, though they need moist but well-drained soils to do so, as do *Actaea simplex* 'James Compton' and *Brunnera*. This is a relatively new planting, and one component is hardly visible: *Galium odoratum*, a low-growing creeping species of woodland habitats which will eventually fill gaps between the larger plants.

Note that this is in Sweden. At higher latitudes, it is often possible to grow species which are thought of as shade plants in higher light conditions, even in full sun. Location: Skärholmen Park, Stockholm, Sweden.

Glowing grasses

The grass in the center here (a chance *Miscanthus* seedling) has just caught the light, making it glow – the real special feature of many grasses from this time of year onwards. The effect tends to be even better later in the year. Behind it are the plumes of *Calamagrostis brachytricha*, in front *Deschampsia cespitosa*. The red flowers in front are those of *Persicaria amplexicaulis* and to the right dark pink *Eupatorium maculatum* 'Atropurpureum'.

This is a late summer going into autumn scene which captures something very specific about this season: the growing predominance of red-russet tones, the incredible variety of grass forms and brown-to-fawn color combinations. Red or pink tones in flowers often pick up related tones in grasses or dying foliage of other perennials. There is also a sense of what might be called the growing chaos of autumn, when the maximum growth of the year is finally reached and then begins to die. Points of definite form and order, such as grass or flower-heads, are important as contrast.

This border at Hummelo is now 25 years old. Some of the original species included have been lost, but it does not seem to matter as it still looks very good. The survivors are obviously long-lived, but for the most part have only spread vegetatively. *Deschampsia*, however, does die after a few years, but has very effectively seeded in gaps and therefore persisted. Surviving perennials are inevitably those which are highly persistent.
Location: Hummelo.

Silhouettes

The perfectly spherical balls of *Echinops* species are irresistible as silhouettes against either the sky or a lighter background, even though they are relatively short-lived, soon shattering into individual seeds. *Echinops* is an example of an almost unique shape in the flora of plants available to temperate-zone gardeners. Another here is that of the branching spikes of *Veratrum nigrum* to the right. Its foliage, though now browned at the edges, is still worth having in the garden – the pattern of pleating is also unique.

This whole, very autumnal scene is lit up by the flowers of *Persicaria amplexicaulis* 'Alba', which reinforce their lightness with a shape that makes them appear to dance. Like nearly all the increasing numbers of varieties of this species, it has a very long flowering season, and may well go on until the first frost. Location: Hummelo.

A rich mix ▸▸ (pages 170–171)

Long, slow autumns can result in some perennials hanging on to their leaves, and even producing a new flush of growth. In west coast maritime and Mediterranean climates this is quite normal, especially for some species of *Geranium*, such as *G. phaeum* here with the spotted leaves. Their fresh green (regrowth after being cut back following early flowering) is a good contrast to the yellowing of the foliage of perennials from more markedly Continental climates such as *Amsonia hubrichtii*, the seedheads of others such as biennial *Eryngium giganteum* in the foreground, and the seasonal coloring of certain grasses like *Panicum virgatum* 'Shenandoah' on the left. The silvery structures at the core of *Lunaria rediviva* seedheads (rear, right) are also visible.

Despite the absence of flowers, such rich combinations of leaf and seedhead can create a remarkable amount of interest in a comparatively small space. Location: Hummelo.

Light and dark

One of the easiest effects to achieve in the autumn or winter garden is the combination of dark, clearly defined perennial seedheads set against a backdrop of pale, wispy grasses. Many late season seedhead effects are dependent on sunlight to look their best, but this is one that does not. Tall *Inula magnifica* 'Sonnestrahl' is here seen against a backdrop of several different grasses, with familiar *Deschampsia cespitosa* on the right – a particularly good species for this effect because of the lightness of its seedheads.

Location: Hummelo.

Classic autumn

Perennials and grasses put on a good show in front of a line of trees and shrubs also developing autumn colors, so forming a unified late season scene. The dark/light effect just discussed can be seen in the foreground, but the main impact here is sunshine on a bank of grasses and perennials, notably *Sporobolus heterolepis*, which can always be relied on for warm autumn shades, and tall *Veronicastrum virginicum* (mid-left). At the rear is some *Eupatorium maculatum*, one of the North American Joe-Pye weeds, which may not be particularly spectacular but whose combination of height/bulk and sturdiness gives them a reliable late season presence, particularly useful for making a visual connection with woody plants; they are also very effective in silhouette.

Location: Hummelo.

Bleached of color

Winter has pretty well set in now. When nearly all the color has been lost from the garden, every last scrap of the differences between the shades of fawn and brown that are shown up by the available light is important, and even more important is plant structure. A line of *Deschampsia* grass makes an effective backdrop for (from left to right) *Veronicastrum virginicum*, *Stachys officinalis* and *Astilbe chinensis* var. *tacquetii* 'Purpurlanze'. Further back are some examples of varieties of the taller grass *Molinia caerulea* subsp. *Arundinacea* and the rather dramatic looking perennial *Veratrum californicum*. Location: Hummelo.

Snow – the great leveller

Snow tends not just physically to level so much standing perennial material but metaphorically too, as anywhere without woody plants ends up looking the same under its blanket of white. Some perennials do stand for longer than others, especially ones like *Peucedanum verticillare*, which is the main feature here; it has a strong, very upright stem and little in the way of surviving leaves to catch snow and so be weighed down. The very upright grass *Calamagrostis* 'Karl Foerster' (behind) is similar. During snow, it is not designed combinations which create attractive features but simple survival. Location: Hummelo.

FOUR

LONG-TERM PLANT PERFORMANCE

Plants have evolved a whole series of strategies for survival in nature – not just of individuals, but more fundamentally of their genes. These survival strategies influence how plants grow in gardens and other designed landscapes. Understanding them is key to appreciating, and making the most of, the long-term performance of our plants.

HOW PERENNIAL ARE PERENNIALS?

Applying language to nature is rarely easy. We humans like to deal in hard and fast categories, and yet nature rarely does. A key concept in understanding nature is the gradient whereby black at one end turns imperceptibly into white at the other through infinite shades of gray. Language led by human understanding has to make decisions about where one category ends and another begins, so inevitably much subtle detail is lost. However, there is a particular failure in our inability to recognize the diversity of plant lifespans in the simple three-part division of plants into annuals, biennials and perennials – a failure which seems to cross languages.

Many gardeners know from experience that some annuals live for more than a year and some perennials always die after three or four years. Research I have undertaken, partly through observation but also through surveying experienced gardeners (66 of whom filled in a detailed questionnaire), indicates that a wide measure of agreement exists about which perennials are really perennial and which might more correctly be termed short-lived.

That some perennials might not live up to their name indicates there is potentially a big problem out there for professionals who wish to use perennials in

◄ Perennials amidst self-sowing grasses.

planting schemes. Writers of reference books and others who have promoted perennials have rarely addressed this problem – indeed, their failure to do so is actually quite shocking. The problem has been compounded by the nursery trade, which, it might be argued, has something of a vested interest in not being too clear about what is really long-lived and what is not. The nursery trade, in fact, tends to be dominated by wholesale producers of plants for the retail garden centers. A great many of their products are quick-impact but short-lifespan plants; professional users and gardeners interested in sustainability are more likely to be interested in genuinely long-lived plants, but much less varietal development goes into these. Or to be more precise, the larger scale nurseries catering for the retail trade do little. Specialist nurseries do more work at this end, with more limited resources – Piet himself being an example; he

has selected out some 70 new cultivars over the years, nearly all of them being naturally long-lived plants, the list including *Aster*, *Eupatorium*, *Monarda*, *Salvia* and *Veronicastrum*.

In our last book (*Planting Design*, 2005), we looked at some basic perennial categories. More recent research and thinking enables us to throw more light on these, and develop some more nuanced categories. One problem is that an enormous variety of herbaceous plants is available, and they simply do not fall into neat categories. There is also a wider variety of shrubs than we like to think. Looking at the problem in evolutionary terms, we can suppose that plants have evolved herbaceous and woody, annual and perennial lifestyles several times over – so there should be no surprise that there is such disparity and no obvious tidy pattern of classification.

LONGEVITY AND SURVIVAL STRATEGIES

In trying to understand how plants survive and coexist in the wild, ecologists have developed a number of different models. One of the most successful is the CSR model, which stands for Competitor, Stress-tolerator, Ruderal. The first two are self-explanatory, while 'ruderal' describes the behavior of short-lived plants which have an opportunist and pioneering lifestyle, such as the weeds which can occupy bare soil in a matter of weeks. The CSR model was developed at the University of Sheffield by J. Philip Grime in the 1970s. It is a way of understanding plant survival strategies – how plants survive and reproduce themselves in the wild or in their colonization of human-made spaces. A lot of this model makes sense to gardeners, and when I first came across it in the mid-1990s I was very impressed by how it explained so much about plant behavior and garden practice. For example, bare soil is important for ruderal growth, which explains why the traditional practice of constantly hoeing bare soil between plants is counterproductive: this is simply making an ideal seedbed for ruderals! The CSR model has had considerable impact in Germany, where it is used to provide a basis for different regimes of planting management. There is, however,

scope for misunderstanding and misinterpretation, and I do feel that too much can be made of it.

Here I will briefly outline the CSR model, primarily because its core ideas provide some useful concepts and labels for us as gardeners and designers and because some discussion of plant performance is now framed in these terms by colleagues. However, little further reference will be made to it.

Competitors do literally this – compete. They are plants of high resource environments (full sun, fertile and moist soils). They are able to make effective use of these resources, and grow fast and spread quickly through spreading roots and side-shoots. All this growth leads them to compete strongly with each other – to the extent that they will often end up eliminating each other. This is why exceptionally fertile, moist habitats can sometimes end up being dominated by only one species. Examples include lush wetland plants, grasses and perennials of fertile meadow and prairie habitats.

Stress-tolerators are survivors where the three vital inputs for plant growth are reduced: solar radiation (light and heat), water and nutrients. They grow slowly and do all they can to conserve resources. Examples

Blue *Symphytum caucasicum*, a species of comfrey, is a very strong competitor and in fertile, moist soils can spread aggressively – perhaps more than any other ornamental perennial – but its blue flowers can be appreciated for several months. Here, however, its growth has diminished over the years, because of the competition of the roots of the tree *Acer griseum*; the building foundations are also probably limiting the plant's availability to access moisture and nutrients. The lesson is that strong competitors may be very dependent on high levels of resources and suffer when they are not available. The silver is *Lamium maculatum* 'Pink Nancy', a much more modest and more stress-tolerant spreader. Also present is *Geranium sanguineum* (foliage left foreground), another modest but steady and drought-tolerant spreader, and a seedling of an *Origanum* species (right foreground), which spreads only minimally but seeds enthusiastically in many gardens.

include tussock grasses of poor soils and exposed habitats, subshrubs in dry or windy places, wildflowers on dry rocky soils, shade-tolerant perennials.

Ruderals 'live fast, die young'. They are opportunists and pioneers, seeding in gaps between other plants or in new environments. They grow rapidly and put a lot of energy into flowers and seed. They are usually short-lived, with the species surviving through its genes being scattered in plentiful seed. Examples are weeds of arable farmland, annuals of seasonally exposed riverbanks, and many plants of waste ground or disturbed places. Many, including a great many of those in cultivation, are annuals from regions with clear wet/dry seasons, such as Mediterranean and semi-desert climates.

It is often very instructive to think about plants in these terms. However, these are *tendencies* and not *categories*. The majority of plants are not pure competitors or stress-tolerators or ruderals; they combine elements of all three. It is not possible to put plants neatly into one category or another. For those involved in practical planting design and management, it is more useful to think about key aspects of plant performance, which I will do here, making reference to the CSR model where relevant.

LONG-TERM PLANT PERFORMANCE INDICATORS

For the practical designer and gardener there are four key indicators of long-term performance. Plant species tend to combine these in different ways.

Inherent longevity: some plants live a long time, while others do not, deteriorating even in ideal conditions. Anyone who has grown hollyhocks (*Alcea* hybrids), the classic English cottage garden flower, knows how in their third year they just look awful – lacking vigor, with woody growth which seems to have no energy for new shoots. That's all there is to it – they are genetically programed to grow rapidly, seed, and then lose vigor and die.

Ability to spread through vegetative growth, not through seeding. Those new to gardening soon become aware that some perennials spread whereas others stay put and do not increase much in size.

Persistence: this is about the ability of a plant to stay in one place, holding its ground. Those who think the definition of a plant is that it does not move around have not had the experience of growing something like monardas, which may be planted in one spot and the following year appear in several places further afield, but often with no growth in the original planting area.

Ability to seed: how effectively a species reproduces itself by seeding in garden conditions.

Now, I will look at these performance indicators in more detail, in particular their implications for planting designers and gardeners.

INHERENT LONGEVITY

Annual, biennial and perennial are three key words we learn when we first take up gardening, but they are in fact arbitrary categories forced on what is actually a whole gradient of different genetically programmed plant lifespans. The table below illustrates the gradient of hereditary longevity among some common garden plants, with an indication of longevity on the middle row, and an example on the bottom. Needless to say, the categories are not clearly defined!

My main interest is in the right-hand side of the table. Frustratingly little research has been done on perennial longevity. Reports from gardeners tend to be consistent that some species do inevitably die after a number of years, but how long plants live can be highly variable. Many species appear to live for three to five years, and others go on for much longer but perhaps do not survive beyond ten. Environmental factors and competition often have a major impact on survival. A good example is the popular *Echinacea purpurea*, which is reported to live little beyond five years in the wild while the related *E. pallida* may survive for up to twenty. The 'true perennials' category contains plants which have a variety of growth habits; the most important distinction (discussed in 'Ability to spread' below) is between 'clonal' perennials (which spread) and 'non-clonal' (which do not).

	Ephemerals	True annuals	True biennials	Functional biennials	Short-lived perennials	True perennials
Life expectancy	A few months	A full growing season	Two years	Two years plus, but deteriorating	Three years plus	Potentially forever
Examples	*Papaver rhoeas*	*Calendula officinalis*	*Digitalis purpurea*	*Alcea hybrids*	*Echinacea purpurea*	*Geranium endressii*

▲

Early morning sun on *Persicaria amplexicualis* 'Roseum' and a *Molinia* cultivar. In the foreground are the deep red button heads of *Knautia macedonica*, a plant which appears to be short-lived, but makes up for this by producing large quantities of seed: self-seeding is needed if it is to persist. Behind it are the heads of *Verbena bonariensis*, an annual of dry-season riverbanks in Argentina, but in cultivation a very short-lived perennial; it almost inevitably self-seeds in gardens, however. August at Pensthorpe in Norfolk.

►► (pages 180–181)

Peucedanum verticillare has a habit very typical of umbellifers. It is monocarpic, which means that it dies after flowering, which occurs after two or three years' growth. However, it self-seeds well in most gardens. Its 2.5 meter high seedheads make a magnificent winter spectacle.

How is it possible to tell whether or not a plant will be a true long-lived perennial? This is where the 'rabbit's eye view' is important. Examine the base of the plant – if there are clearly shoots with their own independent root system, then the plant is clonal, so it is going to spread and be a long-term survivor. A good example is any one of the pink-flowered *Geranium endressii* or *G. ×oxonianum* cultivars. If, instead, all the roots and shoots appear to connect at one point, like a neck, and the shoots do not appear to have their own root systems, then the plant will be non-clonal: it has no ability to spread itself and could be short-lived. The lighter and more fibrous the root system, the more likely it is to be short-lived. Plants with a narrow point of connection between top and root growth but with a substantial and tuberous root system, however, are probably going to be long-lived. It appears that with some perennials the degree to which a plant is short-lived may vary across the species – it is an aspect of genetic variation.

Being short-lived indicates that the plant has a ruderal component to its survival strategy, so it is most likely a pioneer species, only able to survive by constantly seeking gaps or disturbance where existing vegetation is lacking. While most annuals in cultivation are species of seasonally dry habitats, where seedlings can grow in the rainy season and survive as seed when it is dry, short-lived perennials come from a variety of habitats. Many are woodland-edge plants, such as *Aquilegia* and *Digitalis*, possibly *Echinacea* as well – unstable habitats where

change is constant as trees grow or are felled. Others are plants of grassland, where hillside soil slippage or ground disturbance caused by grazing animals is constantly making tiny gaps for seedlings to establish themselves, including *Knautia* or *Leucanthemum vulgare*. Some are wetland plants which take advantage of bare soil left exposed by flooding or seasonal water level changes (*Lythrum salicaria* or *Verbena bonariensis*). All these species are also vigorous growers, and so can be described as competitive-ruderal in CSR terms.

Longevity refers to the expected lifespan of a plant. It can sometimes be confused with speed of establishment; it is the experience of many gardeners that a young plant will often die, so it ends up being written off as short-lived. In fact, it may be a long-lived plant that is slow to establish. One paradox is that some very long-lived perennials spend most of their first years producing roots and making very few leaves; these roots will ensure long-term resilience and survival, but until they are in place, the weak top growth is vulnerable to slugs, drought or being overshadowed by a faster growing plant. They may be thought of as combining the competitive and stress-tolerant strategies. *Dictamnus albus*, originally a wildflower of dry habitats in central Europe, is a good example. Other examples are species of *Baptisia* – key prairie plants which can grow very slowly in their first years but can be immensely long-lived once established – and the prairie grass *Sporobolus heterolepis*.

▶

Aquilegia vulgaris is a good example of a *non-clonal* perennial. This plant is several years old, but there are no shoots with their own independent root system, only one point of connection between the top growth and the roots.

▶▶

A young *Solidago rugosa* shows a mass of shoots and roots, with several new shoots emerging on the right. Because each one of the older shoots has its own root system it can become an individual plant if the clump is damaged – so it is *clonal*.

Euphorbia cyparissias is a notorious spreader, with roots which emerge as shoots some 20 centimeters away from the parent plant. This habit can be useful for filling space, especially since taller plants are liable to suppress it. The emerging shoots are *Baptisia alba*.

Garden uses

A great many popular garden perennials do seem to come into the 'short-lived' category. So, what is the point of growing them? Annuals and biennials put a larger proportion of their energy into flowers to ensure seed for their continued survival – which makes them attractive plants to grow, especially since their flowering season is often longer than that of perennials. It is the same with short-lived perennials – they make a trade-off between flowers/seed and persistent, spreading growth. Many are free-flowering and showy, so of course we want to grow them. This may be fine for the private gardener or the heavily managed and well-resourced public space, but for anyone wanting to plan for the long term or with limited money or resources for propagation, such perennials should be only a small proportion of the planting.

Self-seeding is a major part of the garden at Montpelier Cottage, Herefordshire. Natural methods of increase of vigorous species are encouraged in an attempt to build up a vegetation dense enough to minimize weed infiltration. Here, in early summer, various color forms of *Aquilegia vulgaris* and *Geranium sylvaticum* (foreground) seed alongside steadily expanding clumps of *Persicaria bistorta* 'Superba' (right).

Late summer plantings in the Montpelier Cottage garden include self-seeding *Verbena bonariensis* – an annual/short-lived perennial (foreground) – and traditional cottage garden hollyhocks (*Alcea rosea*), which also seed successfully on a variety of soil types. The yellow is *Rudbeckia laciniata*, a strongly spreading tall and very competitive perennial only suitable for situations where its vigor will be a virtue.

Talk to gardeners with any experience, and they will report that certain perennials have an aggressive habit of spread. *Euphorbia cyparissias* is a good example, with some gardeners regretting ever having introduced it into their patch, whereas others find that its ability to spread is actually very useful. As usual, the tendency of plants to spread is not clear cut; ecologists recognize a gradient, with plants that never produce side-shoots or spread at one end, and species which within the space of a year send out many runners to start new plants at the other. A useful technical word here is ramet – a ramet is a shoot with roots which can become an individual plant.

There is a great deal of variation in the level and type of ramet production. Some perennials produce a few very long ramets (several tens of centimeters), such as *Euphorbia griffithii*, so that it takes many years before the plant forms a clump rather than a scattering of shoots. Others produce a great many which grow a few centimeters a year, such as *Geranium endressii*, resulting in steadily spreading clumps, whereas some grow even more slowly, such as *Geranium psilostemon*. The rate at which the clump breaks up, releasing ramets to lead independent lives, varies. In the case of *Monarda fistulosa* this can happen in a year, but it may never happen with *Geranium psilostemon* except in the case of damage, when a broken fragment can regenerate the plant. One of the most aggressively spreading perennials is *Lysimachia punctata*, a favorite of old cottage gardens in Britain – once planted, or indeed dumped by the side of the road, it never dies; its combination of a high production of ramets several centimeters long and a high level of persistence means that it can form a dense clump impervious to other plants.

Vegetative spread has been described by ecologists as being either phalanx – where a clump expands in all directions at once – or guerrilla, where odd shoots appear at some distance from the parent plant, and are only followed by clump formation if there is little competition. Relatively few garden plants are guerrilla spreaders, since the tendency to send out runners was seen as a problem by traditional gardeners. Today, we might see such selective spreading ability as potentially useful in occupying space left bare by other plants.

Perennials with an ability to spread are classic competitor-strategy plants, fighting to increase the amount of space they control, to spread themselves at the expense of others. In the garden they are reliable long-lived plants, with an ability to recover from damage and often to hold off weed infiltration. Some of the more strongly spreading ones are able to rapidly fill space – a useful characteristic. Many, however, see this tendency as innately worrying, as if they are behaving like 'weeds'. However, some rapidly spreading species are not effective competitors, dying out when they face the competition of others. *Euphorbia cyparissias* (a classic guerrilla) is a case in point: in the wild it appears only as

Pycnanthemum muticum is an example of a strongly spreading *clonal* perennial. Long new shoots can be seen on the left. The rest of the plant is a mass of shoots with their own root systems. Next year the new shoots will look much like the shoot/root mass on the right, and will be sending out their own new shoots.

Emerging among *Deschampsia* shoots in early summer are stems of *Euphorbia griffithii*, a species which spreads slowly in a guerrilla fashion – erratically. These odd clumps appearing among other plants can be very attractive. It is June flowering. *Allium hollandicum* at the rear will repeat flower in many gardens from year to year, and on lighter soils may even self-seed.

odd shoots among grasses and other wildflowers, while in the garden it seems to be out-competed by taller plants (it is only some 30 centimeters tall). Plants which form steadily spreading dense clumps, such as many species of *Geranium*, *Aster* and *Solidago*, are particularly immune to weed infiltration and can self-repair after damage, and so can be seen as the mainstays of long-term plantings. With time, they form such large clumps that they will dominate the border, at the expense of shorter lived but self-seeding plants and non-clonal perennials. This will be the time to intervene, splitting them up to make more room for other plants in order to create variety.

Garden uses

Rapid spreaders have traditionally been regarded as thugs in the garden. However, given what has just been said, this may or may not be a problem, depending on how competitive they are – the problem is that we do not have much data on this. Gardeners can observe, however, how plants have performed in gardens with older plantings and from their own experience. Weak rapid spreaders with low persistence have value for in-filling between larger plants; strong ones which persist or out-compete neighbors have most value in low-maintenance environments where strong weed suppression and minimal intervention are most important. Guerrilla spreaders can create some attractive spontaneous effects in a similar manner to self-seeding plants if only a few stems pop up here and there. Most species which spread like this are not capable of penetrating established clumps, so combine well with others.

Some perennials are potentially long-lived but often fail to do so in garden conditions – and, one suspects, often in the wild too. These include some species of *Monarda* and *Achillea*, which have wandering shoots, and often only live for a year or two. If the new shoots do not find good conditions or run into an established clump of something else, they are liable to die out quickly, although they are not inherently short-lived. Such plants can be said to have a low level of persistence. They could be considered as competitive-ruderals, as they are constantly on the move seeking out new territory. How long these plants survive in the garden is highly variable; soil, climate and the exact nature of the clone all make a difference. Continental climates with clear-cut winters and summers seem to be more favorable to the survival of many *Monarda* and *Achillea* varieties than maritime climates with their unpredictable winters of alternating periods of cold and damp.

Other perennials increase at a slower rate, but seem to march out from a central base, dying out there and so leaving a hole in the middle of the clump. *Iris sibirica* is a good example; old clumps split away, but for a variety of reasons this does seem to be a competitive species, and this habit does not reduce its usefulness as a long-term resident of most places where it is planted.

Most garden clonal perennials have growth which is strongly persistent. Among the most persistent plants are those that form an underground or ground-level semi-woody base. Some can only be regarded as non-clonal, because there seems to be no ability to naturally produce new independent plants; herbaceous species of *Sedum* (*S. spectabile*, *S. telephium*) are a good example. Others are distinctly clonal, but only in the sense that it

may take a very long time (over ten years) for parts to separate, such as *Veronicastrum virginicum*. The hard, woody basal material is reminiscent of the woody plate-like structure which forms at the base of many shrubs. Plants with this structure may live for decades, and it is even possible that some wild clumps are centuries old.

It can be difficult to work out whether a plant has this type of basal structure, as opposed to a thicket of interconnected ground-level stems. It can most easily be found in spring by gently scraping back soil or debris around the top of the plant. A trowel rammed point down into the center of the plant will also produce a distinct 'thonk' if it hits a woody base.

Many bunch or tussock grasses (correctly cespitose species), like *Deschampsia cespitosa* and *Molinia caerulea*, are also highly persistent. They have a particular trick in that they recycle nutrients, their old leaves forming a mulch around the plant that gradually decays to release nutrients to feed new growth. Plants of some wild cespitose grasses are thought to be hundreds of years old.

Perennials with reduced persistence may seem like a bad bet for gardeners, and indeed in modern terms they are. However, many played an important role in the traditional herbaceous border and continue to be valued, largely because of a number of showy species which were used to produce a wide and opulent range of garden hybrids. Of these, hybrids of a North American aster (*Aster novi-belgii*, the New York aster) and of a phlox (*Phlox paniculata* or fall phlox) were both very important; they have a moderately spreading but non-persistent habit. Technically they are competitive-ruderals, their ancestors living in nature in unstable but fertile habitats such as woodland edges, riverbanks, creeksides and other unstable coastal or wetland situations. In such conditions, persistence in one place is a

Strongly persistent perennials (left) form a solid clump and stay like this for many years. Less persistent perennials rapidly break up to form small clumps (right). There is a gradient of behaviour between the two.

Baptisia alba with *Euphorbia cyparissias* and grass *Nassella tenuissima* in late June. *Baptisia*, like several other North American prairie species, is slow to establish, as it builds up a large root system, but is very long-lived.

disadvantage, so evolution has driven these plants to move ever onwards. As garden plants they need high fertility. The conventional wisdom is that they also need dividing and replanting every two to three years to maintain their vigor; in practice this depends on the cultivar. Species which spread only slowly but tend to seed to replace themselves are another popular group: for example, *Delphinium* and *Aconitum*, natives of very fertile but often rapidly changing mountain woodland habitats. Clumps in the garden can rapidly lose vigor, necessitating propation to keep them going.

Garden uses

The value of slowly spreading and persistent plants to the gardener and designer is very clear. They can form a reliable part of long-term plantings, often without the

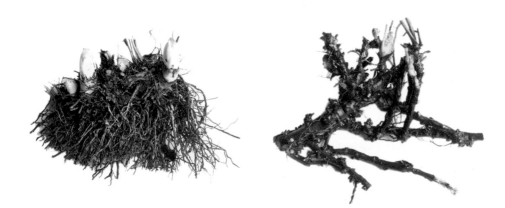

Persistent perennials, produce long-lived growth which lasts for many years in the same position. *Actaea ramosa* 'James Compton' (left) spreads only very slowly, forming a dense mass of shoots and roots. *Geranium sanguineum* (right) is much faster growing and spreads relatively quickly, but as can be seen here from these sturdy, almost woody-looking roots, its growth is durable and persistent, so it forms clumps of solid growth, without dying back.

problems of needing to control them after a few years, which can happen with those which are persistent but spread more strongly. However, whereas the latter can be easily dug up and divided, non-clonal or very slowly spreading persistent plants may not take very kindly to being divided, or division may be very difficult.

Less persistent perennials have a limited value in situations other than the highly managed private garden or public garden with good funding and dedicated staff. However, the genetic variation in some of these species appears to be wide, and may be one of the reasons why they were brought into cultivation in the first place. This genetic variation is not just about the range of flower color and flowering season, but also about habit, height, growth rate and vigor, so potentially there is a wide range of persistence too; as an example *Phlox paniculata* and related species such as the strong-growing *P. amplifolia* still offer a thick seam of diversity for nursery owners interested in making new selections on the basis of persistence and vigor as much as floral qualities.

ABILITY TO SEED

When a species self-sows in the garden it can be thrilling – it is a sign that the plant is happy. Moderate self-sowing of shorter lived species can create the sense of a garden as being a healthy if artificial ecosystem. However, joy can be followed by annoyance if a plant seeds too aggressively and starts to compete with other species, or is in any other way problematic. Although long-lived and persistent perennials tend to have a lower rate of self-sowing precisely because they tend to be competitors, often with extensive or tough root systems, any that do more than very low-level self-sowing may create long-term problems.

Some garden plants are notorious seeders, scattering their offspring everywhere, sometimes to the point of becoming a weed. The level to which species self-seed is very unpredictable; whereas vegetative spread is more or less predictable, seeding is not – it is dependent on a great many factors, such as soil type, temperature and moisture levels in spring.

As a very general rule, the shorter the expected life-span of a plant, the more seedlings it will produce. Biennials are very free with their seed, and the most troublesome if mass germination occurs: species of *Verbascum* are notorious for carpeting all available space with their seedlings, as is *Eryngium giganteum*, known as Miss Willmott's ghost, after the English plantswoman of the early twentieth century who surreptitiously scattered seed in gardens she visited, so the plant would haunt her hosts for evermore. Some short-lived perennials such as *Aquilegia vulgaris* often produce large numbers of seedlings too, but rarely on anything like the same scale.

Biennials and short-lived perennials do not spread vegetatively, so at least the ability of individual plants to physically out-compete other members of a planting is limited. On the other hand, strongly competitive species with an ability to spread vegetatively often produce little seed. Many short-lived, generously seeding species have a narrow and upright habit, so their ability to physically spread over or compete with neighboring plants is relatively limited: large numbers of *Aquilegia* and *Digitalis* plants can grow alongside true perennials and not create problems. The same cannot be said for all, as anyone who has had to cope with the dense basal growth and sprawling flower stems of large numbers of *Knautia macedonica* or *Verbena hastata* will testify.

In planting design, it is questionable whether we can rely on the seeding abilities of self-sowing plants to

Pink *Eupatorium maculatum* 'Riesenschirm' alongside scarlet *Monarda* 'Jacob Cline' with pink *Stachys officinalis* 'Hummelo' in front. *Eupatorium* is long-lived and persistent, only slowly forming clumps, while *Monarda* can survive a long time but only if its highly mobile clumps are able to expand into new territory, so its persistence may be poor.

Allium carinatum spp. *pulchellum* alongside grass *Nassella tenuissima* in May. The grass is short-lived (three years is usual), but in most gardens it self-sows, sometimes extensively. The alliums have also sown themselves here through cracks in paving, a situation which often encourages self-seeding.

regard them as permanent or even semi-permanent components of planting. In smaller gardens where maintenance tends to be more intensive, more perhaps might be allowed; in larger areas one can allow more seeding when the garden has established. Knowledge about levels of self-seeding has never been systematically gathered and is largely anecdotal. While short-lived self-seeding plants can be designed into plantings as minor components, the level at which they will continue to participate will depend very much on the skill, intuition and knowledge of those who manage them. Piet says, 'I have a rule in planting design using biennials and vigorous self-seeders. I hardly use them and if I use it is as an extra in gardens that are established so that there is limited space and enough competition to limit their numbers.'

Garden uses

The sheer unpredictability of seeding makes it difficult to give too many recommendations for its use in management strategies. Most perennials will self-sow better on lighter soils, and some will produce prodigious levels of seedlings in mineral mulches like gravel, but in the final analysis the gardener has to observe, learn the behavior of their plants, and work with the level of seeding of the species. Moderate self-sowing of shorter lived plants is truly a boon, and of long-lived perennials too if they are not strongly spreading. Over-enthusiastic seeding can be a problem, and in extreme cases plants will need to be eliminated. With time, though, as a planting matures and long-lived components spread and monopolize space and resources, the bare-earth opportunities for short-lived ruderals will steadily diminish. Such species seize their advantages in the early years, but unless given active encouragement by the gardener they are bound to reduce as time and more robust, long-lived perennials march on.

▲

Echinacea purpurea 'Fatal Attraction' growing among *Calamintha nepeta* subsp. *nepetoides*, the latter usefully filling out space between *Echinacea* clumps. In time *Echinacea* will die out, although in some situations it self-seeds. Its exceptionally attractive flowers are very popular, though, so its lack of longevity is widely seen as an acceptable price to pay.

► ► (pages 194–195)
Eupatorium maculatum 'Snowball' with *Persicaria amplexicaulis* in the background in August at Hummelo. *Eupatorium* only forms clumps slowly, while *Persicaria* does so at a somewhat faster rate. Like most long-lived perennials, both can seed in the garden but only modestly.

MAKING SENSE OF PERENNIALS –
OR IS IT EASIER TO JUST GROW THEM?

Garden plants, and perennials in particular, are very hard to pigeonhole into categories, but since they behave in so many different ways over time, it is important that we have some way of making sense of their diversity. Realistically, it is best to think of a series of gradients; I have suggested some here related to performance: from short to long lived, from non-clonal perennials which do not spread vegetatively to those which spread aggressively, from those whose clumps are very persistent to those which constantly break up and, finally, the very wide variation in how likely a perennial is to self-seed under garden conditions.

There are relationships between these gradients, and a lot of research needs to be done to improve our understanding of them, and in particular how they relate to each other. It is also possible to set gradients against each other to form a grid.

Such mapping of plant performance characteristics can be very useful in planning for different kinds of planting, and there is definitely scope for research in this area to continue. However, plants are never consistent, which is perhaps part of their interest and attraction to us, so at the moment it is easier to abandon any idea of making categories, which will always be hedged about with 'ifs' and 'buts' and endless exceptions. Instead, think about a plant's position on a series of gradients, which is what we have done in the Plant Directory at the end of the book. Fundamentally, though, the important thing is to enjoy what we grow, and accept the sometimes confused, tangled complexity of nature as part and parcel of our work and our passion.

	Low persistence	Medium persistence	High persistence
Low spreading ability	*Digitalis ferruginea*	*Geranium sylvaticum*	*Sedum telephium*
Medium spreading ability	*Phlox paniculata*	*Iris sibirica*	*Geranium endressii*
High spreading ability	*Monarda fistulosa*	*Euphorbia cyparissias*	*Lysimachia punctata*

Three of the grasses commonly used now in gardens and landscapes: *Molinia* 'Transparent' (top left), *Panicum* 'Shenandoah' (top right) and *Sporobolus heterolepis* in front. Their rate of spread varies: *Panicum* is the most likely to form clumps, whereas *Molinia* is a true cespitose species and will never go beyond a tight tussock. At the very front is *Pycnanthemum muticum*, a perennial which forms large colonies in its native USA, but in cooler summer climates is liable to be much less vigorous.

FIVE

MINGLING CURRENTS IN CONTEMPORARY PLANTING DESIGN

Inspired by nature, planting designers are creating intermingled combinations using either plants or seed. Here we look at some of the most exciting and clearly articulated of these approaches currently being applied by colleagues across three continents.

We have to suppose that there is a zeitgeist at work here. It certainly feels as if many people have had the same good idea at the same time. Inspired by plant ecology science, or just a desire to try to replicate the way plants grow in nature, there are now a number of different but related approaches to creating perennial-based mixes which aim to blend and intermingle varieties. Whereas design in the past focussed on precise plant placement and juxtaposition, these techniques all aim to create the apparent spontaneity of natural vegetation. They do this not by setting out a plan but by planting a mixture – or, to put it another way, they are about creating a vegetation.

◄ The Sullivan Arch Garden in Chicago.

A planting in Noel Kingsbury's garden in Herefordshire on the England/Wales border, in August, illustrating a mix derived from a tall-herb flora model developed for use in public spaces. Very robust perennials are chosen to minimize weed competition on fertile soils in regions with a long growing season. The yellow is *Telekia speciosa*, the mauve-blue *Campanula lactiflora*, the red *Persicaria amplexicualis*, and the pale pink in the foreground *Geranium endressii*.

A version of Prairie Morning, a mix developed by Cassian Schmidt at Hermannshof, Weinheim, Germany, for dry to medium soil. The pink daisy is *Echinacea tennesseensis* 'Rocky Top', the dull purple *Amorpha canescens*, the grass *Nassella tenuissima*, and the pink cup *Callirhoe bushii*.

RANDOMIZED PLANTING

The idea of randomized planting at first hearing sounds strange – almost the antithesis of what design in all about. The immediate analogy is with a wild plant community: a wildflower meadow or prairie looks random. In fact, it is not, because there are what ecologists call assembly rules for how and why plants associate. To our eyes, though, these wild plant communities are effectively random. Creating a deliberately randomized mix is essentially a way of creating a mix of plants which is designed off-site: species are chosen for a given environment, to be compatible at equal spacing, and for particular design criteria, which typically include performance for a given season, color and height. A good mix of different structures is also included. The mix can then be rolled out for any space deemed suitable. It is therefore modular, potentially usable for tens or hundreds or thousands of square meters.

Some in the design community are almost offended by the idea. This may be interpreted as the professional jealousy of those (sometimes not designers but vegetation scientists, entrepreneurs or nursery owners) who have developed the mixes. More crucially, perhaps, there is a sense in which any modular approach is seen as mass-produced, and insensitive to what has become almost a dogma: that of design being site-specific. However, what randomized planting offers is a kind of democratization. Just as industrially mass-produced furniture can bring quality design to people who before could not afford it, sometimes to the chagrin of those who can, so randomized planting brings the possibility of large-scale sophisticated plantings to clients who could not afford to employ someone to undertake planting design on a large scale: local government, not-for-profit organizations, community groups, private gardeners with large or difficult to maintain areas, schools and other institutions.

Many commercial projects tend to squeeze the expenditure for landscape; the building comes first, and cost overruns eat into the landscape budget, and then because the planting usually happens last, resources for this are squeezed further. Bringing down the cost of quality plantings inevitably involves compromises, but randomized mixes offer hope of more visually interest-ing, seasonally changing and biodiverse planting combinations. In particular, they offer the opportunity of visually rich plantings as an alternative to the green cement which in the past has sometimes given the landscape profession a bad name.

The wildflower meadow mixes developed initially by British and German practitioners in the 1970s and the prairie mixes developed during the same period in the American Midwest involve randomization because they are seeded. Seeding is also part of the process used by James Hitchmough and collaborators at the University of Sheffield for creating mixes, each one based on a natural reference model. The idea of applying random mixes to planted combinations was first developed in Germany by Walter Kolb and Wolfram Kircher in the 1990s, with the first public plantings of the mix, *Silbersommer* (Silver Summer), being made in 2001. Since then more than twenty 'Mixed Plantings' have been developed at a number of educational and research institutions in Germany and Switzerland. In addition, other mixes have been developed by garden and landscape designers and individual nurseries.

Here we look at a number of approaches to randomized planting, and then in more detail at the method actually called 'Mixed Planting' in German, which is by far the most deeply researched and influential.

DAN PEARSON – AN EXPERIMENT WITH MODULAR PLANTING

Dan Pearson enjoys a reputation as one of Britain's leading garden designers. The key to understanding him is that he was practically born with a trowel in his hand. Plants and gardening have always been a part of his life, and his design skills have grown out of this personal experience and intimate knowledge. Wild plant communities have always been an inspiration for him; he discovered the limestone meadows of the Picos de Europa mountains in northern Spain as a teenager, and an early experience involved working at the Jerusalem Botanic Garden, which introduced him to the spectacular spring flowers of the Middle East; he has gone on to encounter many other rich wild plant communities.

An excerpt from the plan for perennial mix areas at the Tokachi Millennium Forest (2006). Each block, or panel, indicates one of the plant mixes A to N. Shrubs and large perennials also form another layer to this area, indicated on another plan.

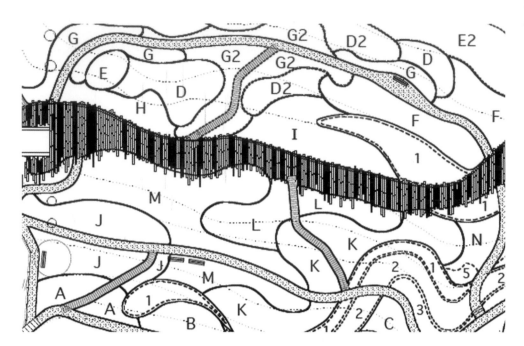

One of the mixes used for the Meadow Garden at the Tokachi Forest. The strip at the bottom is one of the repeating units or modules, analogous to a tile. The cimicifugas (20 percent of the plants), rodgersias (3 percent) and sanguisorbas (10 percent) have flower-heads that function as emergents. The asters (43 percent) and the euphorbias (20 percent) are space fillers, while the two *Paeonia* species (5 percent) are the 'treats'. Spacing is 30 centimeters between plant centers, except for the paeonias and the rodgersias, where it is 50 centimeters. It is instructive to read the accompanying notes on the plan:

• Repeat plant sequence in rows.
• Start each new row at a different point in the sequence.
• Use random number grid to start each new row.
• More random numbers can be generated at www.random.org.
• Apply varying orientation to rows in each of the mix areas.

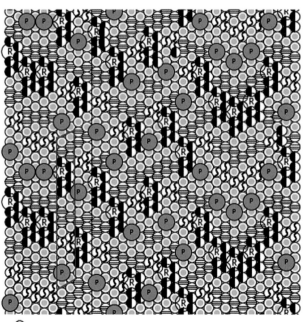

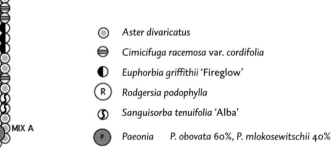

MIX A

⊙	*Aster divaricatus*
⊖	*Cimicifuga racemosa* var. *cordifolia*
◑	*Euphorbia griffithii* 'Fireglow'
Ⓡ	*Rodgersia podophylla*
⑤	*Sanguisorba tenuifolia* 'Alba'
Ⓟ	*Paeonia* P. obovata 60%, P. mlokosewitschii 40%

Like many practitioners he has to tread a delicate balance between designing and implementing tried and tested planting combinations and being experimental. One particular project has allowed him to make what he describes as being 'a risky experiment, not yet repeated', but which so far has seemed successful.

The Tokachi Millennium Forest in Hokkaido, Japan, is a 240 hectare ecological park created by a media entrepreneur, Mitsushige Hayashi, and aims to offset the carbon footprint of his newspaper business. Working with landscape architect Fumiaki Takano, Pearson has helped to create an environment which greets visitors (mostly very urban people) with a gardenesque environment near the visitor center that 'will draw them in, gradually familiarizing them with plants and nature'. The idea is that they will begin to feel more relaxed about exploring the main part of the project, a forest landscape with an immensely rich ground flora recovering from a period of deforestation. This area, the Meadow Garden, uses a modular planting style.

Hokkaido lies on the same latitude as New England and has, if anything, an even more Continental climate, with a short growing season (April to September), cold winters (down to minus 25°C) and a short, hot and humid summer. The 1.2 hectare Meadow Garden is designed to be an attractive experience for visitors, but as the planting uses mostly non-native species, there is a concern that some might escape into the wild. To help prevent this, the garden area is surrounded by hedge walls of pine, willow and other species, some 10 to 20 meters deep, with a thick, weed-free mulch so as to minimize seeding. Within this boundary are a series of 14 panels, each one a mix of 5 or 6 perennial species. Each panel is color-themed, and bands of grass *Calamagrostis* 'Karl Foerster' are used to create screens to avoid color clashes. 'The paths', says Pearson, 'are designed to have the same panel mix on each side, to get a sense of walking through…. Some mixes have an additional component added to get a sense of one panel segueing into another.' A key element in the macro level of design is the use of emergents: shrubs such as *Rosa glauca* or large perennials like *Aconogonon* 'Johanniswolke' 'to bridge the panels and provide a unifying element, and be rocks around which everything flows…. The idea is a river of incidental happenings.'

Each panel mix uses a repeating combination module which Pearson describes as being 'like a strand of DNA…. We have designed a system in which the combination within the mix is never repeated the same way twice so that it is random…. The idea is that the mixes will develop their own balance and rhythms.' A computer program is supplied to the client which is used to generate a pattern based on repeating the modules. The resulting plan can be divided up by a grid, and then the plants set out on to a corresponding grid on the ground.

Different combinations have had different outcomes. In one of the mixes a particular species has become too invasive and has had to be replaced, but the great majority of combinations have been satisfactory and indeed have begun to 'develop their own dynamic'.

As with the Mixed Planting systems developed in Germany, each mix combines plants from several structural categories: what Pearson describes as 'emergents, procumbent [that is, sprawling] plants, space fillers and treats' (treats being occasional unexpected splashes of color or form).

ROY DIBLIK – PLANTING GRIDS

Roy Diblik is a nursery owner in southern Wisconsin. Always something of a pioneer, he was one of the first to grow Midwest natives as containerized plants. Working in a region where there is little history of growing perennials as garden plants, and where many misconceptions exist about the kind and level of maintenance required, Diblik has developed a system called the

▶▶ (pages 204–205)
The Meadow Garden at the Tokachi Forest. Flowering are deep purple *Salvia nemorosa* 'Caradonna', white *Gillenia trifoliata* and blue *Baptisia australis*.

An example of one of Roy Diblik's border planting modules, including both perennials and bulbs. This is 'Elegant #4', for an open site and average soil where a height of 45 to 60 centimeters is required.

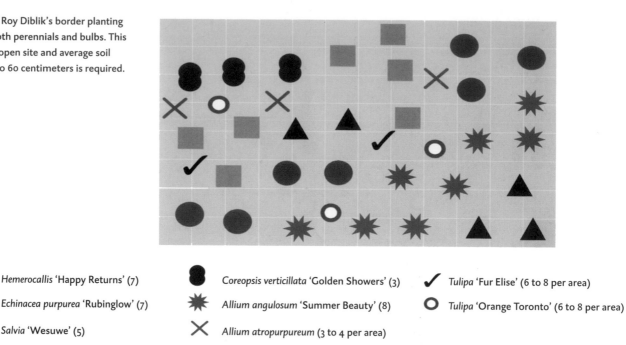

● Hemerocallis 'Happy Returns' (7)

■ Echinacea purpurea 'Rubinglow' (7)

▲ Salvia 'Wesuwe' (5)

◖ Coreopsis verticillata 'Golden Showers' (3)

✸ Allium angulosum 'Summer Beauty' (8)

✕ Allium atropurpureum (3 to 4 per area)

✓ Tulipa 'Fur Elise' (6 to 8 per area)

○ Tulipa 'Orange Toronto' (6 to 8 per area)

'Know Maintenance' planting system. Aimed at homeowners in his Zone 5b area (minimum of minus 26°C), plantings are based on a 'segment' measuring 2.4 by 3.7 meters and divided into a grid of 30 centimeter squares, which can be repeated as a modular system using connecting plants he calls 'Integrated Action Plants' between each module. Outlined in a book (see Further Reading) intended as a manual for domestic gardeners, he sets out some 40 combinations. He does stress, however, that these should be seen as a starting point, and that by using his combinations gardeners can gain the confidence to start making their their own selections.

Among his public works, Diblik has designed a 1,400 square meter planting scheme for the Art Institute of Chicago. A new area at the side of the building, it is within sight of Piet Oudolf's Lurie Garden and consciously makes a connection, but it uses a grid system so it is clearly distinct. Diblik describes how 'I was inspired by the colors of a Pierre Bonnard painting in the collection, "Earthly Paradise". I picked out the color tones in the painting and tried to repeat them in the garden.'

MIXED PLANTING

The Mixed Planting system developed in Germany (and the very similar Integrated Planting System in Switzerland) is an example of public investment (through universities and other institutions of higher education and research) going into research and development for plantings which ornament and improve the public realm. Those in other countries where this does not happen can only look on in wonder and envy. One of the advantages of this work being in the public sector is the fact that trialling can take advantage of a nationally or culturally defined unit and be carried out openly and publicly. Silver Summer, for example, was trialled in 13 different locations in Germany and Austria.

Mixes are developed for different habitats, but are also based on visual themes, particularly color. These themes are especially important for the marketing and public perception of the plantings. The majority of mixes have been created at the Hochschule Sachsen-Anhalt (University of Applied Sciences) at Bernburg in the east of Germany, an area with a marked Continental climate and low rainfall. Other locations in Germany and

June in the Sullivan Arch Garden of the Art Institute of Chicago, Illinois, where Roy Diblik has used a range of about 60 perennials to create an intermingled style planting. The pale yellow is *Achillea* 'Inca Gold', a relatively reliable and persistent cultivar, the pink *Stachys officinalis* 'Hummelo', and the blue *Kalimeris incisa* 'Blue Star'.

By October grasses *Sporobolus heterolepis* and *Eragrostis spectabilis* are much more prominent, especially when laden with morning dew. The yellow is *Rudbeckia fulgida* 'Viette's Little Suzy'.

►► (pages 208–209)
Mixed planting Indian Summer is successful for average to dry and sandy soils. Here flowering in mid-summer the orange *Asclepias tuberosa* is a dry prairie plant well known as being a food source for monarch butterflies. The yellow and brown flower is *Echinacea paradoxa*, the small yellow in the foreground *Coreopsis lanceolata*. The grass is *Nassella tenuissima*.

Silver Summer was the first of the Mixed Planting systems to be developed – intended for dry, alkaline soils. Here it is in the city of Mannheim. The yellow spike is *Phlomis russeliana*, the blue *Veronica teucrium* 'Knallblau' and the white is *Geranium sanguineum* 'Album'.

Switzerland where mixes have been developed have less extreme climates. The support of the German Perennial Nursery Association (Bund deutscher Staudengärtner – BdS) has been vital; clients can buy the mixes from members of the association.

A successful mixed planting is one which can function with relatively little maintenance, almost as an artificial ecosystem. Component plants have to be able to coexist with little input for at least ten years together, while the survival of individual plants is less important than the survival of the whole. The species chosen are overwhelmingly long-lived and resilient, but a minority of shorter lived species may also be included in order to create interest in the early years while longer lived but slower species establish. These shorter lived plants may also self-seed, but over the long term their seedlings will find less and less habitat for their replacement as the more permanent components increasingly dominate the space. The same will also be true of species which spread rapidly through vegetative means such as runners but whose short stature renders them vulnerable to overshadowing by taller plants.

There has to be a structural balance, so the categories of structural, companion and ground-cover plants (discussed in chapter three) are key to building a successful mix. Short-lived filler plants may or may not be in-cluded. Some bulbs or other geophytes may also be included; indeed, in some mixes they play a key role. As a general rule, the summer-aspect perennial components of the mixtures include 5 to 15 percent structure plants, 30 to 40 percent companion plants and at least 50 percent ground cover. Interest through the year is provided by flushes of flower, with some structural interest from seedheads or evergreen foliage for the winter. Floral interest through the year is, however, dependent on the availability of species to choose from for a given habitat. Some conditions, such as shade or dry soil, tend to have fewer species flowering later in the season.

The mixes developed at Hochschule Wädenswil in Switzerland, by Axel Heinrich and others, include annuals which are sown after the completion of the perennial planting; varieties of species such as *Eschscholzia californica*, *Nigella damascena* and *Alyssum maritimum* germinate rapidly from seed, fill gaps between perennials in the first year and may also self-seed for the second year. Short-lived perennials such as *Digitalis lutea* and *Aquilegia vulgaris* are a feature of some mixes – how long they survive in the plantings is dependent on how much they are out-competed by longer lived components. One mix, the most recently developed, Shade Pearl, even includes a shrub, *Diervilla sessilifolia*, which is cut down to the ground every two to three years.

The table below shows the Mixed Planting 'Bernburger Staudenmix Native Perennial Flower Steppe' developed by Wolfram Kircher and his collaborators at Hochschule Anhalt, for dry, open spaces on alkaline soils. *Linum perenne* is short-lived but self-seeding, while *Campanula rotundifolia* runs extensively underground: good at short-term space filling but eventually displaced by larger plants or those, such as *Carex* species, which form densely packed clumps. Numbers given are for plants per 10 square meters.

Seasonal Interest of the 'Bernburger Staudenmix Native Perennial Flower Steppe' planting mix

N°		Spring	Early summer	Mid-summer	Late summer	Early autumn	Late autumn	Winter
	Structure plants							
3	*Stachys recta*		■	■				
	Companion plants							
20	*Allium senescens* subsp. *senescens*			■				
8	*Anthericum ramosum*			■	■			
8	*Aster amellus* 'Sternkugel'				■	■		
5	*Aster linosyris*				■			
8	*Carlina acaulis* subsp. *simplex*		■	■	■	▨	▨	▨
10	*Dianthus carthusianorum*			■	■			
5	*Gentiana cruciata*			■	■			
5	*Linum perenne*		■	■	■			
10	*Pulsatilla vulgaris*	■						
5	*Sedum telephium* subsp. *maximum*				■	■	■	▨
5	*Stipa pennata*		■	▨				
	Ground-cover plants							
5	*Campanula rotundifolia*		■	■	■	■		
8	*Carex digitata* 'The Beatles'	▤	▤	▤	▤	▤	▤	▤
15	*Carex humilis*	▤	▤	▤	▤	▤	▤	▤
8	*Potentilla tabernaemontana*	▤	▤					
5	*Teucrium chamaedrys*		▤	▤				
5	*Thymus praecox*		▤					
8	*Veronica prostrata*	▤	▤					

Flowering

Foliage interest

Structural interest: seedheads, stems, grass flowers

◄◄ (pages 212–213)

A version of Silver Summer developed by Bettina Jaugstetter, for the ABB-Company businesspark. Early to mid-summer sees a strong yellow and blue-violet color scheme with gold *Achillea* 'Coronation Gold' and paler *A.* 'Terracotta', deep blue-violet *Salvia nemorosa* 'Caradonna' and pale blue *Nepeta* 'Walker's Low'. The spherical seedheads are *Allium* 'Mount Everest' and *A.* 'Globemaster'.

■ Flowering

■ Foliage interest

Seasonal Interest of the 'Bernburger Staudenmix Flower Shade' planting mix

N°		Spring	Early summer	Mid-summer	Late summer	Early autumn	Late autumn	Winter
	Structure plants							
3	*Carex pendula*	■	■	■	■	■	■	■
	Companion plants							
5	*Aster schreberi*			■				
10	*Bergenia* 'Schneekuppe' or 'Schneekönigin'	■	■	■	■	■	■	■
10	*Campanula trachelium*			■				
3	*Helleborus* ×*hybridus*	■	■	■	■	■	■	■
10	*Hosta* 'Frances Williams'		■	■	■	■	■	
8	*Smilacina racemosa*		■	■	■	■	■	
	Ground-cover plants							
15	*Convallaria majalis*	■						
20	*Vinca minor* 'Gertrude Jekyll'	■	■	■	■	■	■	■
	Bulbs and other corms and tubers							
100	*Anemone blanda* 'Blue Shades'	■						
50	*Anemone blanda* 'White Splendour'	■						
50	*Eranthis hyemalis*	■						
50	*Scilla siberica*	■						

The table above shows the 'Bernburger Staudenmix Flower Shade', also developed at Hochschule Anhalt, for shade, including (up to a point) dry shade with tree root competition. Numbers given are for plants per 10 square meters. Flowering is heavily concentrated in the spring, as relatively few shade-tolerant species flower reliably in mid- to late summer in central Europe, which is usually dry; however, there is good foliage for the rest of the year. In climates such as the eastern USA or the Far East, where summer rainfall is at least reliable or even heavy, a greater range of species could be used.

Trials have experimented with a range of spacings. Generally, more open spacings (4–6 plants per square meter) have been found to be preferable. Close spacing (8–12 plants per square meter) results in early intense competition with resulting high rates of loss, and the over-dominance of the more aggressively spreading species. Gaps in more widely spaced plantings may be filled temporarily with annuals (as in the Swiss-developed Integrated Planting Systems) or with miniature varieties of *Sedum*, which can be introduced simply by scattering shoots on to the soil surface (at a rate of 30 grams per square meter), as is done for green roofs.

The proponents of Mixed Planting suggest that high numbers of species are a good guarantee of their long-term survival. The mixtures marketed under the name Bernburger Staudenmix contain between 15 and 19 species, while Silver Summer has 30. While plant ecology provides evidence that species diversity improves the resilience of a planting, as losses and gaps are more likely to be filled if there is a wide range able to occupy a variety of ecological niches, as yet no experimental evidence demonstrates that this is so for designed plantings.

How effective mixed plantings are for small areas of just a few square meters is questionable. It is unlikely, and probably undesirable, for plants to be set out at random in such situations, as particular species will be seen as more appropriate for the 'front of border' position: bushy plants rather than 'leggy' ones, for example. The number of species also needs to be restricted, as there will not be enough repetition in a small space if a large number are used.

Mixed plantings are designed for extensive maintenance: management operations that treat the planting as one, with no individual attention for individual plants. The main task is the annual removal of dead material at the end of the year, which can be done with brushcutters or other heavy-duty machinery. Trials in Germany have also experimented with a mid-season mow instead of an end-of-season cut for some mixes, particularly those which flower primarily in early summer (typical of dry habitat combinations). This mimics the mid-summer hay cut of traditional agriculture in much of Europe. There are many advantages: an attractive fresh regrowth of foliage, some repeat flowering, more light for autumn/winter growing bulbs like *Muscari* species, reduced height for late flowering species and easy access for removal of rubbish.

Mineral mulches like gravel and chipped stone add considerably to the cost of plantings but save money by reducing weed infiltration and therefore ongoing maintenance costs – particularly important for public situations where maintenance may be irregular or difficult for access reasons. In high visibility situations such as private gardens, a mineral mulch also creates a tidy appearance and makes an open planting look finished even when it is very young.

The array of Mixed Planting systems developed by 2011 are shown in this table, which is adapted from Norbert Kühn, *Neue Staudenverwendung* (2011).

Brand name of mixture and originating institution*	Visual character	Habitat
Silver Summer, AP (*Silbersommer*)	Mid-height, mostly mid-summer yellows and blues	Dry, calcareous soils, sun
Indian Summer, HHOF	Mid-height, prairie species, range of colors, grasses for late season interest	Dry to average light spaces
Prairie Morning, HHOF (*Präriemorgen*)	As above but blues and purples dominate	As above
Prairie Summer, HHOF (*Präriesommer*)	As above but taller pinks to purples dominate	As above
Native Flower Transformations, AN (*Heimischer Blütenwandel*)	Low, scattered, mid-height, subdued colors in spring	Sun to half-shade

Brand name of mixture and originating institution*	Visual character	Habitat
Exotic Flower Transformations, AN (Exotischer Blütenwandel)	Mid-height, yellows and violets	Half-shade to shade
Flower Border, AN (Blütensaum)	Low to mid-height, subdued blues and violets, spring and early summer	Sun to half-shade
Exotic Flower Border, AN (Exotischer Blütensaum)	Mid-height, wide color range	Sun to half-shade
Flower Shade, AN (Blütenschatten)	Low mix of spring-flowering species with decorative foliage perennials	Underplanting for woody plants, dry to moist
Flower Wave (without summer mowing), AN (Blütenwoge)	Low, scattered mid-height, strong yellow and blue contrast	Dry, sunny
Flower Wave (with summer mowing), AN	As above, but with fresh look in late summer	Dry, sunny
Flower Steppe, AN (Heimische Blütensteppe)	Low, subdued violet-blues and yellows	Dry, sunny, similar to natural steppe habitat
Exotic Flower Steppe, AN (Exotische Blütensteppe)	Low, subdued yellow-greens to blue	Dry, sunny, similar to natural steppe habitat
Flower Veil, AN (Blütenschleier)	Low, gray-leaved, multicolored in spring, later yellows, violets, some pinks	Dry, sunny
Grass Dance, ERF (Tanz der Gräser)	Low perennials and taller grasses, multicolored	Dry to moist, sunny
Veitshöchheimer Flowering Mosaic, VT (Blütenmosaik)	Low, yellows and blues	Dry, sunny
Veitshöchheimer Flower Magic, VT (Blütenzauber)	Mid-height, blue-dominated, later blues, yellows and reds	Dry to moist, sunny
Veitshöchheimer Flower Dream, VT (Blütentraum)	Mid-height, multicolored	Dry to moist, sunny
Veitshöchheimer Colorplay, VT (Farbenspiel)	Low early, later higher, multicolored	Dry to moist, sunny

Brand name of mixture and originating institution*	Visual character	Habitat
Veitshöchheimer Color Border, VT (*Farbensaum*)	Low to mid-height, yellows, blues, whites	Sun to half-shade
Summerwind, WÄD (*Sommerwind*)	Low, pastels – violets, yellows – silver foliage	Dry, sunny
Summerfresh, WÄD (*Sommerfrische*)	Low with some taller, violets, yellows, grasses important	Dry to moist, sunny
Indian Summer, WAD	Warm colors from yellows to oranges, red autumn color	Dry to moist, sunny
Pink Paradise, WÄD	A variety of pinks	Dry to moist, sunny
Summer Night's Dream, WÄD (*Sommernachtstraum*)	Blue-violets with purple foliage, grasses important	Moist
Shade Pearl, WÄD (*Schattenperle*)	Mid-height to taller, yellows and blue-violets, reds, pinks later	Shade, underplanting trees

* German brand names are given in italics. Abbreviations are shown below.

AP = Arbeitskreis Pflanzenverwendung BdS (research group of the German Perennial Nursery Association.

HHOF = Sichtungsgarten Hermannshof, Weinheim (Display Garden).

AN = Hochschule Sachsen-Anhalt, Bernburg (University of Applied Sciences). All mixes produced have the brand name: Bernburger Staudenmix.

ERF = Landesversuchsanstalt für Gartenbau, Erfurt (State Horticultural Research Institute).

VT = Landesanstalt für Wein- und Gartenbau, Veitshöchheim (State Institute for Viticulture and Horticulture).

WÄD = Zürcher Hochschule für Angewandte Wissenschaft, Wädenswil, Switzerland. (Zürich Canton University of Applied Sciences).

The Mixed Planting system is undoubtedly impressive, and appears to be commercially successful. Since 2009, the number of nurseries participating in the provision of plants for the schemes has risen dramatically. At the time of writing, some 40 BdS member nurseries are supplying plants for the older mixes such as Silver Summer, with around 25 for the more recently developed ones. Some non-BdS members are also participating. It is based on an empirical and science-based methodology and extensive trialling, and because it is a product of public funding, the plant mixes are in the public domain. Not surprisingly, it is a concept which is having a growing influence in the countries of eastern Europe, newly emerging into a world where there is more available funding for public and private landscapes.

This mixed perennial prairie planting concept was developed for the ABB-Company businesspark at Ladenburg in the Rhine Valley, Germany, by Bettina Jaugstetter, with a yellow and white color theme. The tall yellow is *Helenium* 'Rauchtopas', the white is *Aster divaricatus*, the silver foliage *Artemisia ludoviciana* 'Silver Queen'. Also present are *Echinacea purpurea* 'Alba', *E. p.* 'Sunrise' and *E. p.* 'Sundawn', *Kalimeris incisa* 'Blue Star', *Liatris spicata* 'Alba', *Pennisetum orientale* 'Tall Tails', *Coreopsis verticillata* 'Grandiflora' and *Sesleria autumnalis* as a ground cover.

HEINER LUZ AND
SEASONAL THEME PLANTS

Related to the Mixed Planting approach is the work of Heiner Luz, a landscape architect who is the third generation of his family to be in the profession. As a design professional, it is not surprising to hear Luz outline his thoughts on planting combinations in clear terms; he stresses the well-known mantra 'less is more', but finesses it to 'uniformity on a large scale and variety on a small scale' as the fundamental principle which underlies all his company's work. The projects for which he designs mixed plantings are on a large scale, primarily garden show sites where several hectares need planting. Garden shows in Germany are a major aspect of the country's landscape and horticulture industry. Sites are chosen for summer-long shows which leave behind a permanent legacy of quality infrastructure and planting, usually as part of urban parks. They are thus a tool of regeneration. Much of the innovation in planting design with perennials in Germany is driven by the garden shows as clients for landscape designers' work.

Luz's key concept is that of *Prinzip der Aspectbildner* – difficult to translate but 'seasonal theme plants' is probably the most descriptive. 'Theme plants' (*Aspektbildner*) are species which visually dominate a planting for a period of several weeks each, making a dramatic large-scale effect. A mix will typically contain 3–6 theme plant species forming around 70–75 percent of the total, and the remainder companion (*Begleiter*) species. Theme plants have to be very distinctive in terms of flower, foliage or structure during the period they are on stage, but may be relatively insignificant before or after. The companion plants play a supporting role, often counterposing or complementing the qualities of the theme plants, or looking good at other times. They make less impact on the large scale because there are more species and so their impact is diluted. However, when the viewer is close to the planting, for example when walking on a path alongside it, they add variety and a sense of constant change – a result of the many different possible combinations that result from their juxtaposition with the theme plants.

Flowering tends to be in flushes, so two to three spectacular periods in the growing season last for several weeks, between which the more subdued companion plants maintain interest. All plants are randomly placed, and for rapid effect planting is relatively dense: 10–12 plants per square meter.

An example of the seasonal theme plant principle is a series of plantings at Landscape Park Riem near Munich, developed from 1995 onwards for a garden show held in 2005, and maintained since then as the park for an exhibition and convention center. Some 2.5 hectares are divided into three areas: the Iris–Mint Meadow, an ornamental reedbed area, and a wet meadow soakaway area. The theme plants for the Iris–Mint Meadow are shown in the table below. The companion plants are *Alchemilla epipsila*, *Camassia cusickii*, *Geranium wlassovianum*, *Lythrum salicaria*, *Mentha pulegium*, *M. spicata*, *M. longifolia*, *Molinia caerulea* subsp. *arundinacea*, *Sanguisborba officinalis* and *Valeriana officinalis*. This project required some 230,000 individual plants – clearly expensive to produce.

The considerable costs of making plantings involving very large numbers of plants at high density can be reduced by using custom-designed seed mixes to reproduce similar proportions to the planted combinations. Maintenance and the future development of plantings and other installations are seen as a key part of all the Luz practice work from the very beginning of the planning process. Annual cutting is done with a mower on a high setting or a brushcutter.

Seasonal Interest at the Landscape Park Riem in Munich

	Spring	Early summer	Mid-summer	Late summer	Early autumn	Late autumn	Winter
Aster laevis				Flowering	Flowering		
Boltonia latisquama			Flowering	Flowering	Flowering		
Iris sibirica		Flowering			Structural	Structural	Structural
Mentha ×speciosa		Flowering					
Nepeta sibirica			Flowering				
Primula veris	Flowering						
Veronica longifolia		Flowering	Flowering				

■ Flowering

▨ Structural interest: seedheads, stems, grass flowers

►► (pages 220–221)
The plantings at Landscape Park Riem, Munich, by Heiner Luz's studio. May with *Iris sibirica* most prominent (top left); August with *Boltonia latisquama* (bottom left); September with the some *Boltonia* still flowering (top right); and December (bottom right).

OTHER APPROACHES TO PLANTING BLENDS

Interest in randomized planting mixes is growing, with every year seeming to bring another gardening practitioner into the marketplace bearing a nursery crate full of plants – each metaphorical crate contains enough plants for one module of a planting system. Criteria for combining plants may be primarily aesthetic, or based on matching soil conditions with appropriate plants. In some cases mixes are being developed by independent garden experts and sold online solely as plans (aimed at amateurs or garden designers), and in other cases by nurseries (aimed at landscape designers and local government managers of public space). The evaluation and trialling of these mixes are almost certainly not as thorough as in the German and Swiss Mixed Planting schemes, if they happen at all, and they are not in the public domain.

Planting blends and mixes are increasingly site-specific, so a mix is designed for one location and not repeated elsewhere; very often these schemes involve several custom-designed mixes for different habitats or particular visual qualities. The always innovative Oehme, van Sweden & Associates of Washington, D.C., are beginning to apply this approach for both private and public commissions. This has also been my own approach for a number of years. I design a mix for a sample area (often 100 square meters) and then replicate it for the whole area. This saves on planning costs, an important consideration for cash-strapped clients – in my case a local government department. A particular concern in my work has been to design planting mixes which are resilient to minimal and unskilled local authority contract maintenance in the south of England, where a long growing season makes for very strong weed growth. Necessity requires a focus on robust clump-forming species.

Site-specific mixed plantings have long been a feature of German garden festivals, with Rosemarie Weisse's work at the 1986 Munich International Garden Show (IGA) being the first to create an impact internationally,

◄
Planting by Noel Kingsbury, working with HTA Landscape, on the Promenade at Bexhill-on-Sea, Sussex, an extremely exposed coastal site with frequent salt spray. Five randomized mixes of species known to thrive in coastal environments are used, each one comprising around 15 species, with around half shared with other mixes. Prominent here are gray *Ballota pseudodictamnus*, *Nepeta* ×*faassenii* and yellow *Achillea filipendulina* and *Rudbeckia fulgida* 'Goldsturm'.

►
At Bexhill, the seafront planting by Noel Kingsbury features pink-flowered *Osteospermum jucundum* with silver-leaved *Stachys byzantina*, *Artemisia* 'Powis Castle', *Phlomis italica* and *Eryngium bourgatii* amongst others. The silver-gray is *Ballota pseudodictamnus*. In the coastal and other exposed situations where these species would naturally grow, plants would be densely intertwined, supporting and protecting each other. The idea here is that with randomized planting a similar meshing together of foliage will occur over time.

◀◀ (pages 224-225)
A planting for the Koblenz Federal Garden Show (BUGA) in 2011, designed by Petra Pelz. The tall yellow spikes are *Eremurus* 'Moneymaker', and the red is *Penstemon barbatus* subsp. *coccineus*; a prominent foliage plant is *Helianthus salicifolius*, with tall stems covered in narrow leaves.

▶

A planting by Sheila Brady of Oehme, van Sweden & Associates Inc., showing an area of the newly redeveloped Azalea Garden at the New York Botanical Garden. Perennials and bulbs have been incorporated to provide context and to lengthen the season of interest. The grass here is *Molinia caerulea* subsp. *caerulea* 'Strahlenquelle', and the blue is *Gentiana makinoi* 'Marsha'.

especially the steppe planting, which is still looking good all these years later. Much work has been done by Urs Walser over the years, and increasingly other designers are working in this style. Prominent among them is Petra Pelz, who for many years used large monocultural blocks of perennials, reminiscent of Oehme van Sweden's work in the US. She is now creating some exciting mixed planting combinations at garden shows.

THE 'SHEFFIELD SCHOOL'

Sheffield is known best as an industrial city, and its increasing profile as a center for horticultural and industrial innovation has come as a surprise to many. This reputation is largely down to two members of the University of Sheffield's Department of Landscape: James Hitchmough and Nigel Dunnett. Both are pioneers of horticultural ecology – the application of plant ecology science to designed plantings. 'I have spent much of my life understanding how to assemble sustainable, designed plant communities that are attractive to the public,' says Hitchmough, 'in particular, how to apply the ecological rules that govern what can be designed....

These rules are universal and blind; they don't distinguish between wild and cultivated plants.' Nigel Dunnett has worked on creating sustainable plantings for a variety of situations, and it is his work with annual seed mixes which has so far created most public interest – an inexpensive way for local government and other managers of public spaces to create vibrantly colorful and wildlife-friendly summer plantings. James Hitchmough's work uses perennials grown from designed seed mixes; these are based on naturally occurring, visually interesting plant communities: central European meadow, North American prairie and South African

A prairie planting by James Hitchmough at the Royal Horticultural Society garden at Wisley, Surrey, in September, created by sowing a seed mix designed to highlight emergent plants – yellow *Silphium laciniatum* is one such. Pink *Echinecea pallida* is a longer lived species than *E. purpurea*, its flowers just topping the main foliage canopy.

montane grassland are three groups he has worked on. Fundamental to the Sheffield School approach is what is referred to as the wow factor: they must be designed to brighten people's lives. As Hitchmough describes one notable public encounter, 'When a massive bloke comes up to you, with no neck and covered in tattoos, with a pit bull terrier on a chain, and says that what you've done is the only thing that gets him out of bed in the morning, you know you're doing something right.'

The use of native plants in Sheffield School plantings is limited to projects where their use is particularly appropriate – a reflection of the very reduced British flora, and the presence in the flora of a number of aggressive species (mostly coarse pasture grasses) which can, paradoxically, if used indiscriminately reduce the potential for supporting biodiversity. In any case, in many urban environments the primary aim is often the creation of relatively stable artificial ecosystems that, in Hitchmough's words, 'meet human and wildlife needs rather than the production of facsimiles of native plant communities'.

Planting aims at matching the fertility of the site with appropriate species. For example, perennial plant-ings on fertile soils are very prone to invasion by weeds, especially since most perennials drop their leaves in winter, and aggressive grasses and others with winter-green foliage are able to take advantage during this period of dormancy. The use of tallgrass prairie plants from an ecosystem with moist, high fertility soils can minimize this, however, as at a high density their leafy shoots and root systems so monopolize light and soil that any unwanted species which establish are often held in check. Conversely, low fertility sites are appropriate for species derived from plant communities which are used to extracting the most out of limited resources, such as European dry meadows.

Central to Hitchmough's designed perennial communities is establishment from seed. Seed-derived plant communities are much more able to resist weed infiltration than those which are planted out, because of their much greater density – up to 150 plants per square meter – at least as long as all sources of potential weed competition are eliminated from the soil on site before sowing. Seed is sown into a 75 millimeter layer of sand or similar material spread over the soil surface. Seed allows for plants to arrange themselves according to natural processes, to sort out their own relationships and ecological niches, rather than have their arrangement imposed entirely on them by the designer. Genetic diversity also allows for greater resilience to stress, pests and diseases, as there will be a variety of levels of resistance to problems. Plantings can be created by a mix of planting and seeding – useful if the seed of certain component species is not available in the quantities needed, or a particular cultivar is required, or the rate of establishment from seed is so slow that such species may be too easily out-competed. Very importantly, planting is also more predictable, something which appeals to risk-averse clients.

Plant community mixes include several foliage layers, which increase the coverage of the soil (reducing water loss, erosion and weed infiltration), increase the value of the planting for habitat and add to its visual richness, and in particular increase length of flowering.

Layers can also be manipulated for aesthetic reasons: low basal foliage with taller emerging naked flowering stems rising out of it is a favorite Hitchmough visual effect. A low canopy layer can include many spring or early summer flowering species (often relatively shade tolerant), with taller emergents for late summer and autumn interest. Grasses are included but only as a minority component, unlike the wild communities from which they are derived, as the high proportion of grasses in wild or semi-natural grassland communities (typically at least 80 percent of biomass) reduces the visual impact. Needless to say, all species used are trialled extensively first to assess their needs in cultivation, and to ensure that they do not show any indication they might become invasive; in fact, the vast majority of species used have either been in cultivation in Britain or have very close relatives which have, and have not shown any inclination to problematic spread.

Layers making up a montane South African community designed by James Hitchmough. The uppermost layer shown is the species-rich base layer to which taller species are added, flowering later but in diminishing frequency through the year, to avoid shading out the shade-intolerant basal layer.

The South African area in London's Olympic Park (2012), designed by James Hitchmough, with white *Galtonia candicans*, pink-red *Gladiolus papilio* 'Ruby', pink *Dierama pulcherrimum*, blue *Agapanthus* varieties and low-growing pink *Diascia integerrima*. The grass is *Themeda triandra*.

An area of British natives at the Olympic Park. These are all 'flowers' – non-grassy species – including white *Leucanthemum vulgare*, pink *Ononis spinosa*, yellow *Leontodon autumnalis* and pale pink *Malva moschata*. Apart from *Ononis*, all were sown.

Maintenance is extensive although the option of additional selective horticultural maintenance is always good to have. Hitchmough says that the planting 'should be designed so that a management operation is applied to all the plants across the whole site and which disadvantages the plants you don't want and advantages those that you do.… This is an alien concept to most designers.' Mowing is an obvious management technique. Mulching is another, to suppress weed seedlings. Burning is also highly effective against the annual weed seedlings which emerge very early in spring in maritime climates, against early leafing perennial weeds, and against slug and snail populations, but has no effect on the largely dormant perennials; it can also benefit the later emergence of seedlings of the component plants. As has been found in Germany with Mixed Plantings, cutting in mid- to late summer also limits the growth of weedy species, and reduces the growth rate of the more competitive components; the disadvantage is that late summer to autumn interest is likely to be reduced.

These artificial plant communities have been developed in the context of researching how to apply a knowledge of plant ecology to ornamental horticulture, and the need to publish data on the results achieved. Having proved they are possible, the next stage might be for other practitioners to mix and match between the different communities, to produce truly global planting combinations.

The table below lists plants used in the Drakensberg South African community designed for one of the gardens in London's 2012 Olympic Park. The numbers refer to how many plants are added to each square meter. The same principle of taller species being used at much lower densities is illustrated. A planting rate of 0.1 means one of these plants every 10 square meters.

Plants used in the Drakensberg South African planting at London's 2012 Olympic Park

Low foliage layer (<30 centimeters tall)	Plants/ square meter
Eucomis bicolor	1
Helichrysum aureum	0.5
Diascia integerrima	1
Haphlocarpa scaposa	0.5
Themeda triandra	1
Carex testacea*	1.5
Berkheya purpurea	0.25
Total	5.75

Medium foliage layer (30–60 centimeters tall)	Plants/ square meter
Agapanthus 'Bresssingham Blue'	0.5
Dierama pulcherrimum	0.2
Gladiolus papilio 'Ruby'	0.25
Tritonia drakensbergensis	0.5
Kniphofia triangularis	1.5
Phygelius aequalis 'Sani Pass'	0.1
Total	3.05

Tall foliage layer (>60 centimeters tall)	Plants/ square meter
Agapanthus inapertus	0.1
Galtonia candicans	0.5
Kniphofia rooperi	0.1
Total	0.7

* Not South African (New Zealand).

Hitchmough's colleague Nigel Dunnett also uses a randomized approach to planting, but with a plant palette that is perhaps more familiar to gardeners as much of it uses species well established in cultivation. His work is particularly geared toward functionality and specific design applications – especially rain gardens and green roofs. At the Olympic Park he has created plantings using plants and seed rather than seed alone, based on Western European hay-meadow and East Asian woodland-edge vegetation. The range of European species available has enabled him to create some color-themed mixes. An advantage of using plants from these areas is that a wide variety are commercially available in Britain and throughout Europe and North America. Rain garden and green roof mixes are designed around very individual environmental conditions; rain gardens need plants with the ability to cope with drought and occasional flooding, whereas green roofs need species which can survive drought, temperature extremes and a root run of limited depth.

The table below shows the Asia garden at the Olympic Park, designed by Nigel Dunnett. Planting densities vary, but the numbers give an idea of the proportions of the plants in the mix. The planting is designed as a series of swathes, each with a specific plant combination.

Plants used in the Asia Garden at London's 2012 Olympic Park

Japanese anemone swathes

TALL EMERGENTS

Miscanthus 'Silberfeder'	2
Miscanthus 'Flamingo'	2

MEDIUM CANOPY

Anemone ×hybrida 'Hadspen Abundance'	1
Anemone ×hybrida 'Honorine Jobert'	1
Anemone ×hybrida 'Prinz Heinrich'	1
Anemone ×hybrida 'Königin Charlotte'	1
Anemone huphensis 'September Charm'	1
Persicaria amplexicaulis 'Rosea'	1
Persicaria amplexicaulis 'Firetail'	1

Hemerocallis/Hosta swathes

TALL EMERGENTS

Calamagrostis 'Karl Foerster'	2
Lilium tigrinum 'Sweet Surrender'	2
Lilium speciosum var. rubrum	2

MEDIUM CANOPY

Hemerocallis 'Joan Senior'	2
Hosta 'True Blue'	2
Hosta 'Tall Boy'	2
Iris chrysographes 'Black Knight'	1
Primula beesiana	1
Sanguisorba officinalis 'Purpurea'	1

Bold swathes

TALL EMERGENTS

Aconogonon 'Johanniswolke'	1
Rheum palmatum	3

MEDIUM CANOPY

Rodgersia podophylla	2
Rodgersia pinnata 'Superba'	2
Euphorbia griffithii 'Dixter'	2
Hakonechloa macra	1

LOWER GROUND-LAYER SPECIES

Primula pulverulenta	1
Bergenia purpurescens	2

THE NEW PLANTING

The planting design style outlined in this book is different to anything which has gone before. But how different? And what do these differences mean for the future development of planting design?

Here I would like to look at the work of Piet Oudolf, and other similar practitioners, in the context of planting design as a discipline which is continuing to develop, to evolve and, we hope, to advance and improve. I would also like to relate it to a wider context – that of our continuing negotiation with nature and the future of the landscapes we design for our cities, suburbs and gardens.

Planting design has, in general, moved from a sense of absolute control to one of negotiating with nature – if not of total spontaneity, then at least of the appearance of spontaneity. However, the precise placing of plants is sometimes as critical to the effect in Piet's work as in more traditional planting. More generally, the spontaneity of allowing plants to move around is, in fact, part of an older tradition. Movements within twentieth-century gardening played with spontaneity: Willy Lange (1864–1941) in inter-war Germany promoted naturalistic planting using native species, while the English cottage

View across Noel Kingbury's Montpelier Cottage garden in autumn where a series of experimental plantings are used to evaluate plant competition. The white (foreground) is *Anaphalis triplinervis*, the blue is *Aster* 'Little Carlow', both very long-flowering and robust perennials.

Sedum 'Herbstfreude' in autumn illustrates the power of intermingled planting as its deep red flower/seedheads and good structure give continued value to this planting at Hermannshof, Germany. *Achillea* 'Coronation Gold' is doing a second flowering. Grass *Chrysopogon gryllus* on the right is a reminder that there are still many good plants in the not-too-distant wild which deserve to be better known in cultivation; it is a central and eastern European species from dry soils but still not much used in gardens.

garden style was an idealisation of the gardens of country people; one of its greatest exponents, Margery Fish (1892–1969), was hugely influential in promoting the idea of covering the soil with a full canopy of vegetation and allowing plants to spread and self-seed.

In April 2011 I visited Piet and Anja in the first phase of getting material together for this book. The weather was clear and sunny, and it was the perfect time to wander around the garden looking at the perennial growth just as it was emerging, making it very easy to see long-term patterns of growth. The conditions were also ideal for Piet to be setting out on a new and very experimental project. The decision to close the nursery in 2010 inevitably left open the question – what do you do with a 6,000-square-foot patch of bare sandy soil? The planting which Piet started to create that weekend was the most radical yet. He set out a selection of perennials and grasses, starting with the main structure using grass *Calamagrostis* 'Karl Foerster', and then sowing a seed mix of Dutch native grasses and wildflowers. My next visit was in August. The perennials were growing strongly and the grasses and the first of the wildflowers were getting established. There were a few spontaneous arrivals, too, including wild chamomile and yarrow. To the uninitiated it looked like a garden had been invaded by wildflowers, or was it the other way around, a wild grassy area being made into a garden?

To design a planting which involved such an element of spontaneity is entirely consistent. Piet's trajectory as a designer has been a continual move away from the ordered to the spontaneous. His earlier work was in the firmly modernist style of Mien Ruys, combining contemporary-style architectural clipping of woody plants with perennials and flowering shrubs. Gradually, the perennials and grasses have taken over, and since around 2000 he has begun to experiment more and more with intermingling. To create something which combines the planned placing of plants with the inevitable randomness of seed sowing can be seen as part of such a journey.

The other interesting thing we did that weekend in April was to look at some of his early plantings, made in the 1980s, which had had very little done to them beyond some weeding and annual cutting back. The number of species had dropped over time – Piet reckoned 'about half' – but the remainder were flourishing and in some cases had spread or sown themselves around. The result was a denser vegetation than is normal in perennial plantings, but the overall effect (visible in late summer) was impressive.

The overriding factor which makes a Piet Oudolf planting work for the long term is that his plants are long-lived. However, simply relying on long-lived plants over time can be remarkably static. Is this what we want? Long-term predictability may work for some situations (rather monumental public ones, say) but is in many ways unrealistic. The number of species which combine longevity with staying in one place is actually quite limited. Fundamentally, though, this staying the same over time is rather boring. Even clipped shrubs tend to change over time – much of the pleasure of historic clipped formal gardens lies in seeing the characterful and sometimes eccentric shapes the plants develop as their nature has gradually asserted itself over the clippers.

In 1994, the year in which I first met Piet and first went to Hummelo, I visited Rio de Janeiro to look at gardens and landscapes by Roberto Burle Marx (1909–94). Having made such a decisive break with traditional geometries of placing plants, Burle Marx had made no such break with the management of time. I was troubled by a static quality to the gardens; every plant had its place, and if it strayed over the line, the effect would be lost. Maintaining such precision could only be achieved through high levels of maintenance, a luxury available in an economy with plentiful cheap labour.

My own gardening is very much about planting and then allowing natural processes of growth, birth and death to take over, or at least to proceed under the eagle eye of my management. The result is a far denser canopy than is considered normal for perennials. The density achieved over time in Piet's garden and in my own approaches James Hitchmough's. High plant density is fundamentally a major break with the past. James's point is that a density approaching that found in natural plant communities is far more resilient than traditional ones with spaces between the plants. Maintenance will be also reduced.

Greater resilience results from:
• reduced space for weeds to infiltrate, and greater competition for them if they do establish
• reduced space for seedlings of the aggressively seeding components

- more competition to limit the aggressively spreading components
- reduced plant size owing to greater competition, resulting in a reduction in top-heavy growth and therefore less need for staking
- support for species with weak stems.

The Sheffield School (James Hitchmough, Nigel Dunnett and those of us who work with them or are graduates of Sheffield) stress ecological process and dynamism – the idea that plantings will change over time and that the role of the gardener or manager is to direct these processes in a way which preserves or enhances their visual qualities and other desired features, such as species diversity.

In chapter five, we saw that James Hitchmough's seed-derived plantings need very different management to conventional ones. Any planting which approaches the density of a natural plant community rather than a traditional garden is going to need a management style which emphasizes operations to the whole rather than to individual plants and to the idea of editing an ongoing process – extensive rather than intensive management.

The skills required by gardeners are clearly different for this new vegetation-style planting. On the one hand, it is probably true that less time for maintenance is needed, but that more skill and expertise is required. On the other hand, for large public areas, the fact that a complex planting can be maintained by simple operations such as mowing or burning means that so long as those responsible for management have the skill, most of the actual physical work can be carried out by relatively unskilled people. The trained gardener or landscape manager of the future will need a grounding in basic ecological science and an ability to use science to guide their intuition in managing complex plantings. There are clearly implications here for the training of horticultural and landscape professionals.

ENHANCED NATURE

A planting style which emphasizes a vegetation – a plant community rather than an arrangement of individuals – is clearly aimed at creating artificial ecosystems. For some this is profoundly disturbing, as there is still a widespread idea that this is something which only nature can do. The problem lies in our attitudes to natural systems and the history of the idea of ecology. Here I would like to look at how the new planting systems we are proposing fit into a broader picture of our relationship with the natural world, and the nature and quality of this natural world.

We have become used to seeing the natural world as pristine, separate from human activity, and in a harmonious balance. We know now that what we thought of as natural harmonious ecosystems are anything but.

When we look at natural vegetation we see only a snapshot in time, and there is a great tendency to interpret this as eternal and everlasting. Now, based on scientific evidence about the past, we have to accept that much of what we think of as nature has often been in a state of dynamic change. Additionally, much has also been human influenced; our distant ancestors, even pre-agricultural ones, made an enormous impact on many natural systems, often over thousands of years, bringing about both mass extinctions of larger animals and huge modifications of ecosystems, largely through the use of fire.

A 1995 book by Stephen Budiansky, *Nature's Keepers: The New Science of Nature Management*, does a very good job of outlining these issues. James Hitchmough says it made a major impact on him when he read it,

▶▶ (pages 238–239)
A pond in the garden at Montpelier Cottage with autumn foliage of *Filipendula camtschatica* and the last flowers of *Aster puniceus* in wet ground behind.

helping to develop his thinking about the creation of artificial functioning plant communities. Budiansky argues that for too long we have confused ecology as a science with ecology as a political philosophy. He confronts the idea that there is an indissoluble and essential link between place and the plant and animal communities which live there. Science, he suggests, now tells us that natural communities are composed of whatever species happened to arrive and establish themselves, and that chance and random events have played a large part in this. Rewind the tape of history, replay it, and communities of different species will result. As an example, two invasive alien species which many in Britain have learnt to hate, *Acer pseudoplatanus* (the sycamore maple) and *Rhododendron ponticum*, may have been native prior to a previous ice age; replay geological history and they might have been natives again.

A more recent book takes this argument further. Piet is not in the habit of recommending books to me (plant recommendations are more likely), so when he told me about *Rambunctious Garden: Saving Nature in a Post-Wild World by Emma Marris* (2011) I immediately went out and bought it. Marris takes a fundamentally optimistic, and at times quite joyful, look at how the massive human impacts on natural ecosystems result not necessarily in a loss of nature but in a new nature as alien and native species adjust to each other, developing entirely novel ecosystems in the process. She likens this to the creation of a garden, where unpredictable and at times almost chaotic processes result in an exuberant floral display. Marris also discusses several ambitious projects at large-scale ecosystem recreation, such as the introduction of African herbivores (zebras, elephants, etc.) to part of the USA to replace the species ancestors of the Native Americans wiped out tens of thousands of years ago.

Anyone who has spent time looking at the wide range of species – often quite rare ones – on abandoned industrial sites will understand Marris's concept of the rambunctious garden. The original spontaneous vegetation of the New York High Line was a good example, with its mix of natives and exotics, and its meagre soil limiting the growth of more vigorous species, so allowing for the expression of a rich and varied flora. This floral diversity is actually very typical of abandoned, and often very polluted, post-industrial environments. Conservationists are beginning to realize, often almost too late, just how biodiverse and valuable these places can be; Germany has led the way, with places like the Südgelände Park in Berlin, a former railway marshalling yard. To see sites like this as nature reserves in the making challenges many of our conventional notions about nature, or what we should consider valuable. The lesson is that nature is very good at fighting back and regenerating, and that we should cherish these examples and perhaps take them as models for future designed plantings.

Reading *Rambunctious Garden*, it is clear where we gardeners come in. We are involved in creating an enhanced nature (the term is from James Hitchmough and Nigel Dunnett). This idea recognizes the importance of visual beauty for human users (the overwhelming majority of whom know nothing of ecology) and the fact that artificial ecosystems can support considerable and valuable levels of biodiversity. There should be no contradiction in pragmatically designing plantings which combine native and exotic and which provide value for human and other users. Piet's work is a notable step forward in creating plantings which appeal not only to our love of beauty and a certain sense of order but also to the high level of diversity and openness to dynamic change that biodiversity needs.

PLANT DIRECTORY

This selection covers the majority of the plants used by Piet Oudolf, plus a selection suitable for maritime climates with relatively mild winters.

There is a bias toward plants of open, sunny conditions. Shade lovers included are those which tend to have some structural interest from early summer onward.

ABBREVIATIONS

General

cvs. = cultivars

M = meters

N° PER M² = number per square meter

spp. = species (plural)

subsp. = subspecies

Height

Plant height varies greatly between different growing conditions. These categories are intended to give a rough indication.

L   Low, less than 0.3 meters

S   Short, 0.3–0.8 meters

M   Medium, 0.8–1.4 meters

T   Tall, 1.4–2.0 meters

VT   Very tall, greater than 2.0 meters

Spread

The approximate diameter of the bulk of a plant's foliage at its widest point after three years, NOT the spread of the base of the plant.

<0.25   Less than 0.25 meters

0.25-0.5   Between 0.25 and 0.5 meters

0.5-1.0   Between 0.5 and 1.0 meters

>1.0   More than 1.0 meter

Numbers per square meter

This is a planting density suggested for commercial and other projects where a full look is wanted within the first year. It is not the same as spread, but takes into account the speed of establishment of a plant.

Piet Oudolf's method is to use 9 centimeter pots for most perennials and 11 centimeter pots for larger ones like eupatorium or miscanthus. If only larger sizes (often 2 liters) are used, he recommends reducing planting density by 10–15 percent.

Foliage

E   Evergreen

S/E   Semi-evergreen

Au   Good autumn color

Architecture

This relates to the plant form as described by the stem-leaf relationships discussed in chapter three. In theory, this is an objective description; here, however, it has been modified to give a more subjective, and arguably more useful, assessment of the basic appearance of overall plant shape.

Li   Linear leaves, virtually all basal

BB   Broad basal leaves

Em   Emergent

LM   Leafy mound

Up   Upright

SM   Stem mound

Br   Branching

In addition:

Pro   Procumbent

For grasses, with reference to page 127, the following descriptions are used:

cespitose

clump or mat

Flower

Color is indicated.

Flowering season

Occasionally also a period of attractive berries is indicated. The flowering season for grasses also includes the period of seedhead interest.

Sp   Spring

Su   Summer

Au   Autumn

Wi   Winter

E   Early

M   Mid

L   Late

Structural interest

See page 132.

9 mths   More than 9 months, implies good seedheads

3-9 mths   3 to 9 months, flowers and seedheads

short   Filler plants or only a short season of structural interest

Long-term performance

Data for performance are based on author experience, and that of colleagues, overwhelmingly in north-west Europe, and also reflect the research survey Kingsbury 2010 (see Further Reading).

Longevity. See pages 178–83.

<5 yrs	Less than 5 years
<10 yrs	Less than 10 years
Per	True perennial
LL	Notably long-lived

Spreading ability through vegetative growth, not seeding, and distinct from foliage spread – see 'Spread' on previous page. See pages 186–87.

None	Non-clonal, not spreading
Lim	Very limited
Slo	Slow
Mod	Moderate
Rap	Rapid

Persistence: lower numbers indicate plants die back in center and new growth is further away from original planting position. See pages 188–91.

V lo	Very low
Lo	Low
Med	Medium
Hi	High

Self-sowing/seeding. See pages 191–92. Note this is notoriously difficult to predict and this is a rough guide only.

Lo	Low, often minimal
Mod	Moderate
Hi	High, occasionally problematic

Garden habitat

LIGHT:

Su	Sun
HSh	Half-shade
Sh	Shade-tolerant

SOIL:

All plants will flourish in average soil conditions, with average levels of fertility and moisture.

We	Some tolerance of wet – in other words, waterlogged soil
Mo	Moist (but not wet) soil preferred, drought not tolerated well
Dr	Drought tolerant, but growth is usually better in conditions of average moisture
Hi	Appreciates highly fertile soils
Lo	Tolerant of poor fertility, but growth is usually better in conditions of average fertility, although lifespan may be shorter

Zone

United States Department of Agriculture Hardiness Zones, minimum recommended.

This is a good guide to winter hardiness for Continental climates, less so for maritime-influenced climates like north-west Europe. Zones describe geographical regions where winter minimum temperatures are the chief limiting factor for the cultivation of particular plant species. For example, a zone 5 plant will potentially tolerate temperatures down to minus 28°C or minus 20°F.

	HEIGHT (M)	SPREAD (M)	N° PER M²	FOLIAGE ARCHITECTURE	FLOWER SEASON	STRUCTURAL INTEREST	LONGEVITY
Acaena spp. and cvs.	L	0.25-0.5	9-11	Colored, pinnate, E **Br, Pro**	Red-brown seedheads **E-M Su**	3-9 mths/ short	Per
Acanthus spinosus	M-T	0.5-1.0	7-9	Dark, deeply toothed, large **LM, Em**	White, purple **M-L Su**	3-9 mths	LL
Achillea filipendulina and cvs.	T	0.5-1.0	9	Dark, very finely divided **Up, Em**	Yellow umbels **M-L Su**	3-9 mths	Per
Achillea millefolium, cvs. and hybrids	M	0.25-0.5	9	Dark, very finely divided **Up**	Various **M-L Su**	3-9 mths	<10 yrs
Aconitum European spp.	M	0.25-0.5	9	Dark, pinnate **Up**	Blue-violet **E Su**	short	Per
Aconitum East Asian spp.	M-T	0.25-0.5	9	Dark, pinnate **Up**	Blue-violet **M-L Su**	short	Per
Aconogonon 'Johanniswolke' (*Persicaria polymorpha*)	VT	> 1.0	1	Dense, dark **SM, Br**	White, pink **E-L Su**	3-9 mths	LL
Actaea pachypoda	M	0.25-0.5	9	Divided **Em**	White berries **Au**	short	LL
Actaea spp. (former *Cimicifuga*)	T	0.25-1.0	9	Divided **Em**	Cream **L Su-Au**	3-9 mths	LL
Agapanthus spp. and cvs.	M	0.25-1.0	7	Wide, straplike **Li**	Blue **M-L Su**	3-9 mths	LL
Alchemilla spp.	S	0.25-0.5	9	Attractive foliage shape **LM**	Lime-green **E-M Su**	3-9 mths	Per
Amorpha canescens	M	0.5-1.0	3	Pinnate, very small leaflets **SM, Up**	Gray-purple **M-L Su**	3-9 mths	Per
Amsonia spp.	M	0.25-0.5	5-7	Small, Au **SM, Up**	Steely blue **E-M Su**	9 mths	LL
Anaphalis margaritacea	M	0.25-0.5	7	Dark gray-green **SM**	White, papery **M-L Su**	3-9 mths	Per
Anemone ×hybrida and similar species	T	0.25-1.0	7	Large, divided **Em**	Pink, white **L Su-Au**	3-9 mths	LL
Aquilegia vulgaris	M	0.25-0.5	11	Divided **Em**	Various **E Su**	short	<5-<10 yrs
Aralia herbaceous spp.	M-T	0.5-1.0	1	Very large, divided **SM**	Attractive heads **M-L Su**	3-9 mths	LL
Artemisia lactiflora	T	0.25-0.5	7	Dark, divided **Up**	Off-white **M Su**	3-9 mths	Per
Artemisia ludoviciana 'Latiloba'	S	0.5-1.0	5	Silver, divided **SM, Up**	Flowers insignificant	3-9 mths	Per

SPREADING ABILITY	PERSISTENCE	SELF-SOWING/ SEEDING	HABITAT LIGHT	SOIL	ZONE	NOTES, ADDITIONAL SPECIES AND FORMS
Mod-Rap	Hi	Mod	Su		6-7	Invasive in maritime climates
Mod	Hi	Lo	Su		7	Can be slow to establish
Mod	Med	Lo	Su	Dr, Lo	3	
Mod	Lo	Mod	Su	Dr, Lo	3	
Slo	Lo-Med	Lo-Mod	Su-HSh	Hi	3	Can be summer-dormant
Slo	Lo-Med	Lo-Mod	Su-HSh	Hi	3	
Lim	Hi	Lo	Su-HSh	Hi	3	A big plant!
Slo	Hi	Lo	HSh-Sh	Mo	3	
Slo	Hi	Lo	HSh-Sh	Mo	3	Some cvs. have bronze foliage
Mod	Hi	Lo	Su		7	Hardier than often thought
Mod	Hi	Hi	Su-HSh		3	
None	Hi	Mod	Su	Dr	2	Bushy habit, good with low grasses
Slo	Hi	Lo-Mod	Su-HSh		4	Clear yellow autumn color
Lim	Hi	Lo	Su		3	
Mod	Hi	Lo	Su-HSh		4	Often slow to establish
None	Hi	Hi	Su-HSh		3	Can be summer-dormant
Lim	Hi	Lo	Su-HSh		3	Collapse with first frosts
Lim	Hi	Lo	Su-HSh		3	
Mod	Hi	Lo	Su	Dr, Lo	4	Can have floppy growth late season

Acanthus spinosus

Amorpha canescens

Amsonia orientalis

Anaphalis margaritacea

Artimisia ludoviciana

	HEIGHT (M)	SPREAD (M)	N° PER M²	FOLIAGE ARCHITECTURE	FLOWER SEASON	STRUCTURAL INTEREST	LONGEVITY
Aruncus dioicus	T	0.5-1.0	3	Divided, elegant **SM**	Cream **E-M Su**	9 mths	LL
Asarum europaeum	L	0.25-0.5	11	Glossy, E **BB**	Flowers insignificant	3-9 mths	Per
Asclepias incarnata	M	0.25-0.5	7-9	Lancelike **Up**	Pink **M-L Su**	3-9 mths	<5 yrs
Asclepias tuberosa	M	0.25-0.5	9	Lancelike **Up**	Orange **M-L Su**	3-9 mths	Per
Asperula odorata (*Galium odoratum*)	L	0.25-0.5	11	Small, pale **Br, Pro**	White **Sp**	short	Per
Aster ageratoides	M	>1.0	5	Small, profuse **Up, SM**	Pale blue **M-L Su**	3-9 mths	Per
Aster cordifolius	T	0.5-1.0	5	Small, profuse **Up**	Blue **L Su-Au**	3-9 mths	Per
Aster divaricatus	M	0.25-0.5	7	Small, profuse **Up**	White **L Su-Au**	9 mths	Per
Aster ericoides	M	0.25-0.5	5	Very small, profuse **Up**	Various **L Su-Au**	3-9 mths	Per
Aster laevis	M-T	0.25-0.5	7	Small, grayish, profuse **Up**	Purple-blue **L Su-Au**	3-9 mths	Per
Aster lateriflorus 'Horizontalis'	M	0.5-1.0	7	Small, dark **Up**	White **L Su-Au**	9 mths	Per
Aster novae-angliae	M-T	0.25-0.5	5	Small, profuse **Up**	Blue, purple, pink **L Su-Au**	3-9 mths	Per
Aster oblongifolius 'October Skies'	M	0.5-1.0	3-5	Small, profuse **Br**	Blue **L Su-Au**	3-9 mths	Per
Aster tartaricus	M-T	0.5-1.0	7	Small, profuse **Up**	Purple **L Su-Au**	3-9 mths	LL
Aster umbellatus	T	0.25-0.5	7	Small, profuse **Up**	Cream **L Su-Au**	3-9 mths	LL
Aster ×herveyi 'Twilight' (*A. macrophyllus*)	M	0.5-1.0	7	Small, profuse **Up**	Purple-blue **L Su-Au**	9 mths	Per
Aster ×frikartii	M	0.25-0.5	7	Small, profuse **Up, SM**	Purple-blue **L Su-Au**	3-9 mths	<5-<10 yrs
Astilbe chinensis varieties	M	0.25-0.5	7	Elegant, divided **BB**	Bright pink **L Su-Au**	9 mths	Per
Astilboides tabularis	M-T	0.25-1.0	7	Large, circular **BB**	Cream **E-M Su**	3-9 mths	Per

SPREADING ABILITY	PERSISTENCE	SELF-SOWING/ SEEDING	HABITAT LIGHT	SOIL	ZONE	NOTES, ADDITIONAL SPECIES AND FORMS
None	Hi	Mod	Su-HSh		4	'Horatio' - hybrid, 1m tall, red autumn color
Mod	Hi	Lo	HSh-Sh		4	Many additonal Asian spp. with good foliage
None	Hi	Lo-Mod	Su		3	Good autumn color
Lim	Hi	Lo	Su	Dr, Lo	3	
Rap	Med	Lo	HSh-Sh		4	Often summer-dormant
Mod-Rap	Hi	Lo	Su		4	'Harry Smith' especially good
Slo-Mod	Hi	Lo	HSh-Sh		2	'Little Carlow' especially good
Slo-Mod	Hi	Mod-Hi	Su-Sh		4	
Slo	Hi	Lo	HSh-Sh	Dr	3	
Slo	Hi	Mod	Su-HSh		4	
Slo	Hi	Lo	Su		3	Branching flower-heads give a bushy habit
Slo	Hi	Mod	Su		2	
Lim	Hi	Lo	Su		3	
Slo	Hi	Lo	Su		4	'Jindai' has especially good autumn color
Mod	Hi	Hi	Su		3	
Mod	Hi	Lo	Su-HSh		4	
Lim	Hi	Lo	Su		5	
Slo	Hi	Lo	Su-HSh	Mo	4	Good autumn color and winter seedheads
Mod	Hi	Lo	Su-HSh	Mo	5	

Aruncus 'Horatio'

Aster cordifolius 'Little Carlow'

Aster lateriflorus 'Horizontalis'

Aster tartaricus 'Jindai'

Aster ×herveyi 'Twilight'

	HEIGHT (M)	SPREAD (M)	Nº PER M²	FOLIAGE ARCHITECTURE	FLOWER SEASON	STRUCTURAL INTEREST	LONGEVITY
Astrantia major	S	0.25-0.5	11	Dark, divided **SM, Em**	Cream, red, pink **M-L Su**	3-9 mths	<10 yrs-Per
Baptisia australis	M	0.5-1.0	1	Grayish, neat **Br**	Indigo blue **E Su**	9 mths	LL
Baptisia alba (B. leucantha)	M	0.25-1.0	1	Neat, tree-like habit **Br**	White **E-M Su**	9 mths	LL
Bergenia spp. and cvs.	L	0.25-0.5	9	Rounded, glossy, E **BB**	Pink, white **Sp**	3-9 mths	Per
Boltonia asteroides	T	0.25-0.5	7	Narrow, grayish **Up**	White daisy **L Su**	3-9 mths	Per
Brunnera macrophylla	S-M	0.25-0.5	11	Large, rough texture **LM**	Blue **Sp**	9 mths	Per
Buphthalmum salicifolium	S	0.25-0.5	7	Narrow **SM**	Yellow daisy **E-L Su**	3-9 mths	Per
Calamintha nepeta subsp. *nepeta*	S	0.25-0.5	11	Small leaves **SM**	Pale pink **M Su-Au**	3-9 mths	Per
Campanula glomerata	S	0.25-1.0	11	Dark, rough **Up, SM**	Violet-blue **E Su**	short	Per
Campanula lactiflora	T	0.5-1.0	7	Light, rough **Up, SM**	Pale blue **M Su**	short	<10 yrs-Per
Campanula persicifolia	S	0.25-0.5	9	Elongated **Em**	Purple-blue **M Su**	short	Per
Campanula poscharskyana	L	0.5-1.0	7	Light green **Br, Pro**	Violet-blue **E Su**	short	Per
Campanula trachelium	M	<0.25	9	Dark, rough **Up**	Violet-blue **M Su**	short	<10 yrs-Per
Centaurea montana and cvs.	S	0.5-1.0	7	Grayish **SM**	Blue, pink **E Su**	3-9 mths	Per
Cephalaria gigantea	T	0.5-1.0	5-7	Dark, rough **Em**	Pale yellow **M-L Su**	short	<10 yrs
Ceratostigma plumbaginoides	S	0.25-0.5	11	Small, Au **Br**	True blue **L Su-Au**	short	Per
Chaerophyllum hirsutum 'Roseum'	M-T	0.25-0.5	5	Very finely divided **LM**	Pink **E Su**	3-9 mths	Per
Chelone obliqua	M	0.25-0.5	9	Dark, profuse **Up**	Pink **L Su-Au**	3-9 mths	Per
Clematis heracleifolia, *C. integrifolia* and hybrids	M	0.5-1.0	3-5	Divided **Br**	Blue, small **M-L Su**	3-9 mths	Per

SPREADING ABILITY	PERSISTENCE	SELF-SOWING/ SEEDING	HABITAT LIGHT	SOIL	ZONE	NOTES, ADDITIONAL SPECIES AND FORMS
Slo-Mod	Hi	Hi	Su-HSh	Mo	5	Performance strongly dependent on habitat Dislikes heat
Slo	Hi	Lo	Su	Dr	3	
Slo	Hi	Lo	Su	Dr	5	Statuesque plant with good autumn color
Mod	Hi	Lo	Su-Sh		3	
Slo	Med	Mod	Su-HSh	Mo, Hi	4	
Mod	Hi	Lo	HSh-Sh		3	Several variegated cvs.
Slo	Hi	Lo	Su	Lo	4	
Lim	Hi	Mod	Su	Dr, Lo	6	
Mod-Rap	Hi	Mod	Su-HSh	Dr, Lo	3	Good ground cover in shade
Slo	Hi	Mod-Hi	Su-HSh	Hi	5	All campanulas have white/pink variants
Mod	Lo	Lo	Su-HSh		3	
Rap	Hi	Lo	Su-HSh		3	
Slo	Hi	Mod	Su-HSh		3	
Slo-Mod	Hi	Lo	Su-HSh		3	Degree of spread varies between clones
None	Hi	Lo-Mod	Su		3	
Mod	Hi	Lo	Su		5	Hardiest of several related spp.
Lim	Hi	Lo	Su-HSh		6	
Mod	Hi	Lo	Su-HSh	We	3	White form good, as are related spp.
None	Hi	Lo	Su		3	Can be allowed to run through shrubs

Baptisia alba (B. leucantha)

Brunnera macrophylla

Chaerophyllum hirsutum 'Roseum'

Clematis heracleifolia

Clematis integrifolia

	HEIGHT (M)	SPREAD (M)	N° PER M²	FOLIAGE ARCHITECTURE	FLOWER SEASON	STRUCTURAL INTEREST	LONGEVITY
Coreopsis tripteris	T	0.25–0.5	7	Divided, elegant **Up**	Yellow daisy **M-L Su**	3–9 mths	Per
Coreopsis verticillata	S	<0.25	7	Dark, fine **SM**	Yellow daisy **M-L Su**	3–9 mths	Per
Crambe cordifolia	M	0.5–1.0	1–3	Very large, dark **BB**	White **M Su**	3–9 mths	LL
Crocosmia hybrids	M	0.25–0.5	9	Upright **Li**	Yellow, orange **L Su-Au**	3–9 mths	LL
Darmera peltata	M	0.25–1.0	9	Large, round, Au **BB**	Pale pink **Sp**	9 mths	LL
Delphinium hybrids	T	0.25–0.5	9	Pale green, lobed **Up**	Shades of blue **E-M Su**	short	<10 yrs
Desmodium canadense	M	0.25–0.5	5	Small leaflets **SM**	Dark pink **L Su-Au**	3–9 mths	LL
Dierama spp. and cvs.	M-T	0.25–1.0	9	Grayish, stiff, bunched **Li**	Pink, purple, white **M-L Su**	3–9 mths	Per
Digitalis spp.	M-T	<0.25–0.5	11	Rosettes **Em**	Pink, yellow, brown **M-L Su**	3–9 mths	<5 yrs
Doronicum spp. and hybrids	S-M	0.25–0.5	9	Lush green **Em**	Yellow daisy **Sp-E Su**	short	Per
Echinacea spp. and cvs.	M	0.25–0.5	9	Large leaves **Em**	Pink, purple, some yellow **M Su-Au**	9 mths	<5-<10 yrs
Echinops spp. and cvs.	M-T	0.5–1.0	7–9	Thistle-like **Em**	Blue spheres **M-L Su**	3–9 mths	<10 yrs
Epimedium spp. and cvs.	S-M	0.25–0.5	11	Glossy, S/E **BB**	Yellow, white, pink **Sp**	short	LL
Eryngium bourgatii	S	0.25–0.5	9	Spiny, gray **LM**	Gray-blue **M Su**	9 mths	Per
Eryngium ×tripartitum	M	0.25–0.5	9	Spiny, gray **LM, Br**	Gray-blue **M Su**	3–9 mths	Per
Eryngium yuccifolium	T	0.5–1.0	9	Spiny, straplike **Em**	Off-white **M-L Su**	3–9 mths	Per
Eupatorium maculatum and related spp.	T-VT	0.25–1.0	5–7	Whorled leaves **Up**	Purple-pink **L Su-Au**	3–9 mths	LL
Eupatorium perfoliatum	M-T	0.25–0.5	7	Narrow, distinctive **Up**	White **L Su-Au**	3–9 mths	Per
Eupatorium rugosum	M	0.25–0.5	5	Fresh green **SM, Up**	White **L Su-Au**	3–9 mths	Per

SPREADING ABILITY	PERSISTENCE	SELF-SOWING/ SEEDING	HABITAT LIGHT	SOIL	ZONE	NOTES, ADDITIONAL SPECIES AND FORMS
Slo	Hi	Lo	Su-HSh		3	
Slo	Hi	Lo	Su-HSh	Dr	3	
Lim	Hi	Lo	Su	Dr	5	*C. maritima* good for coastal situations
Mod Rap	Hi	Lo	Su		5-8	Many varieties but only suitable for mild climates
Mod	Hi	Lo	Su-HSh	We	5	Reddish autumn color
None	Hi	Lo	Su	Hi	3	
Lim	Hi	Lo	Su		3	
Lim	Hi	Hi	Su	Mo	7	Wide range for mild winter areas
None	Hi	Hi	Su-HSh	Lo	7	Variety of spp., varying lifespans
Mod	Med	Lo	HSh-Sh		5	
None	Hi	Lo-Mod	Su		3-5	Range of longevity, *E. pallida* longest
None	Hi	Mod-Hi	Su		3-5	
Slo-Mod	Hi	Lo	Su-HSh	Dr	5	Asian spp. less tolerant of sun and dry soils
Lim	Hi	Lo	Su	Dr, Lo	5	
Lim	Hi	Lo	Su		5	
Lim	Hi	Hi	Su		3	
Lim-Slo	Hi	Lo-Mod	Su	Mo, Hi	4	Some autumn color, statuesque winter silhouette
Slo	Med	Lo	Su-HSh	Mo	3	Many other *Eupatorium* spp. worth growing
Slo	Hi	Lo-Mod	Su-HSh		3	Some cvs. have dark foliage

Coreopsis tripteris

Crambe cordifolia

Echinacea 'Fatal Attraction'

Echinops ritro

Eryngium yuccifolium

	HEIGHT (M)	SPREAD (M)	Nº PER M²	FOLIAGE ARCHITECTURE	FLOWER SEASON	STRUCTURAL INTEREST	LONGEVITY
Euphorbia amygdaloides	S	0.25–0.5	11	Green/red **Up**	Yellow-green **Sp-E Su**	3–9 mths	<10 yrs
Euphorbia characias	M	0.5–1.0	5–7	Grayish, shrublike, E **LM**	Yellow-green **Sp**	3–9 mths	<10 yrs
Euphorbia cyparissias	S	0.5–1.0	9	Gray, fine **Br**	Yellow-green **E Su**	short	Per
Euphorbia griffithii	M	0.5–1.0	7	Dark, narrow **Up**	Red and yellow **E-M Su**	3–9 mths	Per
Euphorbia palustris	M	0.5–1.0	3	Narrow, mid-green, Au **SM**	Yellow-green **Sp-E Su**	3–9 mths	Per
Euphorbia polychroma	S	0.25–1.0	7	Fresh green **SM**	Yellow-green **Sp-E Su**	3–9 mths	<10 yrs
Euphorbia schillingii	M	0.5–1.0	3	Dark, veined **SM, Up**	Yellow-green **M Su**	3–9 mths	Per
Filipendula spp. and cvs.	T	0.25–1.0	3–5	Pinnate, large, Au **Em, Up**	Pink to white **M Su**	3–9 mths	Per
Gaura lindheimeri	M	0.5–1.0	7	Wiry stems **Br**	White or pink **M Su-Au**	short	<5 yrs
Gentiana asclepiadea and *G. makinoi*	S	0.25–0.5	9	Leafy stems **SM**	Blue **M Su**	3–9 mths	LL
Geranium nodosum	S	0.5–1.0	9	Glossy, 3-pointed **LM**	Pink **L Sp-M Su**	short	Per
Geranium phaeum	S	0.5–1.0	9	Lobed **LM**	Pink, maroon **E Su**	short	Per
Geranium pratense	S	0.25–0.5	9	Lobed **LM**	Violet-blue **E Su**	short	Per
Geranium psilostemon	M	0.5–1.0	9	Lobed **LM**	Magenta **M Su**	short	Per
Geranium sanguineum and cvs.	S	0.25–1.0	9	Dark, lobed **LM**	Various shades pink **E-M Su**	short	Per
Geranium soboliferum	S	0.25–0.5	9	Lobed, Au **LM LM**	Magenta **M-L Su**	short	Per
Geranium sylvaticum	S	<0.25	9	Lobed **Em**	Blue, pink **E Su**	short	Per
Geranium wallichianum	S	0.5–1.0	9	Lobed **LM, Pro**	Violet-blue **L Su-Au**	short	Per
Geranium wlassovianum	S	0.25–0.5	9	Lobed, Au **LM**	Purple **M Su-Au**	short	Per

SPREADING ABILITY	PERSISTENCE	SELF-SOWING/ SEEDING	HABITAT LIGHT	SOIL	ZONE	NOTES, ADDITIONAL SPECIES AND FORMS
Lim-Slo	Hi	Mod	HSh		7	
None	Hi	Mod	Su-HSh	Dr	8	
Rap	Med	Lo	Su	Dr, Lo	7	
Mod	Hi	Lo	Su-HSh	Mo, Hi	7	Guerrilla spread
None	Hi	Mod-Hi	Su-HSh	Mo, Hi	7	
Lim	Hi	Lo-Mod	Su		7	
Slo	Hi	Lo	Su	Mo, Hi	7	
Mod	Hi	Lo-Mod	Su	Mo, Hi	3-4	Wide variety of height among spp.
None	Hi	Lo	Su		5	
None	Hi	Lo	HSh	Mo	6	
Mod	Hi	Mod-Hi	Su-Sh	Dr	5	
Mod	Hi	Mod-Hi	Su-Sh		4	Large number of cvs.
Lim	Hi	Mod-Hi	Su		4	
Slo	Hi	Mod	Su-HSh	Mo	4	
Slo	Hi	Mod	Su-HSh	Dr, Lo	4	
None	Hi	Hi	Su-HSh	Mo	5	Red autumn color
Lim	Hi	Hi	Su-HSh		4	
None	Hi	Lo	HSh	Mo	4	
None	Hi	Mod	Su-HSh		5	

Euphorbia griffithii

Euphorbia schillingii

Filipendula rubra 'Venusta'

Geranium phaeum

Geranium sylvaticum

	HEIGHT (M)	SPREAD (M)	N° PER M²	FOLIAGE ARCHITECTURE	FLOWER SEASON	STRUCTURAL INTEREST	LONGEVITY
Geranium ×oxonianum cvs.	S	0.5-1.0	9	Lobed, broad **LM**	Shades of pink **E Su** and **L Su-Au**	short	Per
Gillenia trifoliata	M	0.25-0.5	3-5	Narrow, bushy **Br**	White, red **E Su**	9 mths	Per
Gypsophila paniculata	M	0.25-0.5	3-5	Small, pointed **Em, Br**	White **E Su**	3-9 mths	Per
Helenium hybrids	T	0.25-1.0	9	Lush green **Up**	Yellow, red, brown **L Su-Au**	3-9 mths	Per
Helleborus spp. and hybrids	S	0.25-1.0	9	Palmate, E **BB**	Various subtle colors **Sp**	3-9 mths	Per
Hemerocallis spp. and hybrids	S	0.25-1.0	9	Clump, arching **Li**	Yellow-red, pink **M-L Su**	3-9 mths	Per
Heuchera spp. and cvs.	S	0.25-0.5	11	Lobed, often colored **BB**	Tiny, cream **Sp-M Su**	3-9 mths / short	Per
Heuchera villosa	S	0.25-0.5	9	Lobed, green **BB**	Tiny, cream **L Su-Au**	3-9 mths / short	Per
× *Heucherella* cvs.	S	0.25-0.5	11	Lobed, marked **BB**	Cream, red **Sp-M Su**	3-9 mths / short	Per
Hosta spp. and hybrids	S-M	0.5-1.0	5-9	Large, heart-shaped, Au **BB**	White, lilac **M Su**	3-9 mths	Per
Inula helenium	T	0.25-0.5	7	Large **Em**	Yellow daisy **E-M Su**	3-9 mths	Per
Inula magnifica	T-VT	0.5->1.0	7	Very large **Em, Up**	Yellow daisy **M Su**	9 mths	Per
Iris fulva	S	0.5-1.0	11	Linear **Li**	Copper **E Su**	3-9 mths	Per
Iris sibirica	M	0.25-0.5	11	Tight, upright clumps **Li**	Violet-blue **E Su**	9 mths	Per
Kalimeris incisa	S	0.25-1.0	7	Profuse, small **Up**	Palest purple **E Su-Au**	9 mths	Per
Kirengeshoma palmata	M	0.25-0.5	9	Maple-like **SM**	Butter yellow **L Su-Au**	3-9 mths	Per
Knautia macedonica	S-M	0.25-0.5	9	Elongated **SM, Br**	Dark red-pink **E Su-Au**	3-9 mths	<5 yrs
Kniphofia spp. and cvs.	M-T	0.25-1.0	7	Imposing rosettes **Li**	Yellow, orange **M Su-Au**	3-9 mths	Per
Lamium maculatum	L	0.25-0.5	9	Small, dense **Br, Pro**	Pink, white **Sp-E Su**	short	Per

SPREADING ABILITY	PERSISTENCE	SELF-SOWING/ SEEDING	HABITAT LIGHT	SOIL	ZONE	NOTES, ADDITIONAL SPECIES AND FORMS
Mod	Hi	Mod-Hi	Su-Sh		5	Large group of varieties, mostly very vigorous
None	Hi	Lo	Su-HSh		4	Reddish autumn color
None	Hi	Lo	Su	Dr, Lo	4	Short-lived on damp soils
Slo	Mod	Lo	Su	Mo, Hi	3	
Lim	Hi	Mod-Hi	Su-Sh	Dr	4	Varieties with distinct stem liable to be short-lived
Slo	Hi	Lo	Su		3-5	
Lim	Lo-Med	Lo	Su-HSh		4	H. micrantha more reliable than hybrids
Lim	Hi	Lo	Su-HSh	Mo	3	
Slo	Hi	Lo	Su-HSh		4	
Slo-Mod	Hi	Lo	Su-HSh	Mo, Hi	3	Clear yellow autumn color, very wide range of varieties
Lim	Hi	Lo	Su		5	
Lim	Hi	Lo	Su		6	Magnificent but can flop badly
Mod	Med	Lo	Su	Mo	5	
Slo	Med	Mod	Su		4	
Lim	Hi	Lo	Su-HSh		4	Other spp. also good
Slo	Hi	Lo	HSh	Mo	5	Can be slow to establish
None	Hi	Hi	Su	Dr	4	
Lim	Hi	Lo	Su		6-7	Wide range spp. and cvs. varying hardiness
Slo	Med	Lo	HSh		3	Some varieties have variegated foliage

Gillenia trifoliata

Helenium 'Rubinzwerg'

Iris fulva

Kirengeshoma palmata

Knautia macedonica

	HEIGHT (M)	SPREAD (M)	N° PER M²	FOLIAGE ARCHITECTURE	FLOWER SEASON	STRUCTURAL INTEREST	LONGEVITY
Lathyrus vernus	L	0.25-0.5	9	Small leaflets **SM**	Pink, white **Sp**	short	Per
Lavatera cachemiriana	T	0.25-0.5	1	Lobed, hairy **Up**	Pale pink **M-L Su**	3-9 mths	<10 yrs
Liatris spp.	M-T	<0.25-0.5	11	Narrow, profuse **Up, Em**	Pink **M-L Su**	3-9 mths	Per
Libertia grandiflora	M	0.25-0.5	9	Dark, clumps **LB**	Pure white **E-M Su**	9 mths	Per
Ligularia spp. and cvs.	MT	0.5-1.0	5-7	Large, lush **Em**	Yellow **M Su-Au**	3-9 mths	Per
Limonium platyphyllum (*L. latifolium*)	S	0.25-0.5	7	Large, glossy **Em**	Cloud of lilac **M-L Su**	6 mths	Per
Liriope and *Ophiopogon* spp.	L	<0.25-0.5	11	Linear, E **Li**	Pale purple **L Su-Au**	3-9 mths	Per
Lobelia spp. and cvs.	M	<0.25	9	Fresh green **Em, Up**	Red, purple, pink **M-L Su**	short	<10 yrs
Lunaria rediviva	M	0.25-0.5	9	Broad, green **Em**	Palest purple **Sp-E Su**	9 mths	Per
Lysimachia clethroides	M	0.5-1.0	7	Narrow **Em, Up**	White spikes **L Sp-M Su**	3-9 mths	Per
Lysimachia ephemerum	M	<0.25-0.5	9	Gray, narrow **Em**	White spikes **Su**	3-9 mths	<10 yrs
Lythrum spp.	MT	0.25-0.5	9	Small, narrow **Up, Br**	Pink **M-L Su**	3-9 mths	Per
Macleaya spp.	T-VT	>1.0	5	Grayish, broad **Up**	Wispy heads **M-L Su**	9 mths	Per
Maianthemum racemosa (*Smilacina*)	M	0.25-0.5	9	Dark, elegant **SM**	Cream heads **Sp**	short	Per
Mertensia spp.	L	0.25-0.5	9-11	Grayish, broad **LM**	Pale blue **Sp**	short	Per
Monarda bradburiana	M	0.25-1.0	9	Aromatic **Up**	Pale pink **E Su**	9 mths	Per
Monarda hybrids	M-T	0.25-1.0	9	Aromatic **Up**	Pink, purple, red **M Su**	3-9 mths	Per
Mukdenia rossii	L	0.25-0.5	9	Broad, lobed **BB**	Insignificant	3-9 mths	Per
Nepeta racemosa and similar spp.	L-S	0.5-1.0	5-7	Gray, aromatic **Br, Pro**	Purple-violet **E-L Su**	short	Per

SPREADING ABILITY	PERSISTENCE	SELF-SOWING/ SEEDING	HABITAT LIGHT	SOIL	ZONE	NOTES, ADDITIONAL SPECIES AND FORMS
Lim	Hi	Lo	HSh		4	
None	Hi	Mod	Su		6	
Slo	Hi	Lo	Su		4	Liable to rot in maritime climate winters
Lim	Hi	Lo	Su	Mo	8	Other spp. good in maritime climates
Slo-Mod	Hi	Lo	Su-HSh	Mo	4-5	Size and spreading ability varies
None	Hi	Lo	Su	Dr, Lo	3	
Slo-Mod	Hi	Lo	HSh-Sh		5	Spreading ability depends on climate
Lim	Med	Lo-Mod	Su	Mo, Hi	3-7	*L. syphilitica* can seed strongly
Lim	Hi	Mod	HSh		4	Very good scent, attractive seedpods
Mod-Rap	Hi	Lo	Su-HSh		3	*L. barystachys* similar but stronger spreader
None	Hi	Lo	Su-HSh	Mo	6	
None-Lim	Hi	Mod-Hi	Su	We	3	*L. virgatum* extremely invasive in N. America
Mod-Rap	Hi	Lo-Mod	Su-HSh		3	*M. microcarpa* spreads less
Slo	Hi	Lo	HSh-Sh		3	
Slo	Hi	Lo-Mod	HSh-Sh		3	
Mod	Lo	Mod	Su-HSh	Dr, Lo	3	Autumn color
Slo	V lo	Lo	Su-HSh	Lo	3	
Slo-Mod	Hi	Lo	HSh-Sh		6	
Lim	Hi	Mod	Su	Dr, Lo	4	More *Nepeta* spp. are constantly becoming available

Lathyrus vernus

Lavatera cachemiriana

Lunaria rediviva

Lysimachia ephemerum

Macleaya spp.

	HEIGHT (M)	SPREAD (M)	N° PER M²	FOLIAGE ARCHITECTURE	FLOWER SEASON	STRUCTURAL INTEREST	LONGEVITY
Nepeta sibirica	M	0.5-1.0	5-7	Narrow, aromatic **SM**	Blue **M-L Su**	short	Per
Nepeta subsessilis	M	0.25-0.5	9	Small, aromatic **SM**	Pale mauve **M-L Su**	short	Per
Oenothera fruticosa	S	0.25-0.5	9	Narrow **SM**	Yellow, large **E-M Su**	3-9 mths	<10 yrs
Origanum spp. and cvs.	S-M	0.25-0.5	11	Small, aromatic **SM**	Red-pink **M-L Su**	3-9 mths	Per
Paeonia herbaceous spp. and hybrids	M	0.25-1.0	3-5	Large, deeply lobed **SM**	Pink, red **E Su**	3-9 mths	LL
Papaver orientale hybrids	M	0.5-1.0	7	Hairy, toothed **LM**	Orange, pink **E Su**	short	Per
Parthenium integrifolium	M	0.25-0.5	9	Toothed, dark **SM**	White **E-M Su**	3-9 mths	Per
Penstemon digitalis	S	0.25-0.5	9	Dark, reddish **Em**	White **E Su**	3-9 mths	<10 yrs
Perovskia atriplicifolia cvs.	M	0.25-0.5	1-3	Fine, gray **Up**	Violet-purple **M Su**	9 mths	Per
Persicaria amplexicaulis cvs.	M-T	0.5->1.0	3-5	Large, broad **Br**	Red, pink **M Su-Au**	3-9 mths	Per
Persicaria bistorta	S	0.5-1.0	5	Large, broad **Em**	Pink **E Su**	short	Per
Phlomis russeliana	M	0.5-1.0	9	Large, broad, E **Em**	Soft yellow **E Su**	9 mths	Per
Phlomis samia	M	0.25-1.0	9	Large, broad **Em**	Pink **E Su**	9 mths	Per
Phlomis tuberosa	T	0.25-1.0	9	Dark, veined **Em**	Pink **E Su**	9 mths	Per
Phlox paniculata and *P. maculata* cvs. and hybrids	M-T	0.25-1.0	9	Mid-green **Up**	Pink, red, purple **M-L Su**	3-9 mths	Per
Phlox divaricata and *P. stolonifera* cvs.	L	0.25-1.0	11	Small, profuse **Br, Pro**	Blue, pink **Sp-E Su**	short	Per
Polemonium caeruleum	M	<0.25	9	Pale, pinnate **Em**	Blue **E Su**	short	<5 yrs
Polygonatum and *Disporum* spp. and hybrids	M	0.25-0.5	9	Elegant **Up**	Cream bells **Sp**	3-9 mths	Per
Primula – tall Himalayan types	M	<0.25	11	Rosettes **Em**	Pink, yellow **E Su**	short	<5 yrs-Per

SPREADING ABILITY	PERSISTENCE	SELF-SOWING/ SEEDING	HABITAT LIGHT	HABITAT SOIL	ZONE	NOTES, ADDITIONAL SPECIES AND FORMS
Mod	Med	Mod	Su-HSh	Dr	3	Dislikes heat
Lim	Hi	Lo	Su-HSh		4	
None	Hi	Mod-Hi	Su	Dr, Lo	4	Many other good *Oenothera* spp.
Lim	Hi	Hi	Su-HSh	Dr, Lo	5	
Lim	Hi	Lo	Su	Hi	3	
Lim	Hi	Lo	Su	Dr	3	Summer-dormant
Lim	Hi	Lo	Su	Dr	4	
Lim-Slo	Hi	Lo	Su-HSh	Dr	3	Dark red autumn color
None	Hi	Lo	Su	Dr, Lo	3	Extreme tolerance of severe climates
Mod	Hi	Mod	Su-HSh	Mo, Hi	4	Bushy habit very useful
Rap	Hi	Lo	Su-HSh	Mo, Hi	4	May repeat flower in late summer
Mod	Hi	Mod	Su-HSh		4	Ultra-low maintenance, weed suppressor
Mod	Hi	Lo	Su	Dr	7	
Slo	Hi	Lo-Hi	Su	Dr	5	
Slo	Lo-Med	Lo	Su-HSh	Hi	3-4	Wide range of performance between varieties
Mod	Med	Lo	HSh		3-5	Need humus-rich soils to thrive
None	Hi	Mod-Hi	Su	Mo	4	Dislikes heat
Slo	Hi	Lo	HSh-Sh	Mo	3-5	Some may become summer-dormant
None-Lim	Hi	Mod-Hi	Su-HSh	Mo	3-6	Only *P. florindae* reliable, dislikes heat

Nepeta subsessilis

Persicaria amplexicaulis

Persicaria bistorta

Phlox paniculata

Polygonatum ×hybridum

	HEIGHT (M)	SPREAD (M)	N° PER M²	FOLIAGE ARCHITECTURE	FLOWER SEASON	STRUCTURAL INTEREST	LONGEVITY
Pulmonaria spp. and cvs.	S	0.25-0.5	11	Hairy, broad, often marked **LM**	Blue, pink **Sp-E Su**	short	Per
Pycnanthemum spp.	M	0.25-1.0	9	Gray, aromatic **Up**	White bracts **M-L Su**	3-9 mths	Per
Rodgersia spp. and cvs.	M	0.5-1.0	9	Very large, often bronze **BB**	Large white, pink heads **E-M Su**	9 mths	Per
Rudbeckia fulgida	S	0.25-1.0	9	Dark, broad **SM, Em**	Yellow daisy **L Su-Au**	3-9 mths	Per
Rudbeckia laciniata (*R. nitida*)	T-VT	0.5-1.0	5	Divided **Em**	Yellow daisy **L Su-Au**	3-9 mths	Per
Rudbeckia subtomentosa	M	0.25-0.5	7	Divided **Em**	Yellow daisy **L Su-Au**	3-9 mths	Per
Ruellia humilis	S	0.25-0.5	9	Small, profuse **Br**	Open, purple **E Su-Au**	3-9 mths	Per
Salvia azurea	T	0.5-1.0	9	Grayish **Em**	Blue **L Su-Au**	short	Per
Salvia glutinosa	S-M	0.5-1.0	9	Broad leaves **SM**	Pale yellow **E-M Su**	3-9 mths	Per
Salvia verticillata	S	0.25-0.5	9	Rough texture **SM**	Purple tones **M Su**	3-9 mths / short	<10 yrs
Salvia ×superba, *S. nemorosa*, *S. ×sylvestris*	S	0.25-0.5	9	Matt texture **SM**	Blue, violet, pink **E-Su** and **L Su**	short	<10 yrs
Sanguisorba spp.	S-T	0.5-1.0	3-5	Pinnate, very attractive **Em, SM**	Dark red, white **E Su-Au**	3-9 mths	Per
Saponaria lempergii 'Max Frei'	S	0.25-1.0	11	Small, S/E **SM, Pro**	Pale pink **E-L Su**	short	Per
Scabiosa caucasica	S	0.25-0.5	9	Grayish, lobed **SM**	Pale blue, pink **M Su**	short	<10 yrs
Scutellaria incana	M-T	0.25-0.5	9	Elongated **Up, Br**	Blue, tubular **M-L Su**	3-9 mths	Per
Sedum 'Bertram Anderson'	S	0.25-0.5	11	Gray, rounded **SM, Pro**	Purple-pink **M-L Su**	short	Per
Sedum spectabile and *S. telephium* hybrids	S	0.5-1.0	9	Fleshy **SM**	Pink, red **L Su-Au**	9 mths	Per
Selinum wallichianum	M	0.5-1.0	9	Finely divided **Em**	White umbels **M Su**	3-9 mths	<10 yrs
Sidalcea spp. and cvs.	M	0.25-0.5	9	Lobed **Em**	Pink **M Su**	short	<10 yrs

SPREADING ABILITY	PERSISTENCE	SELF-SOWING/ SEEDING	HABITAT LIGHT	SOIL	ZONE	NOTES, ADDITIONAL SPECIES AND FORMS
Lim-Slo	Hi	Lo	HSh-Sh	Mo	3-4	May become summer-dormant in hot, dry periods
Slo-Mod	Hi	Lo	Su	Dr	3-4	Species vary in drought tolerance
Mod	Hi	Lo	Su-HSh	Mo, Hi	5	Can be slow to establish
Mod	Med	Lo	Su-HSh		3	Very prolific flowers
Mod	Hi	Mod	Su		3	
Slo	Hi	Lo	Su		4	
Slo	Hi	Mod	Su-HSh	Dr	4	
Lim	Hi	Lo	Su		6	Very good for late flowering
Slo	Hi	Hi	HSh	Dr	6	Good in dry shade
None	Hi	Mod-Hi	Su		6	
None	Hi	Mod	Su	Dr, Lo	6	Important group for dry calcareous soils
Lim-Mod	Hi	Mod	Su	Mo	3-5	Many have transparent flower clusters, good foliage
Slo	Hi	Lo	Su		7	
None	Hi	Mod	Su		4	
Slo	Hi	Lo	Su	Dr	5	Good gray seedheads
Lim	Hi	Lo	Su	Dr	5	
None	Hi	Lo	Su	Dr	4	Large number of cvs. and hybrids
None	Hi	Mod	Su-HSh		8	
Lim	Hi	Lo	Su		5	

Pycnanthemum muticum

Rodgersia aesculifolia cultivar

Rudbeckia subtomentosa

Ruellia humilis

Selinum wallichianum

	HEIGHT (M)	SPREAD (M)	N° PER M²	FOLIAGE ARCHITECTURE	FLOWER SEASON	STRUCTURAL INTEREST	LONGEVITY
Silphium spp.	T-VT	0.5-1.0	1	Large, leathery **Em**	Yellow daisy **L Su-Au**	3-9 mths	LL
Solidago and × *Solidaster* spp. and hybrids	M-T	0.25-1.0	7	Small, profuse **Up**	Yellow heads **L Su-Au**	3-9 mths	Per
Stachys macrantha	S	0.25-0.5	9	Broad, chunky **LM**	Purple-pink **L Sp-E Su**	3-9 mths	Per
Stachys byzantina	S	0.5-1.0	11	Silver, hairy **LM**	Insignificant	short	Per
Stachys officinalis and hybrids	S	0.25-0.5	9	Small, dark **Em**	Deep pink **M Su**	9 mths	Per
Symphytum 'Rubrum'	S-M	0.5-1.0	9	Large, coarse **LM**	Red **L Sp-E Su**	short	Per
Telekia speciosa	T	0.5-1.0	5-7	Very large **Em**	Yellow daisy **E-L Su**	3-9 mths	<10 yrs
Tellima grandiflora	S	0.25-0.5	11	Dense, light green **LM**	Pale green **L Sp**	short	Per
Thalictrum aquilegifolium	M-T	0.25-0.5	9	Delicate, tiny leaflets **Em**	Purple-pink **E Su**	3-9 mths	Per
Thalictrum flavum	T	0.25-0.5	7	Grayish **Em**	Pale yellow **E Su**	3-9 mths	Per
Thalictrum lucidum	T	0.25-0.5	7	Shiny, leaflets **Em**	Creamy **E Su**	3-9 mths	Per
Thalictrum pubescens (*T. polygamum*)	T-VT	0.25-0.5	9	Delicate, tiny leaflets **Em**	Cream **E Su**	3-9 mths	Per
Thalictrum delavayi, T. roche-brunnianum and hybrids	T-VT	0.25-0.5	9	Delicate, tiny leaflets **Em**	Purple-pink **M Su**	3-9 mths	Per
Thermopsis spp.	M	0.25-1.0	5-7	Leaflets **Up, Em**	Yellow lupin-like **E Su**	3-9 mths	Per
Tiarella spp. and cvs.	S	<0.25-0.5	11	Good markings **LM**	Cream spikes **Sp**	short	Per
Tricyrtis spp. and cvs.	S-M	<0.25-0.5	9	Elegant **Up**	Spotted **L Su-Au**	short	Per
Trifolium pannonicum	S	0.25-0.5	9	Clover-like **LM**	Creamy **E-M Su**	3-9 mths	Per
Trifolium rubens	S	0.25-0.5	9	Clover-like **LM**	Pink-red **E-M Su**	3-9 mths	Per
Trollius spp. and cvs.	S-M	0.25-0.5	9	Dark, lobed **Em**	Yellow **Sp-E Su**	short	Per

SPREADING ABILITY	PERSISTENCE	SELF-SOWING/ SEEDING	HABITAT LIGHT	SOIL	ZONE	NOTES, ADDITIONAL SPECIES AND FORMS
Lim	Hi	Mod	Su		3	*S. laciniatum* has deeply divided leaves
Slo-Rap	Med-Hi	Mod	Su		3-5	Wide range of flower-head shapes and spread
Slo	Hi	Lo	Su-HSh		6	
Mod	Hi	Lo	Su	Dr	5	'Big Ears' especially good
Lim	Hi	Mod	Su-HSh		5	
Mod	Hi	Lo	Su-HSh	Hi	5	Many other spp. often aggressive spreaders
None	Hi	Mod	HSh		6	Several purple/bronze foliage cvs.
Slo	Hi	Mod-Hi	HSh-Sh		6	Good in dry shade
Lim	Hi	Mod-Hi	Su- HSh	Mo	4	All spp. prefer cooler climates
Lim	Hi	Mod	Su	Mo	5	
Slo	Hi	Mod-Hi	Su	Mo	4	
Lim	Hi	Mod	Su	Mo	4	
Lim	Hi	Lo	Su-HSh	Mo	5	Increasing number of hybrids available
Lim	Hi	Lo	Su		2-4	Some spp. do spread strongly, however
Slo-Mod	Hi	Lo	HSh-Sh	Mo	4	Many new varieties
Slo-Mod	Hi	Lo	HSh-Sh	Mo	4-6	Many new varieties
None	Hi	Lo-Mod	Su		5	
None	Hi	Mod	Su		6	
None	Hi	Lo	Su	Mo	5-6	

Solidago rugosa

Stachys byzantina 'Big Ears'

Thalictrum aquilegifolium

Thalictrum rochebrunnianum

Tiarella wherryi

	HEIGHT (M)	SPREAD (M)	N° PER M²	FOLIAGE ARCHITECTURE	FLOWER SEASON	STRUCTURAL INTEREST	LONGEVITY
Veratrum spp.	M-T	0.25-0.5	7	Pleated, striking **Em**	Green or brown **Su**	3-9 mths	LL
Verbascum spp.	T-VT	0.25-0.5		Rosettes **Em**	Mostly yellow **E-M Su**	9 mths	<5 yrs
Verbesina alternifolia	VT	0.5-1.0	7	Small, profuse **Up**	Yellow, small **L Su-Au**	3-9 mths	LL
Vernonia spp.	VT	0.25-1.0	7	Dark, narrow **Up**	Deep violet **Au**	3-9 mths	LL
Veronica austriaca and cvs.	S	0.25-0.5	11	Dark, small **Up**	Deep blue **E Su**	short	Per
Veronica longifolia and cvs.	M	0.25-0.5	9	Small, profuse **Up, Br**	Blue, pink **M-L Su**	3-9 mths	Per
Veronica spicata	S	0.25-0.5	9	Grayish **Up, SM**	Blue, pink **Sp-E Su**	3-9 mths	Per
Veronicastrum spp. and cvs.	T	0.25-0.5	7	Narrow **Em, Up**	Blue, pink **E-M Su**	9 mths	Per
Zizia aurea	S	<0.25	9	Divided, fresh green **Em**	Green-yellow **Sp-E Su**	3-9 mths	Per

GRASSES

	HEIGHT (M)	SPREAD (M)	N° PER M²	FOLIAGE ARCHITECTURE	FLOWER SEASON	STRUCTURAL INTEREST	LONGEVITY
Andropogon gerardii	VT	0.5-1.0	5	Upright **clump**	Distinctive **L Su**	3-9 mths	LL
Anemanthele lessoniana	S	0.5-1.0	5	Olive to bronze **cespitose**	Diffuse heads **L Su-Au**	3-9 mths	<10 yrs
Bouteloua curtipendula	M	0.25-1.0	9	Upright **cespitose**	Narrow heads **E-L Su**	3-9 mths	Per
Briza media	S	<0.25	9	Grayish, loose **cespitose**	Nodding heads **E Su**	short	Per
Calamagrostis acutiflora 'Karl Foerster'	T	0.5-1.0	1-3	Strongly upright **clump**	Fluffy panicles **E Su-Wi**	9 mths	Per
Calamagrostis brachytricha	M	0.25-1.0	5	Open habit **cespitose**	Fluffy panicles **L Su-Wi**	3-9 mths	Per
Carex muskingumensis	S	0.25-0.5	7	Mid-green, 'tiered' **clump**	Insignificant	9 mths	LL
Carex bromoides	S	0.25-0.5	11	Fine **clump**	Insignificant	short	Per
Carex dipsacea and other New Zealand spp.	S	0.25-0.5	9	Colored, E **cespitose**	Insignificant	9 mths	<10 yrs-Per

SPREADING ABILITY	PERSISTENCE	SELF-SOWING/ SEEDING	HABITAT LIGHT	SOIL	ZONE	NOTES, ADDITIONAL SPECIES AND FORMS
Lim	Hi	Lo	Su-HSh	Mo, Hi	5-6	
None	Hi	Hi	Su	Dr, Lo	4-5	Very large genus Not planted in groups
Slo	Hi	Lo	Su	Mo	4	Has limited ornamental value
Slo	Hi	Lo	Su	Mo, Hi	4	
Slo	Hi	Lo	Su	Dr	4	A range of cvs.
Slo	Hi	Mod	Su	Mo	4	A range of cvs.
Slo	Hi	Mod	Su	Dr	3-4	A range of cvs.
Slo	Hi	Mod	Su		3	Growing range of cvs., autumn color
Slo	Hi	Mod	Su		3	*Z. aptera* is similar
Slo	Hi	Mod	Su		3	
None	Hi	Hi	Su-HSh		8	
Mod	Hi	Lo	Su		4	*B. gracilis* also good ground cover
Lim	Hi	Mod-Hi	Su		4	
Mod	Hi	Lo	Su		5	
None	Hi	Mod-Hi	Su		4	
Slo	Hi	Lo	Su-HSh		4	Unique habit
Lim-Slo	Hi	Lo	Su-HSh	Mo	2	
None	Hi	Mod-Hi	Su		6	

Veratrum nigrum

Verbesina alternifolia

Veronicastrum virginicum

Briza media

Calamagrostis acutiflora 'Karl Foerster'

	HEIGHT (M)	SPREAD (M)	N° PER M²	FOLIAGE ARCHITECTURE	FLOWER SEASON	STRUCTURAL INTEREST	LONGEVITY
Carex flacca	S	0.25-0.5	11	Wiry, E **mat**	Insignificant	short	Per
Carex pensylvanica	S	0.25-0.5	11	Fine, E **mat**	Insignificant	short	Per
Chasmanthium latifolium	M	0.25-0.5	7	Broad **clump**	Oat-like panicles **L Su-Au**	3-9 mths	Per
Deschampsia cespitosa	M	0.25-1.0	5	Dark, glossy **cespitose**	Diffuse heads **M Su-Wi**	9 mths	<10 yrs
Elymus hystrix (*Hystrix patula*)	M	0.25-0.5	7-9	Loose upright **clump**	Open heads **M-L Su**	3-9 mths	Per
Eragrostis spectabilis	S	0.25-0.5	9	Medium width, Au **cespitose**	Diffuse heads **L Su**	6 mths	<5-<10 yrs
Festuca mairei	S	0.25-0.5	1	Wiry **cespitose**	Narrow, wiry **M Su-Wi**	9 mths	Per
Hakonechloa macra	S	0.25-0.5	9	'Combed' look, Au **clump-mat**	Insignificant	3-9 mths	Per
Koeleria macrantha	S	0.25-0.5	9	Bright green **clump**	Light-colored **L Sp-E Su**	3-9 mths	<5-<10 yrs
Luzula spp. and cvs.	L-S	0.25-0.5	9	Broad, E **mat**	Cream, brown **E Su**	short	Per
Miscanthus sinensis cvs. and related spp.	M-VT	0.5-1.0	1	Broad, often with silver midrib **clump**	Silver-red **L Su-Wi**	3-9 mths	Per
Molinia caerulea cvs.	M	0.25-0.5	5-7	Narrow, Au **cespitose**	Fine, diffuse **Au-E Wi**	3-9 mths	Per
Molinia caerulea subsp. *arundinacea*	T-VT	0.5-1.0	1	Narrow, Au **cespitose**	Fine, diffuse **Au-E Wi**	3-9 mths	Per
Nassella tenuissima (*Stipa tenuissima*)	S	<0.25	9	Very fine **cespitose**	Fine, soft **M Su-Wi**	9 mths	<5 yrs
Panicum virgatum and cvs.	M-T	0.5-1.0	5	Broad, Au **clump**	Fine, diffuse **Au-Wi**	3-9 mths	Per
Pennisetum alopecuroides	M	0.5-1.0	1-3	Narrow, Au **clump**	Fluffy heads **L Su-E Wi**	3-9 mths	Per
Pennisetum orientale	MT	0.5-1.0	3-5	Narrow **clump**	Fluffy heads **L Su-E Wi**	3-9 mths	Per
Schizachyrium scoparium	S-M	0.25-1.0	5-7	Narrow, Au **cespitose**	Low impact	3-9 mths	<5-<10 yrs
Sesleria spp.	S	0.25-0.5	9	Dense, blue green **mat**	Insignificant	9 mths	Per

SPREADING ABILITY	PERSISTENCE	SELF-SOWING/ SEEDING	HABITAT LIGHT	SOIL	ZONE	NOTES, ADDITIONAL SPECIES AND FORMS
Mod	Hi	Lo	Su-HSh		4	Suitable for sandy soils and salt exposure
Mod	Hi	Lo	HSh		4	
Lim	Hi	Lo	Su-HSh		3	
None	Hi	Hi	Su-HSh	Lo	4	
Slo	Hi	Lo	Su-HSh		3	
None	Hi	Mod	Su		5	Autumn color
None	Hi	Lo	Su		5	Slow-growing
Slo-Mod	Hi	Lo	HSh	Mo	5	Pale yellow autumn color
None	Hi	Mod	Su		4	
Mod	Hi	Lo	HSh-Sh		6	Often good in dry shade
Slo	Hi	Lo-Hi	Su		5	Some cvs. potentially invasive
None	Hi	Lo	Su-HSh		4	Clear yellow autumn color
None	Hi	Lo	Su-HSh		4	Clear yellow autumn color
None	Hi	Hi	Su		7	
Slo	Hi	Mod	Su		4	Some cvs. have dark red autumn color
Slo	Hi	Mod	Su		6	Autumn color
Slo	Hi	Mod	Su		5-6	'Tall Tails' one of the best cvs
Lim	Hi	Mod-Hi	Su		3	Good foliage plant, can flop, autumn color
Mod	Hi	Lo	Su	Lo	4	S. autumnalis is distinct yellow-green

Eragrostis spectabilis

Eragrostis curvula

Festuca mairei

Hakonechloa macra

Pennisetum viridescens

	HEIGHT (M)	SPREAD (M)	N° PER M²	FOLIAGE ARCHITECTURE	FLOWER SEASON	STRUCTURAL INTEREST	LONGEVITY
Sorghastrum nutans	T	0.25-0.5	5-7	Often grayish **clump**	Brown **L Su-Wi**	3-9 mths	LL
Spodiopogon sibiricus	M-T	0.25-0.5	5-7	Broad, dark **clump**	Brown **L Su-Wi**	3-9 mths	Per
Sporobolus heterolepsis	M	0.25-1.0	9	Fine **cespitose**	Fine, diffuse **L Su-Wi**	3-9 mths	LL
Stipa barbata, *S. pulcherrima*	M	0.25-0.5	9	Fine **cespitose**	Extraordinarily long **E Su**	3-9 mths	Per
Stipa calamagrostis (Achnatherum)	M	0.5-1.0	9	Fine **cespitose**	Soft heads **E Su-Au**	3-9 mths	Per
Stipa gigantea	T	0.5-1.0	1	Fine, E **cespitose**	Very open **M Su-Au**	3-9 mths	LL
FERNS							
Adiantum pedatum	S	0.25-0.5	11	Delicate, tiny leaflets		short	Per
Athyrium niponicum 'Metallicum'	S	0.25-0.5	9-11	Distinct markings		short	Per
Dryopteris spp.	S-M	0.25-0.5	7-9	Deciduous, some spp. S/E		3-9 mths	Per
Osmunda regalis	M	0.5-1.0	5-7	Large, grand, divided		9 mths	LL
Polystichum setiferum and cvs.	S	0.25-0.5	7	Very finely divided, E		9 mths	LL

SPREADING ABILITY	PERSISTENCE	SELF-SOWING/ SEEDING	HABITAT LIGHT	HABITAT SOIL	ZONE	NOTES, ADDITIONAL SPECIES AND FORMS
Slo-Mod	Hi	Mod	Su		3	'Sioux Blue' especially good
Lim-Slo	Hi	Lo	Su-HSh		4	Best in cooler climates
Lim-Slo	Hi	Mod	Su	Dr	3	Can be slow to establish in cooler climates
None	Hi	Lo	Su	Dr	5	Very brief effect
None-Lim	Hi	Lo	Su	Dr	5	Floppy on rich soils
None	Hi	Lo	Su	Dr	5	Well-known transparent heads
Mod	Hi	Mod	Sh	Mo	3	
Slo-Mod	Hi	Lo	Sh		3	
Lim	Hi	Lo	Su-Sh		4-5	Wide range of foliage texture and sizes
Lim	Hi	Lo	Su-HSh	Mo	3	Several other similar spp.
Lim	Hi	Lo	Su-Sh		6	One of the most tolerant of drier sites

Spodiopogon sibiricus

Stipa gigantea

Adiantum pedatum

Polystichum setiferum 'Herrenhausen'

To the annoyance of gardeners and landscape professionals, botanists – or, more correctly, taxonomists – appear to keep on changing plant names, or burdening plants with unfeasibly long ones. Scientific accuracy is important, but sometimes compromises have to be made. In this book, I have largely followed one of the most widely respected naming authorities, that of Britain's Royal Horticultural Society, but in order to avoid confusion please note the following.

Some taxonomically correct names are unfeasibly long for use in diagrams, tables or for marketing purposes. In this book I have shortened the following:
• *Calamagrostis* 'Karl Foerster' is *Calamagrostis* ×*acutiflora* 'Karl Foerster'.
• *Molinia* 'Edith Dudszus', *M.* 'Heidebraut' and *M.* 'Moorhexe' are all *Molinia caerulea* subsp. *caerulea* varieties.
• *Molinia* 'Transparent' is *M. caerulea* subsp. *arundinacea* 'Transparent', the *arundinacea* types being considerably taller.

Taxonomists do change plant names as part of an ongoing process of tidying up or as new knowledge becomes available. It then takes a long time for those in the garden and landscape businesses to catch up, and in some cases changes may not be accepted everywhere. Here I clarify my use of some disputed or changing names.

Aconogonon 'Johanniswolke' is what is called *Persicaria polymorpha* in the English-speaking world. I bow to the taxonomists on the genus name, but since the plant originated as a hybrid at the nursery of Hans Simon, it seems appropriate to use his cultivar name (it refers to the ascent of John the Baptist), which is accepted in Germany.

Asperula odorata is *Galium odoratum*.

The genus *Aster* has been reorganized following recent DNA-based evidence. I stick to the old names as the new ones are not yet that familiar outside the botanical community. New names here follow the United States Department of Agriculture and Missouri Botanic Gardens:

Aster cordifolius is now *Symphyotrichum cordifolium*.
Aster divaricatus is now *Eurybia divaricatus*.

Aster ericoides is now *Symphyotrichum ericoides*.
Aster laevis is now *Symphyotrichum laeve*.
Aster lateriflorus 'Horizontalis' is now *Symphyotrichum lateriflorum* 'Horizontalis'.
Aster novae-angliae is now *Symphyotrichum novae-angliae*.
Aster oblongifolius 'October Skies' is now *Symphyotrichum oblongifolium* 'October Skies'.
Aster umbellatus is now *Doellingeria umbellata*.
Aster ×*herveyi* 'Twilight' (*A. macrophyllus*) is now *Eurybia* ×*herveyi* 'Twilight' (*E. macrophylla*).
Aster ageratoides, Aster ×*frikartii* and *Aster tartaricus* stay the same.

Baptisia alba subsp. *macrophylla* is what used to be *Baptisia leucantha*.

Cimicifuga we include as part of *Actaea*, although this makes little sense to us gardeners! It is also not yet accepted everywhere.

DNA analysis has reorganized *Eupatorium* as well:
Eupatorium rugosum is now *Ageratina rugosus*.
Eupatorium maculatum is now *Eupatoriadelphus maculatus*.

Limonium latifolium is now *L. platyphyllum*.

The larger *Sedum* species are sometimes now regarded as *Hylotelephium*.

The small fluffy grass which went under several names, usually *Stipa tenuissima*, and involved more than one species getting confused, is now *Nassella tenuissima*.

For those interested in keeping up with names the following websites are very useful (even if they do not agree with each other):

For plants in cultivation in the UK:
http://apps.rhs.org.uk/rhsplantfinder/

For US natives and species naturalized in the USA:
http://plants.usda.gov/java/

METRIC AND US EQUIVALENTS

1 millimeter	=	0.04 inch	1 square meter	=	10.8 square feet or 1.2 square yards
1 centimeter	=	0.4 inch	1 hectare	=	2.5 acres
1 meter	=	39.4 inches or 1.1 yards	1 gram	=	0.04 ounce
1 kilometer	=	0.6 mile	1 liter	=	33.8 fluid ounces
			1°C	=	33.8°F

FURTHER READING

I see this book as very much resting on foundations built by our two previous books: *Designing with Plants* (Timber Press, 1999) and *Planting Design: Gardens in Time and Space* (Timber Press, 2005), as well as a monograph, *Landscapes in Landscapes*, for which I wrote the text (Monacelli Press/Thames & Hudson, 2011).

Among colleagues mentioned in this book, Nigel Dunnett and James Hitchmough have an edited volume aimed at those in the landscape and environment management world, *The Dynamic Landscape: Design, Ecology and Management of Naturalistic Urban Planting* (Spon Press, 2004). These two have personal research websites which are of interest:
www.nigeldunnett.info
www.landscape.dept.shef.ac.uk/james

Roy Diblik has written *Roy Diblik's Small Perennial Gardens: The Know Maintenance Approach* (American Nurseryman Pub. Co., 2008) and is (at the time of writing) working on a book for Timber Press.

Possibly to the chagrin of the British, it is German practitioners who have written most about planting design, and who have raised it to the status of a true discipline. Wolfgang Borchardt's *Pflanzenkompositionen: Die Kunst der Pflanzenverwendung* (Ulmer Verlag, 1998) is a classic text, underpinning much work on the structuring of planting; the division of plants into theme plants, solitary plants, etc., was originally his, but articulated more fully by the following authors. More

radical, in English, and a key book for understanding the whole idea of planting communities is Richard Hansen and Friedrich Stahl's *Perennials and their Garden Habitats* (Cambridge University Press, 1993). Most recent is a magisterial textbook on planting design by Norbert Kühn, *Neue Staudenverwendung* (Ulmer Verlag, 2011).

The work on plant performance here has drawn on my unpublished doctoral thesis, 'An Investigation into the Performance of Species in Ecologically Based Ornamental Herbaceous Vegetation, with Particular Reference to Competition in Productive Environments' (University of Sheffield, 2009), and a further study, 'Evaluating the Long-term Performance of Ornamental Herbaceous Plants using a Questionnaire-based Practitioner Survey' (2010), as part of a European Union funded program: Interreg IVb Making Places Profitable – Public and Private Open Spaces (MP4) (not yet published). This, along with a number of 'easy reading' versions, is available from my personal website, which also has links to a number of other studies and sources of information on plant performance:
www.noelkingsbury.com.

For the BUGS project (Biodiversity in Urban Gardens) mentioned in chapter one, see www.bugs.group.shef.ac.uk.

The two books mentioned in the conclusion are *Nature's Keepers: The New Science of Nature Management*, by Stephen Budiansky (Free Press, 1995) and

Rambunctious Garden: Saving Nature in a Post-Wild World by Emma Marris (Bloomsbury, 2011).

I am often asked for reference works on perennials. Until I write my own, almost certainly in collaboration with colleagues, the most comprehensive is the Royal Horticultural Society's *Encyclopedia of Perennials*, edited by Graham Rice (Dorling Kindersley, 2006), although this is of limited use for professionals. The best online source of information is from Missouri Botanic Gardens: www.missouribotanicalgarden.org/ gardens-gardening/your-garden/plant-finder.aspx.

ACKNOWLEDGMENTS

Writing a book like this involves seeking advice from colleagues – the collective knowledge is always greater than the individual. Both of us particularly rely on Cassian Schmidt in Germany and Roy Diblik in the USA for their opinions and experiences in growing and managing perennials. Rick Darke is also someone whose opinion we seek and respect, putting gardens and designed landscapes into a wider ecological context. We would like to acknowledge the wisdom of the following, in no particular order: Yuko Tanabe, Tracy DiSabato Aust, Wolfram Kircher, Neil Diboll, Martin Hughes-Jones, Colleen Lockovitch, Jennifer Davit, Neil Lucas, Jacqueline van der Kloet and Dagmar Hillova.

We would like to thank other colleagues who have let us write about their work in chapter five: Heiner Luz, Petra Pelz, Nigel Dunnett, James Hitchmough and Dan Pearson.

This particular project has been a challenge, and we have relied on passing drafts around to colleagues to reassure us that what we are doing makes sense, and even more importantly to tell us when we are not. Thank you to Daniela Coray and John Marder, to Elliott and Susan Forsyth for your comments and reassurance. Particular thanks to Catherine Lucas for her ability to spot word repetition and to Amalia Robredo for her comments on the intelligibility of some of the plans. Thank you to Ye Hang for being a third member of the team in picture selection, in drawing the diagrams and for working to get our books published in China.

We would like to show our appreciation to Anna Mumford and other staff at Timber Press, and to our agent and facilitator, Hélène Lesger, whose cheerful and efficient competence we both greatly admire. Finally, to our wives, Anja Oudolf and Jo Eliot, for their continual love and support during this project and throughout our careers. Anja's hospitality and constant supply of bread, cheese and coffee are also much appreciated during the days we have worked together at Hummelo.

PHOTO CREDITS

All photographs and planting plans by Piet Oudolf except the following:

Sheila Brady: 226
Imogen Checketts: 42–43
Rick Darke: 14–15
Roy Diblik: 198, 207T
Nigel Dunnett: 8, 11
Joanna Fawcett: 88–89, 91TR
Ye Hang: illustrations on 122–127
Walter Herfst: 40, 44–45, 67B, 107
James Hitchmough: 227, 229

Andrea Jones/Garden Exposures: 22–23, 56–57, 223, 232, 238–239
Noel Kingsbury: 27, 72, 133T, 184, 185, 200T, 222
Heiner Luz Landschaftsarchitekt BDLA DWB: 220–221
Philip Ottendorfer: 193
Dan Pearson: 204–205
Petra Pelz: 224–225
Julie Amadéa Pluriel: illustrations on 188, 228
Amalia Robredo: 18
Cassian Schmidt, Bettina Jaugstetter: 16–17, 30–31, 152–153, 154–155, 156–157, 200B, 208–209, 210, 212–213, 218, 234–235